DEALING
WITH THE
DRAGON

Also by Jonathan Fenby

FRANCE ON THE BRINK:
A GREAT CIVILIZATION FACES THE NEW CENTURY

DEALING
WITH THE
DRAGON

*A Year in the
New Hong Kong*

JONATHAN FENBY

ARCADE PUBLISHING • NEW YORK

To Renée

FIRST U.S. EDITION

Maps by Neil Hyslop

Note: At the time of writing, the currency conversion rate was as follows: US$1 = HK$7.78

Library of Congress Cataloging-in-Publication Data

Fenby, Jonathan.
    Dealing with the dragon : a year in the new Hong Kong / Jonathan Fenby.— 1st U.S. ed
      p. cm.
    ISBN 1-55970-559-0
      1. Fenby, Jonathan—Diaries.   2. Journalists—Great Britain—Diaries. 3. Hong Kong (China).   I. Title.
DS796.H74 F42 2001
951.25'05'092—dc21   00-54307

Published in the United States by Arcade Publishing, Inc., New York
Distributed by Time Warner Trade Publishing

Visit our Web site at www.arcadepub.com

10 9 8 7 6 5 4 3 2 1

EB

PRINTED IN THE UNITED STATES OF AMERICA

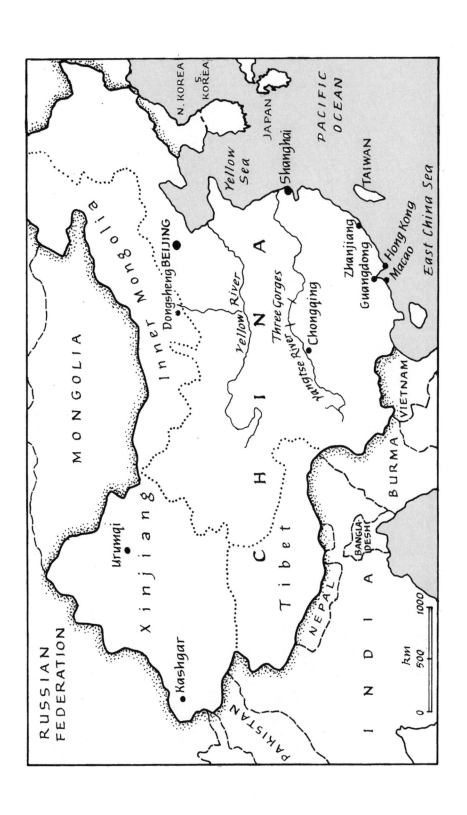

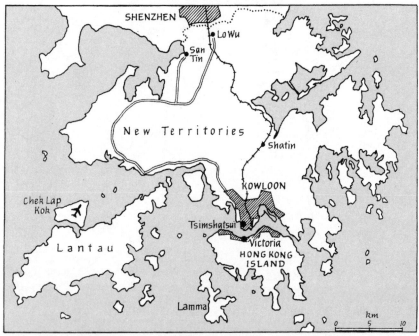

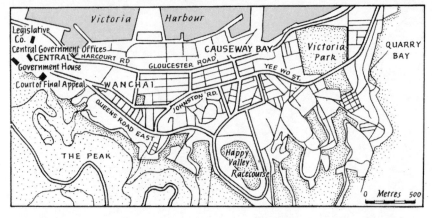

HONG KONG . . .

This is the story of a year in the life of a unique place, long known for its material superlatives but now also the scene of an unparalleled political experiment. It also happens to be the last year of a century in which Hong Kong grew from being a small, unconsidered fragment of the predominant empire on the planet to a treasure house whose wealth was proportionately greater than that of the colonial master on the other side of the globe. More recently, it has undergone a unique passage from being the final major possession of a liberal democracy to becoming the freest city in the last major power ruled by a Communist party. A meeting place of East and West at the crossroads of the twenty-first century, this territory of only a thousand square kilometres and 6.8 million people has a gross domestic product of US$175 billion and the world's fourth largest foreign exchange reserves. An accident of history and geography, it has become a theatre for major questions of our times, not in theory but in everyday life.

Since British rule ceased at midnight on 30 June 1997, the Hong Kong Special Administrative Region (SAR) of the People's Republic of China has been the most advanced and richest city in the biggest developing nation on earth. As it boomed in the 1980s and 1990s on the back of the opening-up of mainland China, what had once been dismissed as a rocky outcrop of little interest to Victorian empire-builders attracted international companies in their thousands to make it one of the great cosmopolitan metropolises. Apart from its 95 per cent Chinese population and its own dealings with the mainland, it has long been the unofficial capital of the diaspora of 100 million overseas Chinese, who see Hong Kong as a safe haven for their money and as a gateway to the mother country. Going in the other direction, it has been the main conduit for funds coming out of China, legally or illegally, some destined for licit investment, others moving through clandestine channels; and for spectacular criminals moving to and from the mainland.

Coming out of a long and deep slump, the SAR still has more billionaires than its former sovereign. Even in the depths of recession, the best-known tycoon, Li Ka-shing, whose empire stretches from property and container ports to supermarkets and mobile telephones, took tenth place in the listing of the world's mega-rich by *Forbes* magazine. Income tax is a flat 15 per cent, and only a quarter of the population pays it. The wealthy are further comforted by the absence of tax on dividends or capital gains. 'Here, the money we make, we keep,' as the owner of a big Chinese herbal pill business puts it. When it changed sovereign powers in 1997, Hong Kong made up 20 per cent of China's wealth, with 0.5 per cent of the mainland's population. The head of its government earns HK$287,141 (US$36,900) a month – more than his counterparts in the US, Britain or Japan. His number two, the Chief Secretary for Administration, who heads the civil service, is paid HK$229,713 a month, and the Financial Secretary, the equivalent of the Chancellor of the Exchequer, HK$217,149. Dwarfing their pay, the golf-champion boss of the central bank gets eight times as much as the chairman of the US Federal Reserve Board. Leading barristers can pull in 45 per cent more than their London counterparts. In the 1997 bull market, the stock exchange was the sixth biggest in the world, and membership debentures at the main golf club cost US$1.5 million.

Despite a poor construction safety record, pollution, and bureaucratic blunders such as paying China the equivalent of US$200 million a year for water which overflows into the sea, Hong Kong is generally a model of urban development. It has a superb infrastructure and a spectacular new airport, reached over the world's longest two-level suspension bridge to the mountainous island of Lantau. The harbour, which has ranked as the world's most used container terminal in all but three of the last twelve years, is a constantly shifting pattern of slow ferries and fast ferries, jet foils, tugs and container barges, cargo ships, rusting liners that ply up the China coast, sampans, powerboats and yachts, cruise liners, corporate entertainment launches, visiting warships, a big brightly-lit blue and white gambling craft which takes punters on trips out of Hong Kong waters, and the emblematic green and white Star Ferry shuttling endlessly between Hong Kong Island and the Kowloon peninsula.

The local anthem is the sound of the pneumatic drill; the national bird should be the crane. Sheer walls of apartment blocks perch on the edge of steep slopes. Plans for new buildings rise a hundred floors up into the sky. Though too many developments are unimaginative concrete, glass and steel towers designed to make the most money from the allotted plot ratio, there is no finer office building in the world than the triangular masterpiece designed by I. M. Pei for the Bank of China which dominates the Hong Kong skyline. If road traffic is increasingly caught in gridlock in busy areas, the territory's transport network encompasses an underground system to put most others to shame, along with surface trains, trams, minibuses, double-deckers, shuttles, ferries, taxis, three cross-harbour tunnels, three tunnels through the mountains, plus the funicular railway up the Peak towering over Hong Kong Island. Carrying half the territory's population each day, the underground Mass Transit Railway (MTR) is the world's most heavily used people-carrier, and probably the most efficient. As for other means of getting around, taxis are cheap, the flat fare on the tram is 26 cents, and you can cross the harbour on the upper deck of the ferry for only a penny more.

Above ground is an amazing array of road bridges, overhead pedestrian walkways and an 800-metre-long escalator system up the slopes above the main business district. The sprawling squatter camps without electricity or running water that once housed refugees and were the scene of massive fires and landslip disasters have long gone. But there are still indigent 'street sleepers' and 'cage homes' occupied by unmarried, unemployed, unskilled men who live in railed-off bunk spaces. The early housing estates with their shared toilets and communal cooking facilities belong to history. Still, space is often woefully inadequate, with an average of under 500 square feet per home. More than 100,000 people live in temporary accommodation. But the vast blocks of public flats built on what were once rice paddies or virgin land have made Hong Kong – for its size – the site of one of the world's major urban housing developments.

Though the potential for fast or long driving is severely limited by the small size and steep geography of the place, there are more luxury limousines per head of population here than anywhere else on earth. The owners of the flat on top of the apartment block my wife and I lived in kept a black stretch limousine waiting permanently downstairs but never seemed to use it. The son of the house switched between Porsches and Ferraris with the occasional Maserati thrown in. The last time we visited the home of the leader of one major political group, he had a large Mercedes, a Porsche and a Ferrari in the driveway, and a Rolls inside the garage.

Real-estate and textile barons rendezvous in secluded coves in the South China Sea on Sunday afternoons aboard huge, personally designed luxury boats made in Italy, with resident chefs and dining rooms as big as the average flat: one can seat eighteen. Although the boats could sail the globe, they generally don't venture far for fear of pirates, and watchful crew members keep their eyes open for kidnappers. One younger socialite doesn't go anywhere at all. He keeps his yacht permanently moored in a bay on the south side of the island to be used as a floating dining room: the champagne is Dom Pérignon and the cheese is flown in from France to order.

Hong Kong is home to more luxury hotels than any other place of its size, and almost certainly holds the record for atrium space. With one eating establishment for every 650 inhabitants, it may well also have the highest restaurant penetration, including five of the ten busiest McDonald's outlets. Times Square in the Causeway Bay district of Hong Kong Island is one of the world's two busiest shopping centres, and few other cities have such a concentration of retail outlets – from the luxury stores of the Central District and the jostling shops of Tsim Sha Tsui across the harbour to the streets round the Wanchai market with their stalls selling meat, vegetables, fruit, dried fish, shoes, women's panties, videos, watches, nuts, flowers, towels and food from all over South-East Asia.

The streets are alive not only with the sound of people, but with signs jutting out overhead: in the first hundred yards of Mody Road in Tsim Sha Tsui, you walk under signs for Baron King's Tailor, Rio Pearl, Nikon, Surge Restaurant, Hong Kong Fur, Spring Deer Restaurant, Kam Chien Shoe Store, Tourist House, Maclary Fashions, Holdrich Guest House, Laser People, Club 38, Sandalwood Club, Fantastic Beauty and Image, Home Town Guest House and the Choy Kee Cleaning Service.

While under British rule, Hong Kong created templates for popular culture – Cantopop and kung fu – that had absolutely nothing to do with the colonisers, even if some of the stars took names like Bruce, Aaron and Lionel. The territory's take-no-prisoners crime epics made directors like John Woo into post-modernist icons. Though the film output is only a quarter of what it was in the early 1990s, the major attraction, Jackie Chan, is one of the most popular stars in the world. Chow Yun-fat, who was voted *Premiere* magazine's 'sexiest action star of 1999' before becoming the King of Siam to Jodie Foster's Anna, was striking serious attitudes with a matchstick in the side of his mouth well before Quentin Tarantino drew his inspiration for *Reservoir Dogs* from Hong Kong gangster flicks.

This is media city incarnate. With a population equivalent to that of London, it supports no fewer than fifteen newspapers. In the go-go years around 1997, the dominant English-language daily made a pre-tax profit equivalent to US$90 million. Hong Kong is awash with magazines, and the air buzzes with in-your-ears radio: one leading talkshow host so offended somebody that he was the target of a severe attack with a chopper that left him badly maimed. As for television, an executive reckons Hong Kong's programmes are watched by 16 million people across the border.

Business rules, and its practitioners are lords of the universe. There is nothing new about this: the only public statue in the Central District is of a Victorian general manager of the Hongkong Bank. Names of firms and buildings translated from Chinese reflect the aspirations and preoccupations of owners and inhabitants – Brilliant

Trading, Joyful Construction, Good Luck Corrugated Carton, or Tycoon Court, Wealthy Heights, Good Results, Prosperity Centre and Everprofit.

A ranking of top wealth creators in Asia at the end of 1999 placed seven Hong Kong firms in the top ten. Business figures regularly lead polls of the territory's most admired people, and their interests stretch across the globe. Apart from major investments on the mainland of China, they own real estate by the Thames, the Hudson and the Pacific coast of North America, luxury hotels from Tokyo to Knightsbridge, textile works in Cambodia and Pringle knitwear in Scotland, the Harvey Nichols store in London, sheep farms and electric power stations in Australia, palm oil plantations in Indonesia and container ports in Felixstowe and the Panama Canal. Hong Kong entrepreneurs turn out goods for top American brand names, operate casinos in North Korea and ski resorts in Canada, and bankrolled Donald Trump's latest development on the West Side of Manhattan.

They are renowned as flexible, on-the-ball traders. Few restrict themselves to a single line of activity. Property, garments, shipping, the Internet, mobile phones, retailing, the stock market and mainland China: mix and match to maximise profits. As middlemen, they set up deals around the globe at the drop of a fax, an e-mail or a telephone call. They employ millions of people at factories in China turning out export goods that have fuelled the mainland's economic rise. Costs at home are too high to allow Hong Kong to compete. So what was once a low-cost centre turning out cheap clothes, toys, watches, wigs and a hundred other products has seen its manufacturing shrink dramatically, leaving a pool of middle-aged and elderly men and women without work or a future.

The destiny of the once mighty textile industry stands as a measure of the changes in the last two decades, and of the flexibility of Hong Kong's business culture. In 1980 textiles accounted for 23 per cent of the economy; now this is down to 6.5 per cent. The industry's workforce of 93,000 in 1995 was 58,000 two years later. Holding a quota licence to export textile goods to the West remains a ticket to riches, but the sweaters and jeans and T-shirts do not have to be made in Hong Kong. So the quota-holders either moved their factories to

southern China where wages were far lower, or subcontracted production to others and pulled down their factories to make way for
real-estate developments.

From the heights of the Peak to people scrabbling with bank over-
drafts to get on the escalator to wealth, property dominates. Go out to
a friendly dinner, and the prices of flats – there are few houses here –
will inevitably come up at some point. Property tycoons are the masters of the city. Li Ka-shing is known simply as 'Superman'. Lee
Shau-kee of Henderson Land earned a cool US$1.1 billion from divi-
dends alone in 1997. A real-estate heiress, Nina Wang, was listed as the
richest working woman on earth with US$7 billion to her name.
Property companies constitute 30 per cent of stock market capitalis-
ation. Solicitors become multi-millionaires on conveyancing fees. Ask
many a Rolls-Royce or Mercedes owner where his money comes
from: he will name his business, but then add, 'Of course, the real
money's from property.' The Mass Transit Railway system is building
massive office and apartment blocks on top of its stations; the latest
project is for a 102-storey office tower in Kowloon. After the territory's
leading gangster was caught in 1998, he was found to own thirty-one
pieces of real estate. At the other end of the scale, tenants of public
housing are being urged to get into the game by buying leases on their
homes. In any case, demand usually exceeds supply. Apart from the
Anglican cathedral, all land belongs to the government, and it parcels
it out carefully at land auctions, drawing 40 per cent of its revenue from
sales of leases, redevelopment fees and stamp duty.

The result is both some of the highest prices in the world and great
population density. The Kwun Tong area of Kowloon has 54,000 people
per square kilometre. In slum blocks elsewhere, average living space is 21
square feet, and more than a dozen people share a toilet. Such is the
pressure on space that Hong Kong is riddled with 6,000 illegal struc-
tures. The soaring property prices and the government's income from
them are the territory's hidden tax. Real-estate inflation is a big element
in the high cost of shopping, eating out or doing business.

Speculation is not confined to the rich. Visiting flats is a local pastime. Foreign property is snapped up sight unseen at exhibitions in
plush hotels. A software salesman and his secretary wife I know had

three flats in Hong Kong during the mid-1990s bubble, plus a house in Beijing. They also bought a one-bedroom flat in the former County Hall in London at a property road show in Hong Kong, but soon sold it, never having set eyes on their place by the Thames. Li Ka-shing tells of being approached during an early morning golf round by a greens sweeper wearing the traditional wide-brimmed hat of the original inhabitants of Hong Kong, the Hakkas. She said the flats she had bought from his company had been hit by the slump, and asked him not to sue her if she fell behind with the payments. How many flats had this woman bought? Four. 'I bluntly told her that she should not do that with her income level,' Li concluded. 'And I asked her not to disturb my golf game.'

Between 1984, when an agreement between Britain and China removed uncertainty about Hong Kong's future, and the great Asian crash of 1997, property values rose by 2,000 per cent, with the average price of luxury accommodation hitting US$2,250 a square foot. High inflation meant low, or even negative, real interest rates. The currency was rock solid, pegged to the US dollar. Demand was booming. No wonder that this small parcel of land bereft of natural resources and without enough food or water to sustain itself came to outstrip its colonial sovereign in the wealth stakes.

Geography has always been a key to success here. As the estate agents say, what counts is location, location and location. Perched on the flank of the great dragon of China, Hong Kong has been perfectly placed as an entrepôt city, a channel for goods, people and services. As an outpost of Western good practices, with a clean civil service and a reliable legal system, it has benefited from a trust that the West is still hesitant about extending to the mainland. Hence its eminence as a container port, and its position as the centre for financial, legal and managerial services for companies operating in China. If Hong Kong became part of the People's Republic in 1997, geography still gives it the destiny of being a bridge between the mainland and the rest of the world. But that location also makes Hong Kong much more fragile than such a rich and successful place should be. It is at the mercy of events it cannot influence, far away in America, nearer at hand in Tokyo, or across the border in the rest of China.

The currency link to the US dollar means that monetary policy is made by the Federal Reserve in Washington. Changes in US policy towards Beijing have major consequences for Hong Kong. Japan's enormous weight in the Asian economy cannot be escaped. Most of all, there is the China factor: increasingly, it cuts both ways. If mainland economic development stalls, Hong Kong will feel the repercussions first. If Beijing devalues its currency, could the Hong Kong dollar resist the pressure to follow suit? If, on the other hand, the looming superpower-in-the-making relates to the world and ploughs its own furrow in the international economy, there will be much less need for the Hong Kong bridge.

If that happens, how many firms will follow the example of the French communications company Alcatel, which has made Shanghai its regional headquarters, or the electronics division of Philips, which has moved its top management executives to the mainland? If Shanghai can reinvent itself as a great world centre, with double the population and the huge backdrop of the Yangtze basin, who needs this pimple on the backside of the dragon to the north? If container ports in southern China can undercut Hong Kong, why transport goods through the SAR? An artificial place, created by refugees and colonialists, Hong Kong could then move to the wings of China's evolution. An early beneficiary of globalisation, it could be margin-alised by the biggest global link-up of all between 1.2 billion consumers and the rest of the planet.

Like any people living on the edge, the inhabitants of Hong Kong have more than their share of contradictions. They are famed for their entrepreneurial spirit, but local Chinese firms are run on a strict top-down basis. Bosses command huge deference, and do not expect to be argued with. Delegation is seen as a potential source of weak-ness. The result can be a stultifying absence of initiative as decision-making is referred upwards and executives avoid taking responsibility for fear of incorrectly anticipating the wishes of the man on high. Within companies, 'little potato' employees know their place, though the more adventurous waste no time in striking out on their own to fuel the constant flow of new businesses which give Hong Kong its special dynamic.

However sophisticated the city may be, it is still subject to old superstitions and new scares. Women with big mouths are considered bad news because they 'eat' the family's luck and money. Various foods are imbued with special powers. Eat lotus seeds to have a child within the year; water chestnuts promise good fortune; candied coconut stores up family togetherness down the generations; peach blossoms denote longevity, jonquils prosperity, and camellias rebirth.

A massive apartment block on the south side of Hong Kong Island has a large hole in the middle to allow evil spirits to pass through without causing any damage. An executive of a start-up software firm pointed down from his twenty-sixth-floor office at the traffic coming and going on an expressway below as a sign that if money flowed out it would certainly return. In 1997, Hong Kong's Chief Executive used the supposed bad feng shui of the residence of the former colonial governors – which has the sharp edge of the Bank of China building pointing directly at it – as an excuse for not moving in. Asked by the *South China Morning Post*, the main English-language newspaper, to rate major buildings in the middle of Hong Kong, an expert who says he advises film stars, banks and the Hong Kong Futures Exchange found that the Hongkong and Shanghai Banking Corporation would benefit from the air passing beneath Sir Norman Foster's building for its headquarters in Central, which has the additional safeguard of escalators running diagonally to the sea so that the money will not go out to the water.

The tradition of lucky and unlucky numbers is alive and well. Eight is prized because it sounds like 'wealth' in Cantonese, and 9 is good too because it sounds like the word for 'long-lasting'. But 4 is to be avoided at all costs since it sounds like death. The lease of our flat – number 4B – said it was also known as 3F, which does not exist. An apartment block opposite has an Upper 3 floor, Upper 13 and Upper 23 – anything to avoid the dreaded 4.

There have been times in the past few years when Hong Kong has needed all the good feng shui it could get. The handover year of 1997 saw a mysterious outbreak of a lethal virus called bird flu, carried by poultry: all the chickens were slaughtered to stop the spread of the disease. 'Red tides' swept down the Pearl River from China from time to time and killed the fish. In 1999, three people died from virulent bacteria called *Staphylococcus aureus*, for which there is no known treatment.

As befits a place that fancies itself to be at the cutting edge of modernity, Hong Kong puts a premium on smartness, not only among the middle and upper classes who throng the charity galas and fashion shows but also among office workers who preen themselves in their frequently fake designer labels. Mingle with the lunchtime crowd in Central and you will not see a hair out of place or a shoe unshined. 'I can't imagine anybody getting married at this time of year,' says a young woman before going to a wedding in hot and humid June. 'Their make-up just has to run.'

The mood-swings from depression to optimism are extreme – and extremely swift. Launch a new cake or a fresh brand of sunglasses and the queues will form. Nobody wants to miss out anything, from the crowds which besieged McDonald's to buy cut-price Snoopy dolls, to the property companies that rushed pell-mell into Internet offerings and the sober-suited bankers who lined up to lend money to less than transparent mainland enterprises. When would-be immigrants from the mainland formed a long line outside a government office in 1999 seeking authorisation to stay in Hong Kong, several locals joined the queue in case something was being given away.

The essential attribute of the modern Hong Konger is, of course, possession of a mobile phone. Only the Nokiaworld of Finland has more per head of population. Hong Kong people simply cannot live without them. The outcry when mobile phone companies owned by some of the city's biggest tycoons tried to raise rates at the beginning of 2000 was such that even they had to retreat. Ringing so disrupted the opening night of *Othello* by the Royal Shakespeare Company in 1997 that the actors threatened to walk off if there was a repetition during the second performance. A hospital surgeon was suspended after being accused of discussing the purchase of a silver BMW with another doctor over his mobile while operating on a patient's polyp; distracted, he allegedly pierced the man's colon.

Not all the smart objects are genuine: this is a mecca for counterfeit watches and imitation fashion goods, run up for a fraction of the price of the real thing here or over the border in China. Half the people of Hong Kong admit to buying fake goods. Forty per cent of home videos sold in the SAR are rip-offs: in one raid police made what they called the world's biggest seizure, of 22 million pirate video compact discs. Some eighty factories churn out counterfeit music, videos and software. In 1999, copies of the new *Star Wars* epic were on sale within a day of the film's release in the USA.

In a different domain, it is increasingly hard not to see democracy in Hong Kong as something of a counterfeit, too. At the apex of the extraordinary political system under which Hong Kong has lived since 1997 stands the Chief Executive, chosen by a carefully constituted and Beijing-friendly committee. He is advised by a secretive Executive Council whose membership is for him to determine. Then there is a raft of senior civil servants running government departments. That may seem a quite straightforward example of an executive-led government, perpetuating the old colonial system for the benefit of Beijing rather than London. But then there is the legislature, which is meant to represent the democratic element in the way Hong Kong is run.

The Joint Declaration on Hong Kong's future signed by Margaret Thatcher in Beijing in 1984 after tortuous negotiations said that the Legislative Council (LegCo) was to be 'constituted by election'. That formulation was acceptable precisely because it could be interpreted differently by each of the consenting parties. When the agreement was presented to the House of Commons, the British government could allow MPs to imagine that 'election' meant Westminster-style polls. The Chinese, for their part, could be reassured by the fact that in their many elections since 1949 no Communist candidate had failed to be returned. As one former senior colonial official noted, the Chinese didn't mind elections but they rather liked to know the result in advance.

The pressure to introduce democracy became overwhelming in Hong Kong in the late 1980s, particularly under the impact of the massacre of demonstrators in Beijing's Tiananmen Square on 4 June

1989. There was a timid move to bring some independent voices into the Legislative Council, which was appointed by the Governor and used to sit in a government building. Then the last British Governor, Chris Patten, delighted local democrats and horrified Beijing by introducing genuine democracy at elections in 1995, which produced a triumph for pro-democracy parties critical of China. It was a key sign of how Hong Kong was growing up politically, of how it was no longer simply an economic city, but was able to embrace modern accountability, even if the administration continued to keep a careful check on the powers of the legislature.

But the looming date of the handover meant that Patten's experiment was bound to be short-lived, a bouncing baby condemned to death by its morally laudable but practically untenable conception. In the early hours of 1 July 1997, the elected legislature was dissolved and replaced by a body with no popular legitimacy picked by a Beijing-approved committee. Ten months later, in May 1998, a degree of democracy crept back with a newly constituted legislature of sixty members. But only twenty were elected by popular vote, the others representing professional groups (known as functional constituencies) or picked by yet another committee of friends of Beijing and the local administration.

To limit the chances of its pro-democracy opponents in 1998, the government introduced proportional representation and large constituencies designed to handicap them. In most of the functional constituencies, voting was handed back to professional organisations rather than following the one-person-one-vote arrangement brought in by Patten. All the same, and despite a tropical downpour, Democrats took 70 per cent of the poll. But the system meant that, for all their votes, they made up only a minority in the chamber and, even then, were hamstrung by procedural rules which gave the functional constituencies effective veto power.

Thus Hong Kong finds itself with a system in which candidates who got nearly three-quarters of the popular vote are consigned to opposition. At the same time, though the administration can count on general support from a pro-Beijing group and many functional constituency representatives, there is no government party as such.

LegCo members have the power to summon officials and to quiz them, but nobody expects anything to result. Legislators may censure handling of the opening of the new airport or the health scares or the lack of information supplied by the administration on major projects, but the top civil servants who were responsible never resign. The largely toothless body that resulted from the carefully undefined elections promised in 1984 is not quite an empty vessel full of sound and fury and little else, but it comes pretty close. At the time of the 1998 election, I asked Martin Lee Chu-ming, leader of the main democratic party, what he would do with a majority of the votes but no power. 'Make noise,' he replied. No wonder that some of Hong Kong's brightest pro-democracy politicians are turning against running for re-election, preferring to pursue their goals outside the legislature – and that the countervailing powers of the judiciary came to be seen as the bulwark of the high degree of autonomy promised at the handover.

The SAR's constitution, the Basic Law, lays down a ten-year road from 1997 to the prospect of the popular election of a chief executive and the legislature. Even that timetable may be delayed, and, as we will see in this book, the tide since the handover has flowed towards the strengthening of executive power and the marginalisation of anything which might stand in its way. At the forefront of this process is the Chief Executive, a shipping magnate called Tung Chee-hwa, selected at the end of 1996 by a 400-strong committee approved by Beijing. An avuncular figure with brush-cut hair who was formerly the honorary consul for Monaco in Hong Kong, Tung studied at Liverpool University, and supports both that city's football team and the San Francisco 49ers. His father set up a firm called Orient Overseas which made the family extremely wealthy, with assets of US$1 billion. Among his other business ventures, the elder Tung bought the *Queen Elizabeth* liner, intending to convert it into a floating university, but the ship sank in unexplained circumstances in 1971. He died of a heart attack in 1982 while hosting a visit to Hong Kong by Princess Grace of Monaco.

Three years later, the company nearly capsized in the deep waters of a shipping recession. Some pin the blame on the father's over-expansion; others say his sons bought too many ships before the market peaked. The firm had to be bailed out with help from the Hongkong Bank and a loan from China organised by a long-time friend of Beijing called Henry Fok Ying-tung. It was one of the biggest corporate restructuring rescues seen up to that time, and inevitably raises the question of whether Beijing thought it had Tung in its debt as a result, making him an even safer choice to run Hong Kong.

There is a duality about the tycoon chosen to run the SAR. He celebrates two birthdays each year, on 27 May according to the Chinese calendar and then again on 7 July according to the Western calendar used in Hong Kong. Asked how his family described the Communist entry into Shanghai in 1949 which sent them fleeing to Hong Kong, Tung says that they called it both 'liberation' and 'fall' – 'it depended on whom we were talking to'. He has strong links in the West, and the family firm used to be close to Taiwan. But he exhorts Hong Kong to be 'more Chinese', which gave a special edge to a remark by Bill Clinton at a dinner party in 1998 about how pleased he was that all the Chief Executive's children were US citizens.

Tung believes in running things the old way according to 'good traditional Chinese values'. One of his officials describes him as a 'righteous' man in the Confucian tradition. More to the point, perhaps, is that he was brought up in a prosperous family firm, assured of wealth, a man who ran a company which would wait upon his decisions, and who moved in a small and cosy circle where favours were exchanged and the mutual well-being of the plutocracy was paramount. In keeping with that background, he came to office on the basis of a public handshake from Chinese President Jiang Zemin and the support of a section of the business community led by Li Ka-shing, who had taken Tung's family firm as his partner in the Felixstowe container port – a connection which worried those who thought that Hong Kong's 'Superman' already had quite enough influence.

Nobody knows how much Hong Kong's leader consults the mainland. Some stories say his telephone line only connects him with middle-ranking functionaries in the central capital; but others say he has the rank of a provincial governor. Senior members of his administration insist that they rarely contact their colleagues in Beijing. They contrast the old colonial days, when the telegrams came in from Whitehall in the morning and had to be answered by the evening, with the new situation in which, they say, they never hear from the new sovereign power. But would they really act off their own bat in ways that would annoy the central government? Not if one is to go by examples that arose during the year described in this book.

The duality persists in the public and private faces of the man in charge of the SAR. Tung works long hours, earning the nickname of 'Mr Seven-Eleven', and listens politely to whoever is talking to him. But he seems to find it hard to make decisions, and reserves the right to take no notice. If he cannot make up his mind, nobody else in Hong Kong can decide for him. When he seeks counsel or support, it is from a small, select circle drawn from the business establishment and made up of people trusted by Beijing, or international business magnates. The awkwardness and irritations and demagogy of democracy are not for him. Nor is the assertion that ordinary people have as much right to determine their futures as does the elite. He has a talent for sounding the wrong note, as when he says the Tiananmen massacre belongs to the 'baggage' of history. Too often, his reactions to events are slow, evasive or formulaic. Popular leadership is not his forte. Tung is a patriarch, and patriarchs are there to be respected: the people should acquiesce or, as the Cantonese put it, shoe-shine, as an increasing number of civil servants do with growing acumen.

This paternalistic style does strike a chord with one strand of Hong Kong's mentality. Though they are cosmopolitan and international, people here keep up traditions of deference and strong family loyalties from the bottom of the social scale to the boardroom of one of the biggest property firms, where the chairman's brother, sister, daughter, two sons and son-in-law sit as directors. The elderly get respect, and children are treated with a pride and affection that has grown rare in the West. 'Uncle Tung' fits neatly into this pattern, the Chief Executive who is also chief executive officer of Hong Kong Inc. and aspires to be head of its six-million-strong family.

But that chord is becoming increasingly outdated. The family structure is fraying and the social environment changing. The number of recorded child abuse cases doubled between 1996 and 1999: a third involved sexual abuse. Marital strains and the emotional problems of parents were blamed. Fewer than 40 per cent of children under five are looked after by their parents during the day. Though Hong Kong feels a safe place, crime rose by 4 per cent in 1999. There were kidnappings, including a spate of child abductions, and domestic murders of horrifying violence. The city is a centre for some fifty Triad gangs, operating in legitimate business as well as the traditional pastures of extortion, prostitution, illegal gambling and drugs – and with links across the globe. In 1999, police busted a protection racket run in school playgrounds by apprentice Triads as young as twelve. There are court cases that come straight out of 1920s Chicago: in one, a string of key prosecution witnesses suddenly all lost their memories as they went into the box, and the accused businessman drove away in his gold Rolls-Royce with a starlet girlfriend. Lower down the scale, local government workers have been found stealing valuables from coffins, and a conman bamboozled three women to pay him HK$660,000 for pills he said would protect them from the Y2K bug.

Violent, pornographic Japanese comics are sold freely. Chinese dailies print pictures of dismembered bodies or corpses stuffed into cardboard boxes which would never figure in British or American tabloids. Press photographers snapped the head of a woman who had been decapitated by her son, and the skinless skull of a teenage kidnap victim whose body had been found on a hillside. Prostitution by local women and mainlanders thrives in Triad-run 'vice villas' or the bars and karaoke clubs of Yeung Long, Kam Tin and Mongkok, where the going rate is HK$400 a trick. The women serve a dozen clients a day. After one early morning raid, a policeman sighed and said, 'They'll be back in business tonight.' Until recently, two leading popular newspapers ran regular reviews of the sex services on offer.

At the same time, the establishment and those connected with it can be decidedly prudish. On one evening in 1997, a prominent pro-China figure presided over an evening of French culture. Visiting Paris, he had been much impressed by the spectacle at the Crazy Horse Saloon, so he decided to bring this particular aspect of Gallic art to Hong Kong for a gala charity evening in the ballroom of a major hotel. Leading businessmen paid large sums to take tables. The Deputy Director of the Xinhua News Agency, China's *de facto* representative office in Hong Kong, was the guest of honour, seated at the top table right in front of the stage.

Twenty-four hours before the occasion, alarm bells started to ring. What if the press photographed the Xinhua man with bare Crazy Horse bosoms beside him? The dancers were told to cover up. The photographers who normally immortalise such occasions for the society pages were banned. As the show began, the embarrassment level mounted. The diners were with their wives and found it difficult to show enthusiasm for the showgirls, whose idea of a cover-up was hardly modest. To make things worse, they strutted out in one politically incorrect number wearing busbies and very scanty costumes as British Grenadiers.

The applause grew increasingly tepid. When the interval came, coffee was suddenly served, and the Xinhua official was called up to pick the lucky draw. That traditionally marks the end of a charity do in Hong Kong. So everybody was free to leave. On the way out, I passed the man who had thought up the idea of bringing the Crazy Horse to the party. 'I hope you enjoyed yourself,' he said. 'And I hope you did, too,' was all I could reply.

A watchdog body called the Obscene Article Tribunal once fined a newspaper for running an advertisement showing Michelangelo's statue of David. Faced with an outbreak of women being touched by men on the underground railway system, a police chief advised them to wear 'conservative clothing'. Rock concerts are banned from the open-air Hong Kong Stadium because they might make too much noise. When an Elton John performance was mooted, the local council suggested that the sound should be piped to the audience through headphones, and that gloves should be issued to muffle any clapping. The concert did not go ahead.

The Cantonese, among whom the people of Hong Kong count themselves despite their highly varied origins, are not generally seen as having played much of a role in China's history. This is unfair. Some researchers believe the first inhabitants of the country arrived from the west in the Pearl River Delta, but that is heresy to official thinking, which insists that the Chinese sprouted up in China and owe their origins to nobody else. A Dominican friar, Gaspar da Cruz, who visited Canton – now known as Guangzhou – in the sixteenth century, noted their prowess at duck farming and their taste for tea, 'a kind of warm water which they call *cha* . . . made from a concoction of somewhat bitter herbs'. He also observed foot binding, blind prostitutes and the prevalence of 'unnatural vice'. Intrepid sailors and smugglers from the Pearl River opened up Asian trading routes. A Cantonese scholar called Kang Yu-wei drew up the first coherent programme to modernise the collapsing Qing dynasty, which led the last but one Emperor of China to issue twenty-seven decrees in a hundred days before the fearsome Empress Dowager had her son imprisoned and probably poisoned while ordering Kang to suffer death by a thousand cuts, a fate he avoided by escaping to Japan.

Soon afterwards, another Cantonese, Sun Yat-sen, who used Hong Kong as a refuge, headed the revolutionary movement to establish a modern republic in China, which led to the establishment of the Kuomintang (KMT) government and the rise of Chiang Kai-shek. The KMT's main power centre, Canton, was the scene of bloody internal battles between different factions of Sun's movement. It was from the great southern trading city that he set out on his last voyage to Beijing before dying of cancer in the old imperial capital, and it was from there that Chiang led the Northern Expedition of 1926–28 which made him ruler of China. Twenty years later, the KMT found its final redoubt in the South before the retreat to Taiwan.

The Cantonese are not much loved outside their home region. They have the reputation of being rude, and interested only in commerce. Their slang is known for its inventiveness and its use of sexual references: a local editor, Terry Cheng, reckons it may be the dirtiest dialect in China. Their cockiness gets up the noses of northerners, who may envy their material success but harbour no warm feelings for the country's newest region. 'How can you live with such people?' asks a snooty Beijinger. 'The Shanghainese are bad enough, but all the

Cantonese think about is making money.' Or as Jonathan Mirsky, the former East Asia editor of *The Times*, put it in one of his last dispatches from the city: 'The Cantonese are used to living and working in cramped and crowded conditions. They give no mercy to each other and are no more courteous to tourists.'

Sure enough, Hong Kong people work hard: a report by the International Labour Organisation found that they averaged 2,287 hours a year, or 44 hours a week. Between 1980 and 1996, their productivity rose by 90 per cent. They also count the dollars and cents assiduously, and, for all the conspicuous consumption, put a lot aside – the savings rate is double that in Britain. But they are also great gamblers, wagering tens of millions of dollars on an ordinary mid-week race meeting. Even in the depths of recession, the average bet was $318 (US$40), and the big dividend on the last day of racing brought $2.15 million for a $10 stake. Betting tax contributes 5 per cent of government revenue, covering expenditure on housing, the police and the environment. On top of this, the Jockey Club foots the bill for extensive spending on schools, clinics and charities. Legal betting is restricted to the horses, a weekly lottery and a few licensed mahjong parlours. Anything else entails a trip to the former Portuguese colony of Macau or further: a couple who run a garment factory flew to Las Vegas and lost US$4 million in two weeks; they then went to court claiming a 50 per cent discount on their losses.

You certainly have to watch your place in Hong Kong queues, and know what you want when you reach the counter. Getting on and off the MTR underground, or into a lift, can test both willpower and endurance. In business, the game is played to the bitter end, and there may still be a twist in the Cantonese tail. Getting repairs done to a rented flat can be a marathon process that only ends when you withhold the rent: one tenant I know refused to pay for thirteen months until he got some action from the landlord.

On the money-making front, the inhabitants live up to their reputation all through the social scale. Many have two jobs, or more – the Financial Secretary says that if they have only one nine-to-five job, they get withdrawal symptoms. They play the markets and watch interest rates like hawks. Early on in my time in Hong Kong, I learned that I had better know the late-morning close on the Hang Seng index before I went out to meet anybody for lunch: a quick discussion of how the market is doing takes the place of the weather in Britain as a conversational ice-breaker. Even at the depths of the 1999 recession, there was a constant buzz about the place. Taxi drivers don't wait for a tip; they are too busy driving off after the next passenger.

But this temple of wealth and conspicuous consumption is also a city of rag pickers and old women who scrape a living collecting waste paper and discarded soft-drink cans. At a landfill on a hillside in the New Territories which receives 8,000 tonnes of waste a day, dozens of men paid the equivalent of US$45 for a twelve-hour shift sort their way through the rubbish, retrieving anything which can be recycled for a profit by their employers: they call their pickings 'curry'. One early sign of the economic crisis was when the people who comb through the garbage by the old airport reported a distinct decline in the quality and quantity of what was being thrown away.

The income disparity is among the highest on earth as shown by the tax figures. Six per cent of the population pays 80 per cent of the total income tax bill, while a similar proportion of corporate tax comes from 5 per cent of taxable businesses. It is not simply that the poor are poor (and sometimes do not claim welfare for reasons of pride), but that the rich are so rich. The mansions on the Peak are huge and protected by security systems costing hundreds of thousands of dollars; the public housing estates elsewhere on the island or across in the New Territories contain some of the most crowded accommodation in the world.

Contrasts are everywhere. Sandwiched between shining high-rise towers of chromium and glass stand tenements with peeling walls and washing hanging out of the windows. Small stalls of while-you-wait cobblers and locksmiths line an alley beside some of the city's smartest stores. Near gleaming skyscrapers, a 76-year-old woman pays HK$700 a month for a tiny space in which she keeps a kerosene stove, cooking utensils, clothes, plastic bags stuffed with her belongings and a big metal box. She has never fully stretched out her legs when she sleeps. Her cubicle is part of a 500-square-foot unit where thirteen other people live.

The pay of company directors races far ahead of inflation: in the boom time of 1997, it jumped by an average of 42 per cent. But a survey by the Hong Kong Social Security Society the next year reported that 856,700 people – 14 per cent of the population – were below the poverty line, double the number a dozen years earlier. And that was before unemployment hit a record 6 per cent under the impact of the recession.

As the economy dropped, loan sharks thrived, often using brutal methods to recover their money. Debts were the motivation for a growing number of suicides: in one case in the summer of 1999 a market cleaner and his wife asphyxiated themselves and their three children with the smoke from a charcoal fire because they could not pay back their loans. Their neighbours quickly collected HK$20,000 to pay for a spirit-cleansing ceremony outside the flat where they died.

Personally, I find the people of Hong Kong invigoratingly up-front, smart and anxious to get on with life, rather like the Parisians, who attract similar reactions from Anglo-Saxon visitors and superior French provincials. Yes, they hustle and keep their eye on the main chance. True, commercialism and the making of money are the main reasons for most people's existence. Yes, the very rich can show an ostentatious superficiality as they parade their wealth, but that can also have its endearing side: the his and hers Rolls-Royces, the real pleasure at showing off a US$12,000 magnum of claret in the cellar, the surge of power as the Italian-made boat kicks into top gear and everything on deck goes flying, and the endless glossy charity balls that fill the society pages but do raise a lot of money for good causes.

It is perfectly true that the inhabitants can be insensitive and intolerant as they bustle and jostle their way through life. Hong Kong funeral parlours are brusque, vertically integrated industrial establishments, from the white-garbed professional mourners on the ground floor to the coffins being made on the roof. The religious service at a cremation I attended in the New Territories was interrupted halfway through by a manager who told us our time was up and we should make way for the next body. In a different register, a television network ran a promotion in the mid-1990s saying that advertising with it could have helped Hitler to achieve his 'final solution'. Prejudice is alive and well: many Chinese take a dim view of Indians. In 1999, a survey of people aged between twelve and twenty-five reported that a quarter regarded homosexuals as abnormal or mentally disturbed. A report in the *South China Morning Post* revealed that six funeral parlours were refusing to handle the bodies of people who had died with HIV, while local residents in one part of Kowloon waged a long and bitterly abusive campaign against a nursing home for Aids sufferers in their street, driving a third of the nurses away with their abuse.

On the other hand, their trading links make the business people of Hong Kong admirably internationally minded, a trait strengthened, for some, by the acquisition of foreign passports in case things went wrong after the return to China: at the last count, Hong Kong contained 32,500 people with Canadian passports as well as 29,000 American and 20,000 Australian. They cannot afford to be insular: their *raison d'être* is bound up with the wider world, over the border in China for some but through the rest of Asia, in North America and Europe for many more. While the tycoons are the big players internationally, ordinary Hong Kongers often have property abroad, plus relations across the Pacific and in the Chinatowns of Asia and Europe. The airport has a special importance as the gateway to an outside world that cannot be reached in any other way. The goods they buy, the fashions they wear, the food they eat, make the people of the SAR citizens of the globalised world with an immediacy which ensures the liveliness of the place: if Hong Kong lacks depth, skating across its surface is nevertheless exhilarating.

One result of the concentration on the here and now, rather than on the past or future, is a notable lack of care for the physical environment. Air pollution regularly reaches dangerous levels. The harbour is a sewer strewn with waste. All the assurances from colonial and post-handover administrations that something must be done have not halted, or even slowed down, the degradation: the fine for smoking in a taxi is HK$5,000, but the penalty for the vehicle emitting filthy diesel-fume exhaust is less than a tenth as much.

The march of development has left precious little room for the preservation of history. Elegant books of photographs of old Hong

Kong sit on coffee tables, but just 70 out of an estimated 7,000 pre-war buildings have been granted official protection from destruction. There is a 'heritage trail' which visitors can follow: but, as a local historian, Jason Wordie, says, it consists largely of a series of signs telling you what used to be.

Here and there, you find survivors amid the tower blocks. Elegant white Flagstaff House is the oldest colonial building still standing, dating from 1846. The former home of British military commanders, it is now a teapot museum on the edge of Hong Kong Park, surrounded by skyscrapers. Outside, you can sometimes catch a glimpse of white cockatoos descended from birds that escaped from a Japanese aviary during the occupation of 1941–45. Down below, along busy Queen's Road East, which used to mark the waterfront before reclamation stretched Hong Kong Island out into the harbour, Tai Wong temple constructed back into the hillside has stood its ground since the 1840s. At the end of a nearby cul-de-sac is a small shrine to the Earth God, who sits in a three-sided red wooden box with a taper burning in a two-handled cup: it has been in this spot for more than a century, a relic of the village customs of people from southern China, like a wayside cross in Catholic Europe. Further along Queen's Road East, the old one-storey whitewashed post office has been preserved as an environmental centre and there are a few 'shop houses', built in the 1920s and advertised at the time as being rat-proof. Off on the right as you head towards the bustling market streets, a corner of four-storey houses has survived from the turn of the twentieth century, with grilled balconies, high ceilings and staircases going straight to the first floor without taking a turn.

Further up the hill, at the top of a long flight of steps, past a restaurant that serves only snake dishes, there stands a fine brick mansion with an arched gateway, colonnaded balconies, floors of patterned tiles, and round Chinese windows. A high wall shelters it from the outside world. Once the home of a wealthy family, it was used as a 'comfort house' brothel for Japanese officers in the Second World War. Now, it is abandoned, the wallpaper is peeling, a bathtub stands in what was the dining room, graffiti surrounds the doorway, and the garden is a wilderness. A similar house, used by the Japanese for the same purpose for ordinary soldiers, has been demolished; all that remains is the retaining wall and the balustrade that bounded its grounds. Thus does Hong Kong treat its past.

This lack of concern was only to be expected of a population whose main priority was to establish itself, make a living and raise a family. There was little time to worry about the environment, about whether a colonial mansion should be preserved rather than being torn down for housing, or about the way new high-rise blocks blotted out the views of the mountains. If some old tenement buildings survive alongside new towers, it is often because ownership is fragmented between warring family clans or has simply been obscured amid waves of migration. Reclamation of the harbour has enabled the main business district and the container port facilities to expand, to the general well-being of the community as a whole. Several huge apartment blocks stand on what were oil depots, shipping terminals and power stations whose disappearance nobody can lament. The enormous shopping-hotel-office complex of Pacific Place was built on the former British military cantonment. I. M. Pei's Bank of China tower stands on what used to be the soldiers' Mess.

Traditions are not destroyed as easily as buildings. Chinese festivals are celebrated, temples kept up, and graves swept on the appointed dates. Models of jumbo jets, limousines, and houses with furniture and cardboard figures of maids are burned after funerals to accompany the departed to the next world. The clatter of mahjong tiles is one of the sounds of the place. Individual streets remain the home for certain trades, as they have done for a century or more: flowers in Mongkok, dried fish in Western, furniture on Queen's Road East.

Though an overwhelmingly Chinese city, Hong Kong has a vivid mix of other races which adds to its internationalism. Some are second and third generation – Eurasians, Indians, Pakistanis and Sri Lankans, Parsees, the Jewish community that came largely from Shanghai, and, older than any of those, the Scots and the English who sailed here for profit and to join in the opium trade in the mid-nineteenth century. Then there are more recent arrivals, from Japan, the Americas, Australia, New Zealand and Europe. And almost 150,000 serving maids, mainly from the Philippines.

Another sign of Hong Kong's internationalism is the range of food on offer. Chinese cuisine naturally predominates, but the dishes of the rest of Asia are readily available, not to mention American fast-food outlets, steak houses, sports bars and an English fish and chips establishment. On Hanoi Road in Tsim Sha Tsui, across from Hong Kong Island, a short stretch takes you past La Pasion de España Bodega, the Biergarten German pub and the Valentino Ristorante Italiano. The Trou Normand with its exposed brickwork and red and white striped tablecloths stands nearby at the corner of Carnarvon Road.

The prosperity on which all this rests is supposed to have been built on an economic policy of 'positive non-intervention'. Developed in the 1970s by a long-time Financial Secretary and Chief Secretary, Philip Haddon-Cave, it made Hong Kong the idol of free marketeers round the globe. Haddon-Cave, who disliked Chinese food and insisted on eating steak at banquets, earned the nickname of Choy Sun, God of Fortune. In fact, the non-interventionism has not been as simple or as all-embracing as its boosters like to proclaim.

The colonial administration pursued an active public housing policy, which was taken up in 1997 by the new Chief Executive with a pledge of 80,000 new units a year. Its ultimate ownership of land means that the government has always had its grip on a key element in Hong Kong's economy. The sale of most of that land to a small set of developers has given them a stranglehold, and untold wealth into the bargain. Far from opening up the market, the government's non-intervention precluded it from taking measures to break up the cartels that riddle the city. Interlopers are sent packing if they try to break cosy retail arrangements. When a freebooting entrepreneur tried to undercut the supermarket duopoly by direct home sales, some wholesalers simply refused to supply him with goods.

An entente among banks to avoid competition over mortgage rates will only be dismantled in 2002. A year later, controls on rice imports, introduced during the Korean War, will finally end. At the New Year of 2000, five of the six mobile telephone networks raised fees on the same day and by the same amount: pure coincidence, they insisted before cancelling the increases amid public anger and after the Director-General of Telecommunications had identified 'a tacit understanding among them'. Soon afterwards, it emerged that Hong Kong had the world's highest pre-tax petrol prices, which might not be unconnected with the way in which three companies own 80 per cent of the filling stations and charge the same rates.

But all this is done between consenting businessfolk and, for many abroad, the headline appeal of 15 per cent income tax seems to count for a lot more than the dominant power of a business establishment for which economic freedom often simply means the freedom to play the game by their own rules. As we will see, the year in question shows quite vividly how far the reality is from the image that wins Hong Kong awards as the world's freest economy.

This is just one of a set of contradictions that spring up at every corner, even setting politics and economics aside. A first-world city in many respects, the SAR has third-world population growth due largely to immigration: 89 per cent of the increase of 500,000 inhabitants since 1995 is due to the influx of mainlanders and to Hong Kong emigrants returning home. Though the birth rate is low, these factors are expected to push the population up to 8.9 million by 2016. The United Nations says Hong Kong is about to age rapidly, with the median age shooting up from the present 36.2 to 52.2 by the middle of the twenty-first century. At 78.5 years, life expectancy is high, and infant mortality among the lowest on earth.

How the ageing squares with the official vision of a bustling young city is an open question. But then age has never been an incentive to relinquish power and authority here. Just look at the serried ranks of tycoons in their seventies, or go to a lunch where the assembled company sits in silent deference to the old man at the head of the table.

The local food is good and healthy, but affluence has boosted meat consumption and medical problems. Western fast food is making big inroads. The cholesterol level among seven-year-olds is the second highest in the world. Almost a fifth of Hong Kong babies are overweight and 13 per cent of boys between six and eighteen are classed as obese. An expert estimates that 90 per cent of university students suffer from myopia, and that the proportion in the population as a whole is 50 to 60 per cent – double that in New York. Perhaps as a result of the demand resulting from the high incidence of weak eyesight, this is one of the cheapest places in the world to buy spectacles.

The position of women involves another of the many paradoxes of Hong Kong. Concubinage was abolished only in 1971. But there is a distinct tradition of what might be called open marriages Chinese-style. A landmark legal case in 1999 showed that SAR men had fathered scores of thousands of illegitimate children on the mainland. Back at home, the power of the matriarch remains strong inside many households, even if proper deference is paid to the menfolk in public. Daughters-in-law are traditionally kept at the bottom of the pile, patiently waiting their turn to lady it over their sons' wives one day. Despite the flashing female stars in retail, fashion and the charity round, business remains almost exclusively male-dominated. There are very few women at the top of companies, though the daughters of dead tycoons form discreet networks: the four daughters of the late shipping magnate Sir Y. K. Pao are married respectively to the chairman of a major conglomerate founded by their father, the head of his tanker company, a Japanese businessman, and the director of the government's policy unit who previously chaired the stock exchange.

On the other hand, the top levels of the administration show no shortage of women in high places, known, inevitably, as the 'handbag' brigade. Two years after Hong Kong rejoined China, the Chief Secretary for Administration, the Secretary for Justice, the Secretary for Security and the directors of education, health and trade were women. So was the President of the Legislative Council and three leading pro-democracy politicians, the head of the Urban Council, and four members of the Chief Executive's inner council, not to mention the Director of Broadcasting and the head of the powerful anti-corruption commission.

The physical surroundings are not all they may appear to the casual visitor. It is easy to get the impression that Hong Kong is just a place of concrete and glass, of soaring towers and crowded tenements, of often foul air and jostling crowds. Still, 40 per cent of the land area lies in twenty-one country parks. There are more than 200 outlying islands, mostly uninhabited. Mai Po marshes, up by the border with the mainland, are a major staging post for bird migration, with at least

325 species having been recorded in the 300 hectares of mangroves. The flora and fauna of both Hong Kong Island and the New Territories are exceptional. Householders on the Sai Kung peninsula find their birdcages raided by snakes, and there are quiet walks, tropical trees and temples hidden along narrow paths only a few hundred yards up the hill from the teeming streets of the Central District.

Just before writing this, I went on a four-hour hike with friends up steep slopes, along ridges and down to the sea opposite a suburb of the mainland city of Shenzhen. Across the water were garish pink towers and lines of cranes to unload containers; over the hills behind them loomed high-rise buildings. From the revolving restaurant on the top of one, you get a 180-degree vista of a classic modern urban landscape, followed by 180 degrees of empty countryside. The first is Shenzhen; the second the New Territories of Hong Kong. Not what you might expect if you spent all your time in the SAR amid the canyons of Central.

On that walk, the path led through small villages with old women straight out of a photograph of Imperial China. The rice paddies were overgrown with lush green vegetation. We could still make out the walls that once divided them, and the lines of agricultural terracing on the hillside. The mountains soared into the clouds. The butterflies were enormous. There were wandering water buffalo and packs of stray dogs. In one stream, we counted the crabs and the shrimps and the crayfish. By the sea, three men and a woman sat playing mahjong alongside an abandoned school, one room of which had been turned into a temple. At the top of a hill, graves and small mausoleums stood up from the long grass. In the whole four hours, we passed one Chinese walking group and a solitary Westerner.

. . . CHINA

The country across the heavily guarded frontier with Hong Kong has more than its share of superlatives and contradictions, too. This is the nation that considered itself the centre of the world for centuries, and whose first Communist leader was responsible for the deaths of more of his fellow citizens than any other ruler in history. The size of a continent and symbolised by the figure of the dragon, China is bounded in the west by the Himalayas and in the east by the seas of the Pacific. Stretching from steamy southern jungles to the frozen frontier with Russia, it is a country of mountains and deserts, rice paddies and soaring cities. Despite a long campaign of birth control and limiting urban families to a single child, its population of more than 1.2 billion rose by almost 12 million in 1998 alone, an increase equivalent to all the people of Belgium.

Although Beijing's time zone rules throughout its 3.7 million square miles, China is a collection of vast regions held together by a power structure that can often have only a hazy idea of what is going on in its domain. Immense distances and the backwardness of much of the countryside mean that, even in an age of air travel, many places are cut off from the rest of the nation – villages like Liuyi in southern Kunming province, where the women went on binding their feet a generation after the rest of the country had given up regarding a 7.5-centimetre-long 'Golden Lotus' foot as the epitome of desirability.

The tradition of paying obeisance to the emperor over the mountain, and then getting on with your business locally, is deeply entrenched. So is the often futile attempt by central governments over the millennia to pretend that their people are animated by devotion to the rulers in their palaces in the capital, be they dynastic tyrants or Leninist apparatchiks in business suits.

Half the nation which Hong Kong re-joined in 1997 is populated by people of different race, culture, traditions and religion from the dominant Han Chinese. On one side, Shanghai, with its soaring skyscrapers, the world's biggest trading floor and the highest per capita income in the country (equivalent to US$3,100 a year); on the other, the backward settlements of the interior, the laid-off factory workers with no jobs to go to, and the village in Anhui province where 60 per cent of the girls have moved to work as entertainers in the southern boom city of Shenzhen. On the eastern coast, get-rich-quick entrepreneurs hustle deals on mobile phones. Thousands of miles to the west, poachers roam roadless mountain plateaux where there is no water and the temperature falls to minus 45 degrees centigrade in winter.

This a country where the fiftieth anniversary of the Communist victory is marked by the execution of 200 people in one province alone, and where the livers of the dead are offered for sale to patients from Hong Kong for HK$300,000 (US$38,500) a time. Television stations transmit celebrity game shows and soap operas inspired by Hollywood while old women scour the banks of the Yangtze river for coal dropped from barges and children aged under ten sing for their supper at flashy restaurants. In Beijing, Cherie Booth and other British legal luminaries attend earnest seminars on spreading the rule of law, but down south in Guangdong province, a shop security manager armed with a kitchen knife hacks off four fingers from a woman accused of shoplifting a packet of ginseng – two of the fingers were later re-attached in hospital. The 'little emperor' sons of single-offspring families lord it in the cities, while in the countryside, children are kidnapped and sold as farm labourers. The new rich aspire to smart modernity as they crowd into techno clubs and sweeten their vintage claret with Sprite, while stolen cats are served at Beijing restaurants and the Handsome Wild Life Farming and

Development Park outside the tourist centre of Guilin fed live pigs and calves to tigers in front of spectators before killing the tigers to offer their meat and distilled 'restoration bone wine' to the visitors.

Outside the Han domain, Tibet and the Xinjiang region in the west cover 2.4 million square kilometres, or almost half the land mass of China. The province of Inner Mongolia has more goats than Australia has people. The repression of Tibet is one of those things that the world's leaders have decided they can do nothing about whatever the pressure from Hollywood stars and street demonstrators, the twinkling appeal of the Dalai Lama, the destruction of a traditional culture (including its serfdom and superstitions), the blatant abduction of the child who was to be divine and the decision of the third-highest-ranking spiritual leader to walk across the Himalayas in the depths of the winter to refuge in India at the age of fourteen. In Xinjiang, where the army keeps watch and Beijing tries to dilute the Muslim natives by shipping in Han Chinese, there are occasional ethnic riots, bombings and the execution of separatists.

All of which raises the question of what constitutes 'China' and 'the Chinese' – and where the new SAR of Hong Kong fits into it. Is China a purely geographical entity which has regained Hong Kong and Macau but still has to pine for Taiwan? In which case, what about the many millions of overseas Chinese who think of themselves as Children of the Yellow Emperor even if they live in Soho, Manchester or Vancouver? Are the Chinese a single people? If so, what about the Uigurs and Tibetans and all the other fifty-four minorities living from the frozen north to the sweaty border with Burma? Is it a culture bound by a single language? But, though China has a national written language, there are still a multitude of dominant dialects, the Cantonese who cannot understand the Beijingers, or the inhabitants of coastal towns who speak more easily with second-generation emigrants to Singapore than with their compatriots in Sichuan province. And if being Chinese means belonging to an ancient culture and society, what about the growing gulf between the Confucian tradition and the children of the computer age?

Faced with so many questions to which there are so few answers, it is not surprising if the believers in scientific socialism who hold the reins of political power fall back on dogmatic statements about national unity and lock up anybody who asks what it means to be Chinese today. But until such questions can at least be broached, the prospects of China unravelling must be all the greater as economic progress, social unrest and the Internet eat away at the glue of totalitarian nationalism.

The nationalist spirit is something that the powers in place play on at regular intervals in their desire to lead a reversal of the decline and shame which enveloped the country with the decay of the nineteenth century, the loss of Hong Kong and the Treaty Ports to rapacious Westerners, and the humiliation by the Japanese conquest of great swathes of territory. Four centuries ago, China was the biggest and most advanced nation on earth, with a finely developed bureaucracy and an intricate imperial system. But then the country that had invented silk, gunpowder, paper and porcelain fell steadily behind the fast-developing West and its eager pupils in Tokyo. Mao restored national pride at an unacceptable cost in lives; the next paramount leader, Deng Xiaoping, moved to the market with all the prestige of a Long March veteran. Now their successors have to maintain the country's status and self-belief while making it a big international player.

The debate about the scope of the mainland's progress in the past two decades remains open, particularly when comparisons are made with the advance of the economy and living standards in the United States. For all the leaps forward since Deng led the way to market, its problems are still as great as its achievements. Does that mean China is a 'theoretical power', as the late British commentator Gerald Segal put it, exercising diplomatic theatre to give an impression of strength that does not exist in reality? Despite 2.5 million men in uniform and the testing of neutron bombs and intercontinental missiles with minia-turised warheads, China's military power lags far behind the military might of the West. The heirs of the Middle Kingdom live in a sea of outdated dogma, nationalistic pretensions and doctored economic statistics. The question is whether this will always hold them back, as they cling on to power, or whether they can enable the country to make a decisive – and highly dangerous – move towards modernity, giving teeth to the warning delivered by an imperial minister to a

British envoy: 'You are all too anxious to awaken us and start us on a new road, and you will do it, but you will regret it for once awakened and started, we shall move faster and further than you think; much faster than you want.'

Such matters will be a key element in the rest of this book. The vital point as the new century begins is that, for the first time in its history, China is engaging with the world in politics, economics and other domains. The relationship is prickly, constantly thrown off course by Beijing's reluctance to give ground and by enduring, and often well-founded, suspicions about its motives. As we will see, conservatives in Beijing are anxious to slow down the process of entering the inter-national mainstream. But the dynamic unleashed by Deng Xiaoping in the late 1970s seems unstoppable, even if the speed of change has been considerably over-estimated by optimistic Western businessmen and politicians dazzled by the potential of this mystery wrapped in an enigma rendered unique by the sheer numbers involved.

At lunch in Beijing one day, the Education Minister spoke about her domain: a mere 230 million school pupils and university students, 10 million teachers and 1 million education establishments. China has the biggest army in the world, and a steel industry with 6,000 separate firms. The state employs 8 million civil servants. The Three Gorges Dam project along the Yangtze is the biggest development on earth, and the new boundaries of the city of Chongqing upstream on the river have turned it into the largest city on the planet, with 30 million inhabitants.

China faces environmental and natural problems on a massive scale. Eight of the ten most polluted cities in the world lie within its borders. Beijing is surrounded by 4,700 rubbish dumps. Hundreds of lakes in Qinghai province which feed the Yellow River have been reduced to caked mud with devastating effects on the country's second longest waterway, whose silt has traditionally provided land for crops along its course. In Tibet, glaciers have disappeared, leaving only boulders and pebbles. Parts of northern China are becoming danger-ously short of water in a country where 70 per cent of cereal output is from irrigated land. Elsewhere, flooding makes millions homeless most years, claims thousands of lives and causes damage running into billions of dollars. Mining in river beds and deforestation could well be adding significantly to the man-made disasters looming over a land where environmental concerns have taken second place to crude economic development.

On the human front, the number of migrants moving about in search of work is estimated at 100 million; about the same number are unemployed in rural areas; by coincidence, around 100 million Chinese are reckoned to suffer from hypertension. HIV victims are put at 1 million. China has as many smokers as all the people in Britain, Germany, France, Italy and Spain: unless abstinence spreads, 3 million are likely to die of tobacco-related illnesses each year by the middle of the twenty-first century.

China manufactures half the world's output of kettles, and is the fastest growing market for mobile telephones – the government expects 200 million to be in use by the year 2010. The Communist Party has as many members as there are inhabitants of France. Despite the atheist credentials of the regime, officially approved Protestant and Catholic churches count as many adherents as the population of Canada, and there are reckoned to be at least as many others who worship unofficially. By the middle of the twenty-first century, 440 million Chinese will be aged over sixty, and there will be 70 million young people without siblings as a result of the one-child policy. When the government ordered a campaign against crime in 1999, it was estimated that it would have to target no fewer than 7,000 underground gangs, some with as many as 30,000 members. An anti-prostitution drive two years earlier led to the arrest of a quarter of a million women.

The programme to reform state enterprises has no parallel in its scope and social implications. The share of the economy represented by the state sector has fallen to 42 per cent from 56 per cent when Deng Xiaoping's reforms began in the late 1970s. But there are still a multitude of mammoth enterprises which act more as sources of employment than as competitive enterprises. If they now have to shed their excess labour, will this mean another three million people out of work, or five million, or even more? What is to become of the one million workers being laid off by a single oil company? How will cities and towns which depended on the old state sector survive? No wonder that the 'remnant Maoists', as the old men are known, have been mounting a rearguard action, seeing mass unemployment as the greatest threat to the Communist Party's grip on power.

They could be right. After Mao won in 1949, the Chinese lived with an 'iron rice bowl' of cradle-to-grave protection guaranteeing food, accommodation, education, health care and other benefits. The food may have been of low quality, the housing in dormitories and the hospitals primitive. But the system was there, to be relied on in bad times. Now, the safety net is being taken down, and hundreds of millions fear the chill.

The scale of economic and social re-engineering surpasses anything else seen in the world since the initial revolution in China. The market reforms introduced by Deng under the banner of 'Socialism with Chinese characteristics' require formidable levels of growth to be maintained into the new millennium. Given the extent of the problems China accumulated for itself through the twentieth century, there can be no letting up. But even the most determined cyclist may run out of energy, lose control and hit a brick wall.

The reform drive has to deal with an economy whose main aim for half a century has been to maintain the public sector, whatever the price and however badly it was serving consumers. Official reports say that twenty years after Deng launched his changes in the late 1970s, subsidies to the state sector were still three times as big as its profits. When it announced China's largest stock market flotation at the end of 1999, a state oil firm disclosed that 70 per cent of the money to be raised would be used to pay off debts and fund lay-offs. At the other end of the industrial scale, seventy-nine of the eighty-one state enterprises in the county town of Fengje in Sichuan province were reckoned to be losing money. Excess capacity in factories may be as high as 60 per cent. A Western consultant tells of going to inspect a steel plant in the middle of China. He calculated that the plant could run with 2,000 workers. It had 15,000 and, through their families, supported 50,000 people in all.

China probably has some 50 million workers who are surplus to its requirements, not to mention hordes of local officials who are, at best, in make-work jobs. Once it was a factory's business to keep the

surrounding town in work, and to support the families of its employees as well, floating, if necessary, on a sea of state cash. Now, a new
logic prevails. Tens of millions of would-be workers move around the
country illegally, congregating at railway and bus stations in Shanghai,
Guangzhou, Beijing and scores of other cities. A report by the New
York-based organisation 'Human Rights in China' says that several
million are locked up each year in 700 detention centres, where conditions are filthy and inmates are physically abused: one man was
battered to death after he tried to bargain down the price of a cardboard box which the warders were selling him to sleep in.

Out in the vast rural spaces of China, where 60 per cent of the population still lives, often on unproductive soil and facing harsh climates,
the disparity with urban progress and the rich coastal regions is even
greater. The government in Beijing says 42 million people live on less
than 66 US cents a day while the latest estimate from the World Bank
put the number subsisting on under $1 a day at 106 million, or 11 per
cent of the population, at the end of 1998. Some 25 million women in
rural areas aged between fifteen and forty are illiterate. According to
one expert at an anti-poverty workshop in Beijing, more than 20 million people lack proper water supplies. In some areas, villagers pay the
equivalent of several dollars a month to live in caves.

Given the uncertainties of the present and future, it is not surprising that savings rates are astronomical, reaching an estimated US$720
billion in 1999. 'We have to keep as much money as possible for our
children's education, and in case we fall ill,' as a young and upwardly
mobile professional in Shanghai put it to me. Thanks to all that saving,
domestic demand is not as high as it should be to fuel the growth
China needs. The property boom on which so much was banked is
hollow. One of the first Dengist development zones, on the island of
Hainan, had 7 million square metres of empty space by the end
of 1999. In the showpiece city of Shanghai, 60 per cent of office
buildings in the new business district of Pudong are unoccupied,
together with 150 million square feet of residential accommodation.
Completion of what was to have been the world's tallest building, the
94-floor Shanghai World Financial Centre, has been delayed for at
least four years.

As factories close, disgruntled workers increasingly stage public protests at lay-offs and delayed wage payments. In Beijing at the end of 1999, dismissed staff shut down a department store by occupying the building for five days, something which would have been unthinkable a few years ago. Elsewhere, workers have blocked railway lines and roads, staged marches and held local officials hostage to show their discontent. In one case, farmers who had lost their money in failed government-backed investment funds were suspected of having removed the bolts on the track of the main north–south railway, derailing a train.

'Workers are no longer as docile as before,' President Jiang noted at an economic meeting, according to a source quoted by Willy Lo-Lap Lam of the *South China Morning Post*. 'In many cities, they barge into government offices, smash things up and paralyse the local administration . . . Should the disturbances recur, the party and state may be dealt a fatal blow.'

But a multitude of individual entrepreneurs still prosper. There is Nian Guangjiu, the melon-seed king, who experienced a switch-back of fortune and political persecution before building up a chain of ninety-six shops across the country; and Chen Jiashu, who produces badges in an eastern coastal town for US police forces, Lions clubs and Ghana's customs officers. Shen Qing is making a fortune marketing a patented baked pig's head. Zhang Ruimin, president of the German-sounding Haier household appliance group, has gone beyond his initial leap into the US and European markets in the 1990s by building a factory to turn out the company's goods in South Carolina. And then there is Liu Chuanzhi of Legend computers, the best-selling brand in Asia outside Japan, which more than trebled profits in 1998–99 as sales soared by 60 per cent in six months.

The new breed of businessmen look to a huge national market to replace the old system by which provinces produced and sold within their own boundaries, sheltering local industries from competition. They are penetrating the international market, too, and have no doubts about China's ability to become an economic superpower in the new millennium. 'The twentieth century was the American century, the twentieth-first will be ours,' a young entrepreneur told me as we left a crowded restaurant in Beijing where he had joked about police listening devices in the overhead lights. This is the new world in which China's central bank invests in the Long Term Capital hedge fund in the United States. The personal opportunities offered by the opening up of the economy provide the only reason to live with the antiquated political structure: following Deng Xiaoping's dictum, it is now officially glorious to become rich, and some have made the most of their positions to live up to his urgings.

Contacts – or *guanxi*, as they are known – are one of the keys to the Chinese way of doing business, built up and exploited by perfectly honest companies as well as by people on the make. Family connections are important, so it is not surprising to find the son of the President running a nascent telecommunications empire out of his father's power base of Shanghai, or the son of the former premier chairing a power company with an American listing. With parentage like that, they can attract investors and surf through the bureaucracy. There is nothing illegal in any of this; it is simply that the clout of having a powerful father counts for even more in the Chinese system than it does in the West (though nobody has suggested that Jiang Zemin's son might run for the office his father holds, Bush-style).

Corruption has been a tradition of Chinese life from the days of the emperors. It ran rampant under the Kuomintang, went into hiding during the early days of Communism and then reappeared, boosted by a two-tier price system under which officials could buy subsidised goods cheaply and sell them on at a profit. Now, graft has emerged as a major obstacle to the government's drive to reform industry and agriculture, and induces a weary cynicism throughout society. China as a whole is, indeed, getting a lot richer, but too much of the wealth is going to those who use their official or party status to fill their own pockets while hundreds of millions of the poor remain stuck at the bottom of an increasingly unforgiving social and economic system. The government is busy injecting money into backward provinces to try to spur growth, but it does little good if it ends up in the bank accounts of Communist cadres. The figures involved are staggering for a country that is still relatively poor.

Individual cases run into the equivalent of tens of millions of dollars.

Overall, audits of graft reach tens of billions. In Guangdong, across the frontier from Hong Kong, six officials from the state Bank of China used their position to conspire with the manager of a bowling alley to make the equivalent of US$150 million in a foreign exchange fraud. In the city of Wuhan, four people earned $165 million from a scam involving fake receipts for non-existent imported chemicals. A story in the Asian *Wall Street Journal* in 1999 quoted a report to the Prime Minister as estimating that enough money had disappeared in the grain sector alone to build a million schools, 10,000 factories or a second Three Gorges Dam.

Grain officials at one town in the north-east siphoned off the equivalent of US$5 million by faking 3,000 receipts for purchases that were never made. In central Shaanxi province, a manager of a grain warehouse embezzled US$3 million. In the spring of 1999, a Shanghai newspaper quoted government figures showing that shoddy public building projects cost the country the equivalent of US$11 billion a year, and that a fifth of those still standing do not meet state quality standards. A hundred thousand cases of corruption had been uncovered involving public projects, 63 per cent of them in construction.

Vice-Premier Li Lanqing calls the amount of money involved in graft 'shocking' and warns that 'the manner in which the violations occur is getting increasingly covert'. In Guangxi province alone, more than 400 officials were put under investigation in 1999, including a vice-chairman of the Chinese parliament, the former chairman of the provincial government and a police chief alleged to have received bribes worth some 10 million yuan (US$1.2 million). Nothing was sacred. The national auditor's office discovered that funds earmarked for flood-prevention measures had been misappropriated by officials, who set up a bank account, invested in property and shares, and converted a flood-monitoring centre into a hotel and commercial offices. Such is the endemic nature of corruption that when a 6,000-strong security force was formed to combat smuggling, watchdog units were installed to make sure that it was free of graft.

'Not fighting corruption would destroy the country; fighting it would destroy the party,' a Communist Party elder of the Maoist days, Chen Yun, remarked. The huge sums raked off by officials contrasts with the abysmally low salaries of most Chinese. What can the hundred million living on under US$1 a day think when a former vice-chairman of the Chinese parliament is found to have accepted US$5 million in bribes, or officials in coastal towns are accused of taking part in a smuggling ring that netted US$10 billion or more? Though some may dream of emulating the fast-money men riding in limousines and sipping claret, the very legitimacy of the all-embracing party is at stake as the government is forced to get to grips with the graft.

In the most spectacular case to date, the former Beijing mayor and party chief, Chen Xitong, was sentenced to sixteen years in jail in 1998 for corruption and dereliction of duty. The assumption is that he used the threat of disclosing embarrassing dirt to avoid the death penalty. Aged sixty-seven, he certainly looked unconcerned when the sentence was passed.

The mayor, who had played a role in the Tiananmen massacre, was once talked of as a possible national leader after rising under Deng Xiaoping. Some of Hong Kong's biggest property developers worked with him on their projects in the capital. Following an investigation led by a Communist Party graft-buster in her sixties, he was specifically accused of misappropriating twenty-two gifts worth the equivalent of US$60,000. His deputy, who died in a mysterious shooting incident, is said to have spent the equivalent of US$10 million on a house. A woman with whom Chen was involved fled to Hong Kong and the United States reportedly with US$40 million. Chen was also alleged to have conspired to use public funds for two luxury villas at which, according to the Chinese news agency, he enjoyed 'extravagant wining, dining and personal entertainment'. He also became the central figure in a book published at the time which did not mention him by name but was generally taken as an officially approved *roman à clef*. In the book, the central character is in love with his sister-in-law, a lion-tamer who appears in figure-hugging sequin costumes and puts her head into the mouths of the animals at the Municipal Circus: she eventually dies when a lion bites off her head after its senses were irritated by a chemical mixed into her hairspray by persons unknown.

If prominent mayors can be the target of attack, so can the once invulnerable police, who are listed by a popular verse as one of the 'seven vicious wolves' of China, alongside judges, prosecutors, state and local taxes, Triads and bar hostesses. At the end of 1999, the Minister of Public Security acknowledged that members of the 1.5 million-strong force were guilty of accepting bribes, abusing their power, negligence, illegal use of weapons, dereliction of duty, incompetence, protecting smugglers, drug-trafficking, torture, collusion with criminals, and corruption ranging from arbitrarily stopping cars and demanding money to involvement in major graft. He added that 3,000 officers had already been fired. In one city in Sichuan, 586 guns were confiscated from police who were 'subject to irritable temper and alcoholism'.

In such an atmosphere it is not surprising that get-rich-quick scams have proliferated. Fly-by-night finance outfits masquerading as officially approved companies offer depositors interest rates as high as 48 per cent and then go bust, or make off with the money. In one northern province, 10,000 people signed up for a short-lived scheme which promised payments of 100 yuan every five or ten days to investors who put up 300 yuan to enable a stuffed pancake company to use a 'new business practice imported from Japan'. At the end of 1999, three women were sentenced to death in coastal Zhejiang province for an illegal savings fund that netted 200 million yuan (US$24 million). More than 100 people were reported to have been sent to prison for such scams in the Yangtze city of Chongqing, some of them local officials. Bilked investors stage regular protests. In Chongqing, they blocked train lines and organised a 2,000-strong rally; the city government promised to arrange compensation. In eastern Henan province, a train conductor who tried to sue over a 900 million yuan scam was less lucky. He was locked up in a mental hospital and only freed after protests by fellow investors.

Enterprises are floated with little more motive than the desire of officials and their friends to get rich. Sales of state land offer big opportunities to siphon off cash. So does the flotation of companies like Tibet Holy Land. Its shares were 400 times oversubscribed, but the firm still ran into financial trouble after its scheme to make a smart new drink out of holy water from a spring beneath a mountain monastery went wrong. In the countryside, meanwhile some rural officials have taken to selling jobs in the bureaucracy to people who then exploit their new position to squeeze money out of locals.

Some of the money has gone abroad, or been recycled through banks in Hong Kong. One estimate puts the amount exported illegally from China in recent years at the equivalent of US$50 billion. After a large investment trust crashed in 1999 with a gap of US$2 billion between assets and liabilities, I asked a lawyer in China who follows such things where he thought the missing money had gone. He suggested that it would be interesting to trawl through the land registries in Southern California.

Up and down the country, rural credit establishments which were meant to fuel the growth of local enterprises are going out of business because of poor investments or fraud. The losers are the peasants who entrusted their money to such organisations. Managers of some state enterprises have also played fast and loose with pension funds, using them to cover their firms' losses or to speculate in shares and property. As a result, their retired workers have had to wait months for their pension payments – when they got them at all – provoking demonstrations that represent a further threat to President Jiang Zemin's dreams of social stability.

The extent of government concern about corruption is shown by the way stories about it now appear frequently in the press, such as the saga of the port city of Zhanjiang in Guangdong province. With the best deep-water harbour on China's southern coast and access to sugar and rubber crops, oil, coal and timber, Zhanjiang became one of the first fourteen mainland cities opened to foreign investment in the 1980s. Instead of turning into a boom industrial city, it grew into a honeypot for corruption and contraband. Local businessmen say virtually anything could be purchased at a discount through the government-backed rackets. 'They would come around and ask us what we needed,' one local manufacturer told Matthew Miller of the *South China Morning Post*. 'It was quite simple – you paid them and they provided fake invoices.' After raids in September 1998 involving thousands of police, more than sixty officials were arrested and found guilty, among them the former Communist Party secretary, the customs chief, the deputy mayor and leading members of the police. Six were sentenced to death. Apart from the illegality, corruption on such a scale shelters inefficient industries. When the bubble bursts, the effects are catastrophic. In Zhanjiang's heyday, its biggest company, a car firm called Three Stars Enterprises, assembled 25,000 vehicles a year. Visiting the city a year after the police raid, Miller reported that the factory, with its 3,000 workers, stood idle. So did the second-biggest state enterprise, an electrical appliance outfit.

Take any big project and you are likely to find at least a whiff of corruption in the air. 'To get rich, first make the holes,' as a comment on an Internet site in Guangdong put it. Or, in the official words of the Chinese news agency, Xinhua: 'A large number of projects, which should have gone through extensive processes of design, feasibility study, experts' studies and approval, were built purely because some senior bureaucrats had given their endorsement. This has opened the door of convenience to those cadres who have fallen because of their greed to deal with unscrupulous contractors.' The extent of poor work has given rise to a new phrase, 'tofu' constructions, as if they had been made of bean curd, such as a 72-kilometre highway in the south which gave way eighteen days after it was opened.

No project is as big as the Three Gorges Dam on the Yangtze, the pet scheme of the former Prime Minister Li Peng, who is pictured on cruise ships beaming as he observes the great walls of concrete going up on the river. The total cost will be more than US$55 billion, and anywhere from 1.5 to 2 million people will be moved as the waters rise to create a huge reservoir, flooding towns and cities and covering 30,000 hectares of agricultural land. Environmentalists worry about its effects, particularly a build-up of sediment on the river bed which will push up the water level and make flooding of the surrounding area more likely. Human-rights monitors say many local residents are being moved against their will.

Massive destruction of forests which used to absorb monsoon rainfall upstream of the dams has increased the danger of catastrophic flooding. The electricity generated from the project may not find the expected number of customers since provinces due to use its energy are building their own power stations. Even the tourists seem to be growing cool about the trip through the 100-metre-high gorges. When we made the voyage in 1998, the boat was full of people. Now, the ships are three-quarters empty. 'Tourists have concluded that the Three Gorges have already disappeared,' says the captain of the *Yangtze Angel* cruise boat.

But whatever the doubts, the project has been a godsend for some. The corporation running it has reported a 25 billion yuan (US$3 billion) shortfall, equivalent to one-third of the budget needed to complete the second phase, due for 2003. One report says that at least 232 million yuan (US$28 million) has been diverted from resettlement funds alone. The *Nanfang Weekly* recounted how a local office pocketed one-third of the funds allocated by Beijing for building road bridges. Contractors have used poor materials for dams, and paid the peasant workers half the stipulated amount. One builder had been constructing roads and bridges for thirty years, but had never been subject to any quality checks.

The bigger the job, the greater the take. So some officials simply enlarge projects under their control. Buildings have been erected on ground which could not properly support their weight. Investigations showed that seventeen out of twenty bridges in one area in Sichuan province had 'quality problems'; five were so dangerous that they had to be destroyed. Such scams arouse the particular anger of the Prime Minister, Zhu Rongji, who insisted in 1999 that officials must 'not divert funds to other uses'. He was a bit late, but his ire mounted as inspection trips uncovered more and more of what he called 'constructions made of beancurd and turtle eggs'. 'How can corruption reach such a stage?' he exclaimed on one trip. Another time, he sacked 100 officials on the spot.

This is typical of a man dubbed a fellow reformer by Tony Blair. Zhu himself says he is an 'ordinary Chinese with a bad temper'. His nickname in Hong Kong is 'iron face', and he can bear a distinct resemblance to the fierce and implacable gods of classic Chinese sculpture. He is said to have been the target of several assassination attempts.

Not known for his willingness to take prisoners, the Premier is a

man in a hurry. When he got the job in 1998, he vowed to surmount
'a multitude of minefields and 30,000 abysses' in his drive to reform
the economy and cut the 8-million-strong civil service in half. A
quip circulating in Beijing about Zhu and his predecessor, Li Peng,
says that 'one guy with middling intelligence has left the State
Council, to be succeeded by a smart madman'. How far the 'smart
madman' can go in reforming China will be a theme of the year of
1999, with deep implications not only for Hong Kong but also for the
mainland's whole relationship with the rest of the world.

Born in Hunan province in 1928, Zhu had a hard childhood: his
father died before he was born and his mother when he was nine. She
was buried under a simple heap of soil – in keeping with his austere
image, Zhu has given orders that the family graves are not to be
adorned in any special fashion. Married in 1956, he was purged
during the Cultural Revolution as a rightist and reduced to menial
work. Rehabilitated, he became a key lieutenant to Jiang Zemin
when the future President was Mayor of Shanghai. Zhu then became
mayor himself before being called to Beijing to squelch China's gal-
loping inflation. Gaining the sobriquet of 'economic tsar', he prepared
a massive programme to carry on Deng's crusade, and was the obvious candidate to succeed Li Peng as head of the government, though
he has still not been able to rout critics who hanker for the Maoist
ways.

Hong Kong's Chief Executive likens a session with the Prime
Minister to a manager meeting his sharp-eyed, no-nonsense company
chairman who has the accounts open in front of him and will pick up
on any weakness. The reformist, market-minded character of Zhu's
economic policies has done nothing to diminish his orthodoxy in
other domains. He is the embodiment of the regime's insistence that
economics and politics can be kept apart and, understandably, hates to
be described as China's Gorbachev.

To make reform meaningful and produce a more level playing
field, Zhu and Jiang have had to attack one of the sacred elements of
the system – the People's Liberation Army (PLA) and its involvement
in industry and business. Ranking just below the Communist Party at
the historic pinnacle of the regime, the military–commercial complex

was reckoned to stretch over 50,000 companies with earnings of more than US$5 billion. One major enterprise, China Poly, built up more than 100 subsidiaries. The PLA's General Political Department bought an Australian mining firm as well as companies listed in Hong Kong and Toronto. The Logistics Department runs a big pharmaceutical enterprise, and the Staff Department is into electronics and telecommunications.

As a sop for their drive to take the army out of business, Jiang and Zhu boosted the military budget to ensure the loyalty of officers who claim the heritage of the Long March and the victory of 1949 – and their sons: China Poly is headed by the offspring of a revolutionary elder. The President, in particular, went out of his way to listen to the generals, to safeguard their powers and privileges, and to sing the PLA's praises. Dealing with the army was also vital to Zhu's drive against corruption and smuggling. Army officers had grown accustomed to using their position to cover part of China's vast contraband network, which is estimated to have been costing the central government as much as US$32 billion a year in customs revenue, taking in everything from tobacco and drinks, food oil and machinery to Viagra and pornography, not to mention human cargo shipped out in containers for a new life in North America or Australia.

Apart from getting the army to clean up its act, the campaign is confronting some of China's toughest nuts. In the port of Leizhou, a local gang thought nothing of shooting policemen and attacking customs officers; finally, more than a thousand security men had to be sent in to arrest the underworld bosses, three of whom were executed. Pirates regularly board ships and kill the crews before smuggling the cargoes. In one attack in 1998, they beat the twenty-three sailors on a Hong Kong-owned ship to death one by one and threw the bodies into the sea off the Shanghai coast. Less lethally, pirates stole a couple of cars in Taiwan in 1999 and smuggled them across the Strait, complete with the sleeping drivers, who were so drunk that they didn't know what was happening until they came round on the mainland.

Cracking down on corruption and smuggling is essential if China is to regain its lure as the last great business frontier for Western companies. The statistics of the past two decades are impressive enough, with 324,000 foreign-investment projects that will involve a total of US$572 billion if they are all completed. But few businessmen now share the starry-eyed vision of the late chairman of Coca-Cola of the profits to be made from putting a drinks can into the hands of everybody in China. For much of the 1990s, foreign investment rose by 40 per cent or more a year. In 1993, it almost tripled as China accounted for nearly half of all foreign investment in developing countries. But in 1999, the inflow of funds began to fall.

The question being asked in boardrooms in New York, Tokyo, London and Paris is very simple: where are the returns and when are they going to start showing up? The turn of the century saw a frenzied rush for China-related Internet companies. But for more mundane goods, there are even cheaper manufacturing centres than China these days: for really cut-price labour go to Cambodia. The low level of domestic spending on the mainland, the rudimentary distribution system, and mentalities bred by decades during which production took precedence over the wishes of consumers mean that the market is still something of a mirage for many searchers after the Chinese holy grail. A study by City University in Hong Kong has found that while new private Chinese companies had a return on equity of 19 per cent, foreign firms were making just a sixth of that. The consultants A. T. Kearney report that only 41 per cent of firms which have invested in China say they are showing a profit, and that about a quarter of multinationals are pulling out of at least one mainland venture.

After the collapse of the big Gitic investment trust in Guangdong province in 1999, foreign bankers have become all too aware of the dangers involved in pumping money into Chinese companies, even if the state body they wrongly thought was acting as a guarantor rejoiced in the acronym of SAFE – the State Administration of Foreign Exchange. To add to the worries, the huge state banking sector is awash with debts after decades of being used to keep public sector enterprises afloat. A junior banker from Fujian province was singled out in 1999 as the 'national model of the financial system' because there had not been a single default on any of more than 3,000 loans he approved in an eighteen-year career. But Moody's Investment

Services estimates that bad loans issued by less rigorous managers could amount to a trillion yuan, or US$120 billion, equal to the mainland's entire fiscal revenue for 1998.

For optimists, the conversion to market economics and growing internationalism will produce a new China. Despite the backwardness of vast regions, there is no doubt of the enormous social progress in the last decade; or of the earlier advances in education, health, welfare and the equality of women. Despite the oppressive political rule of the Communist Party, most individuals are now far freer in their everyday lives than they have been for four decades. For many Western businessmen investing in China, the stability provided by one-party rule is greatly preferable to the uncertainties of democracy. On such a view, modernity will sweep the country along with it, a new generation of leaders will shake off the heritage of Mao, a thousand efficient factories will bloom, Taiwan and the mainland will co-exist, and the world will acquire a new major partner to balance the power of the United States in a positive manner.

Pessimists see a paranoid, self-centred state which will not give up an inch of its internal power, a government intent on exerting its authority over free and democratic Taiwan, a regime incapable of real evolution. As for the economy, consider two sets of statistics: official annual growth is put at 7 to 8 per cent, but electricity consumption, a good gauge of economic expansion, is only rising by 2 per cent. And with three-quarters of state firms surveyed in 1999 admitting to falsifying their figures, who can believe in the statistics in any case? As one banker remarked: 'It's the last great illusion.' But great illusions live by their own logic, and China's logic is all its own. So, welcome to China and its administrative region of Hong Kong, and to the concept of one country, two systems.

ONE COUNTRY, TWO SYSTEMS

A t the stroke of midnight on 30 June 1997, China regained sovereignty over the mountainous island of Hong Kong, the bigger area of Kowloon and the New Territories, and the 235 outlying islands scattered round one of the world's finest harbours. The Chinese national flag was raised at midnight, and the soldiers of the People's Liberation Army rolled into Hong Kong standing ramrod stiff in the rain on the back of their trucks. But life went on as usual the next morning in the new Special Administrative Region of the People's Republic of China as Deng Xiaoping's formula of one country, two systems was put to the test.

The soldiers were quickly hidden away in their barracks. Democratic critics of Beijing climbed to the balcony of the Legislative Council building in the early hours to make defiant speeches for the crowd below and the television cameras of the world. The President and Prime Minister of China came and sat on the platform at the ceremonies. The Prince of Wales sailed off into the humid night with the last Governor on the Royal Yacht. And, up the road through the New Territories, past the paddy fields abandoned by owners who make more from leasing them out as container dumps, the border remained as closely guarded as ever. But still the illegal immigrants kept heading for the mecca of Hong Kong, following a pattern which gave a special irony to the decolonisation.

Most inhabitants of the new SAR are of refugee stock. The country which they, or their parents, fled was China, particularly after the Communist victory of 1949. Some came legally; others were smuggled in by land or sea, or swam across to the New Territories. More recently, Hong Kong has taken in 150 mainlanders a day. Families from China have dominated Hong Kong for years. Many come from Shanghai, Asia's most international city in the days of the defeated Kuomintang: textile tycoons who brought their machinery with them, shipping magnates like the Chief Executive's father, film producers and entrepreneurs by the thousand. Before the handover, all but one of the four serious candidates for the post of Hong Kong's first Chief Executive traced their roots back to the city which loomed as an eventual rival to Hong Kong.

Other refugees came from Fujian up the coast, or from the neighbouring southern province of Guangdong whose dialect is the territory's principal tongue. Fleeing China did not mean rejecting mainland roots. Apart from Cantonese, some dialects from across the border still enjoy more currency in the SAR than the official mainland language of Putonghua. There are mutual aid organisations for those from the different provinces. Restaurants offer the cuisine of all parts of China; only the traditional food of the original Hakka inhabitants of Hong Kong, with its salt-baked chicken and marinated fatty pork, is hard to find.

The feelings of this essentially refugee population about returning to the sovereignty of the country which they or their parents fled have been more mixed than the patriots would like to pretend, even if the term 'reunification' has come increasingly into official vogue. There was a notable absence of rancour towards the colonialists who were leaving after 156 years, or of any great rush to follow the Chief Executive's exhortation to become more Chinese. True, a few commentators and a couple of politicians did play the anti-colonial card, and some of those who had gratefully accepted knighthoods stopped calling themselves 'Sir'. Memories of the opium trade and the construction of great Scottish and English fortunes were evoked repeatedly in the more mainland-minded media at the time of the handover. Beijing suspected that lucrative contracts had been given to

British firms in order to sluice money out of the territory, though there proved to be no foundation to rumours of a submarine hidden in a secret dock beneath the Hong Kong and Shanghai Bank, ready to spirit away its wealth to London at midnight on 30 June. And yes, over the decades, Hong Kong had served as an easy source of enrichment for second-raters from the colonial power immortalised in the acronym FILTH – Failed In London, Try Hong Kong.

But although the British influence never reached deeply into the lives of the mass of the population, too many members of the territory's establishment had ties with the former sovereign power for the usual end-of-empire sentiments to take much hold outside old leftist circles. The movers and shakers of Hong Kong have homes in London, children at public schools, links with the City, horses running at Ascot. Lower down the social scale, however badly the British had behaved towards the Chinese earlier in the century, the freedom to live as one wished meant that there was little reason for resentment. It wasn't even as if the departing power had converted most of the people of Hong Kong to speaking its language, the low level of English fluency being a constant source of surprise to visitors and concern to the administration and internationally minded businesses.

In a display of political correctness before the handover, officials referred to Hong Kong as a 'territory' rather than a colony. One seasoned British official says this was not so much out of respect for the colonised natives as to avoid antagonising Beijing, which did not wish to be reminded that part of China was still held by European imperialists. What used to be the Royal Hong Kong Golf Club has dropped the adjective. The flag is no longer hoisted at dawn at the Cenotaph in Central, built as a replica of the memorial in Whitehall, nor does the government arrange a Remembrance Day ceremony there.

Still, the relics of the past are all around. A leading hotel has kept its Churchill Room. A large portrait of the Queen and Prince Philip in ceremonial dress hangs in the Windsor Room of the Hong Kong Club. The table mats in the dining room at the Chief Executive's offices during the handover showed English hunting scenes. An elderly radio presenter called Ralph Pixton continued to run a Sunday phone-in show redolent of the Light Programme of the 1940s. The official residence of the Chief Secretary of the Special Administrative Region is still called Victoria House. Ladies in white hats enjoy games of bowls at their club in Kowloon; the police band in Macintosh tartan plays traditional British tunes at national day ceremonies, and you can post letters in boxes with the royal crest (even if the paint has been changed from red to green or purple). At the military head-quarters building, the metal lettering of the name on the cream tower has been removed, but the words – The Prince of Wales Building – can clearly be read from indentations in the concrete as if carved there for perpetuity.

Anglican services are celebrated in the Gothic-revival Cathedral of St John's. The quiet residential streets of the Kowloon Tong district still bear the names of English counties; in the Central district there is a street called Lambeth Walk. The new office complex in which I used to work has towers with the names of Dorset, Somerset, Devon, Warwick and Lincoln. In a nearby club, old *Punch* covers hang in the men's lavatory. A British company, Stagecoach, runs many of Hong Kong's buses. The underground rolling stock is from Cammell Laird. The Hongkong and Shanghai Banking Corporation and Standard Chartered Bank, both with their ultimate headquarters in London, issue banknotes for the SAR as they did for the colony. And when it comes to the world game, Manchester United are the most popular team, drawing a capacity crowd in high summer heat in 1999.

For individuals, adopted English names persist, though some would raise eyebrows in London. The head waiter at the Hong Kong Club is called Paprika. Two women flight attendants on a trip to Shanghai had name badges telling passengers they were Keith and Aegean. Then there are Fruit the film director, Garidge and Diesel the pho-tographers, Starboard the yachtsman, Charcoal the businessman and Garment and Echo the television executives. One of the two public statues on Hong Kong Island is of Queen Victoria, in a park which still carries her name. At the fashionable China Club, the telephone in the library is an old British apparatus in black Bakelite, its dial engraved with 'Emergency Calls for Fire Police Ambulance Dial 999' and the number Barnet 8235. Two of the senior officials shaping the government's legal policies are British, and one of them found himself acting as Solicitor-General when the administration failed to come up with a local candidate for the job. Most High Court cases are still heard in English before judges wearing horsehair wigs.

The colonial era was not democratic until the last gasp of Chris Patten's opening-up of the electoral franchise. But British rule was generally benign in its later days, particularly compared with what was going on across the border. As the Queen's portrait was taken down at the Central Post Office, few people could remember the days when Chinese had not been allowed to live on the heights of the Peak, when a magnate bequeathed money to a hospital on condition that it would not treat Chinese patients, or when senior civil servants could not take local wives.

The key difference from other colonies from which Britain withdrew was that Hong Kong did not move to independence. Instead, London handed it over to the sovereignty of another nation. Indeed, it can be argued that what happened on 1 July is best seen as a transfer of colonialism with the old system of government that had pertained before Patten's reforms. In that scenario, the Chief Executive of the SAR became the heir of the pre-Patten Governor, with institutions like his Executive Council, the civil service and the legislature carried on intact from one era to another and a business elite calling the shots when it mattered. The provisional legislature sworn in to replace the elected body of late Patten days echoed the era when the Governor appointed legislators. The difference is that before 1997, the man in charge had been the emissary of a liberal democracy ultimately responsible to the House of Commons; now, the line runs to the Communist rulers in Beijing.

Nobody could pretend that the choice of Tung Chee-hwa as Chief Executive in 1997 was a matter of popular consultation. If they had had a free choice, the people of Hong Kong would almost certainly have picked Anson Chan Fang On-sang, the first local Chief Secretary appointed by Patten to head the civil service. But that was not to be, as Tung moved smoothly to centre stage, resigning from the Governor's Executive Council and hewing to the party line on any controversial issues. When one criticised the extremely restricted nature of the selection committee that chose Tung to rule Hong Kong, the response was that at least they numbered 400 and were from Hong Kong. Critics of the Patten reforms rarely miss an opportunity to point out that Britain had left it till the very last moment to introduce democracy, and had been unable to do anything to ensure its preservation. At one point, Margaret Thatcher had wondered wistfully if Hong Kong could, indeed, be given its freedom when Britain's treaties or ownership expired in 1997. But China would never have agreed, and would British troops have been deployed to hold back the PLA? Not a chance, as was brought home forcefully in 1996 when the American fleet sailed through the Taiwan Strait after China staged war games to try to intimidate the breakaway island. Who could imagine *Ark Royal* dropping anchor in the harbour to defend Hong Kong?

Power politics aside, there was the simple fact that the territory depended on the mainland for its water and most of its food. The contents of the beautiful Plover Cove reservoir in the New Territories come from over the border – 770 million cubic metres a year compared to 280 million cubic metres collected from rainfall. Economically, the link has been with China since Deng launched the move to the market in the south. Hong Kong companies have signed some 180,000 investment contracts in the mainland amounting to the equivalent of US$15 billion, most of it in the Pearl River Delta, where they are now reckoned to employ about three million people. Property companies from the SAR have put up towering office and accommodation blocks in Beijing and Shanghai. One of the big conglomerates set out to turn the city of Wuhan into 'China's Chicago'. Others constructed mainland expressways and shopping malls. Tycoons went back to their native towns and villages and spread the manna of capitalism in the form of hospitals and schools. SAR residents make 40 million trips across the frontier each year. Some 50,000 vehicles will cross each day by the year 2005.

At the same time, the Hong Kong establishment did not wait for the handover to move closer and closer politically to the mainland. The British could no longer offer anything, and one country, two systems covered the disparity between Hong Kong's capitalism and the creed still professed up north. If the date for change had not been fixed, there might have been more equivocation. But 1 July was set, and, since Beijing would be in the driving seat, it was clearly advantageous to board its vehicle. Soon after arriving in the territory in 1995, I naïvely asked a local businessman one evening on his corporate boat how he thought Britain was handling the change of sovereignty. 'But it is us and Beijing who are handling the handover,' he replied with a smile.

If few people actively disliked the departing colonial power, there was no definable 'pro-British' sentiment. Nor did independence figure high in the polls. Even the most died-in-the-wool democratic opponents of Beijing could not deny that they were Chinese. What mattered was what you meant by that description: could a line be drawn between belonging to the Chinese race and counting yourself a subject of the Leninist Yellow Emperors in Beijing? In all the celebration of the preservation of the Hong Kong system it was easy to forget about the first two words of the formula – one country – but nobody who knew how the People's Republic functioned could doubt that the new sovereign power would give them precedence.

Opinion polls in 1997 showed a high degree of anxiety about how Beijing would act. There was little of the popular exuberance that accompanied the end of colonialism in Africa. For all the official rejoicing, the SAR has no Reunification Square or Motherland Avenue. Rather, there was a general recognition in the public that a historic turning point had been reached, a tentative welcome at re-joining the Chinese nation, but also an insistence that Hong Kong must remain Hong Kong, and a corresponding concern about the behaviour of the new sovereign and whether the Tung government would stand up for its citizens. Such concerns had fuelled a rush for foreign nationalities and passports after Britain imposed strict immigration restrictions on Hong Kong people. For many, however, acquiring a passport was an insurance policy, not a final decision to live in Canada, Australia or the USA. Though some made the move permanent, many others went for long enough to qualify for passports, and then returned.

The worry about what Beijing would do had been a significant factor in the emergence of the Democratic Party as the main political force after the Tiananmen Square massacre of 1989. Equally, its main rival, the Democratic Alliance for the Betterment of Hong Kong (DAB), suffered from being seen as a 'pro-Beijing' movement. To vote Democrat was also to vote for Hong Kong's separate identity, epitomised by the way people tend to describe themselves. Opinion surveys carried out in 1999 by an academic group called the Hong Kong Transition Project showed that 46 per cent regarded themselves as 'Hong Kong people', 27 per cent as 'Hong Kong Chinese' and 21 per cent simply as 'Chinese'. In another poll among 6,500 students, those who regarded themselves as being purely Hong Kongers outnumbered those who saw themselves as solely Chinese by nearly three to one.

Just as the government in Beijing describes the mainland's hybrid state-market economy as 'socialism with Chinese characteristics', so the best description of the inhabitants of Hong Kong may be 'Chinese with Hong Kong characteristics'. Those characteristics enjoy the underpinning of the agreement reached in 1984 between China and Britain, known as the Joint Declaration, and of the Basic Law which acts as Hong Kong's constitution. There is to be a fifty-year span in which the concept of one country, two systems will prevail, with Beijing taking charge of foreign and military affairs but otherwise leaving Hong Kong with its way of life basically intact. This gives the Special Administrative Region of the People's Republic of China a degree of autonomy unknown anywhere else in the world.

Which other region of a unitary state has its own constitution, central bank, legal code, tax system and civil service structure? Or a currency pegged to that of another country, and note-issuing banks with their group headquarters on the other side of the world? In which other region do you have to dial an international code to telephone the capital? Where else does only 1 per cent of the population use the national language as its usual means of expression, and where else would a poll show 90 per cent of teachers against the idea of conducting lessons in the national tongue?

Over the border, you cannot move about legally without a permit, let alone travel abroad; in Hong Kong, you go to the airport and fly wherever you like. There, the currency is not convertible; here, you dial instructions to your bank to move your money into US dollars, euros or whatever. There, the stock market is in its highly volatile infancy and the banking system opaque; here is a world-class, largely transparent financial structure. On the mainland, corruption has been a way of life as a means of supplementing low official salaries; in Hong Kong, civil servants are among the highest paid on earth and investigators of the anti-corruption body haul in eminent suspects at will. In the rest of China, freedom of political expression is severely limited; here you can say what you want. On the mainland, any airing of the Taiwanese government's point of view is taboo; in Hong Kong, the idea of a ban on such views attracts only 20 per cent support. The Beijing government has an awful human rights record; despite criticism from a United Nations hearing in 1999, a poll in the SAR showed that 94 per cent of people thought human rights were being respected.

The mainland lives with a heavy burden of history; in Hong Kong, Tiananmen apart, there is little feeling of the past, no legacy of emperors, civil war, the Communist victory, the Great Leap Forward, famine, the Cultural Revolution or the Gang of Four. And as for the instant history providers of the media, on the mainland they are part of the political apparatus run by the state and the Communist Party; in Hong Kong, most are commercially driven. There, the media hail the patriotism of the army in 1989; here, newspapers run huge front-page photographs of the Hong Kong vigil to commemorate the dead of 4 June. There independent media politics are still taboo; here a lead letter in the main English-language daily declares: 'The Chinese Communist Party is a failure. It has lasted fifty years only through dictatorial rule, employing tactics of terror, secrecy, suppression and fear.'

In China, tiny groups of dissidents are subject to persecution and long prison terms: the authorities say 2,000 people are locked up for subversion but human rights groups put the number at 10,000. In Hong Kong, anti-government demonstrations are a regular occurrence, and democrats attack the regime in the Legislative Council rather than in jail. On the mainland, the parliament is a one-party body; here, despite large imperfections in the electoral system, anti-government candidates won most of the popularly elected seats at the first post-handover poll. On the mainland, the Communist

Party rules; here the Chief Executive cannot even count on a pro-government party, while the Communists have no official status and are run by a secret cell in a liaison office. For China, the idea of an independent judiciary is strange and foreign. In Hong Kong, it is central. On the mainland, freedom of worship is strictly controlled, and the government insists that the ordination of Catholic bishops is a matter for the Patriotic Catholics' Association, in which the Vatican has no say. In Hong Kong, religions of all kinds flourish. The Financial Secretary and several senior government colleagues are Catholics, as is the leading opposition figure.

In the summer of 1999, the mainland authorities banned a mystic, deep-breathing sect which claims 70 million members in China; in Hong Kong, local practitioners sat freely in the lotus position outside the Chinese news agency in protest. Across the border, urban couples were for years only allowed to have one child; here you can have as many offspring as you wish. In China, despite the lessening of state control in recent years, everything from possession of satellite dishes to the permitted size of dogs is subject to official restrictions. Even the weather reports were doctored to pretend that the heat never rose above 37 degrees. In Hong Kong, the administration cannot even clamp down on illegal smoky exhausts, and regularly loses in court when it tries to impose laws against spitting.

All this is summed up in the concept of one country, two systems launched by Deng Xiaoping as the panacea for the intractable problem of how to recover Hong Kong without undermining its success, which would add so much to China's wealth. The concept was both a recognition of reality and a bargain. Hong Kong would be left to pursue its internationalist, capitalist ways, but at the same time, it would become part of China, and so must not threaten the system on the mainland, in particular the primacy of the Communist apparatus. In one place, freedom was to go on as before; in the other, an autocratic, outmoded power structure was to be preserved based on a mix of oppression and economic opportunity.

Then politics raised its head. This was most troublesome, for Deng had decreed that Hong Kong was an economic, not a political, city. But the demonstration and ensuing massacre at Tiananmen Square changed Hong Kong for ever. A fifth of the population took to the streets in support of the protest. Large amounts of money were raised. Tents and aid flowed north to give fresh resources to the students. After the killings, Hong Kong became a key staging post for dissidents smuggled out of the mainland.

What 4 June 1989 brought was the chilling realisation that eight years, three weeks and five days later, Hong Kong would become part of the country whose leaders had called in the army against their own citizens for daring to challenge their power. But the handover clock could not be stopped. Nobody in London was going to go back on the Joint Declaration. Just two years after the killings, Britain's Prime Minister was the first Western visitor to go to Beijing since the massacre, shaking hands with the Chinese as he signed an agreement on Hong Kong's new airport and inspected an honour guard of the army that had crushed the demonstrators.

One man came to symbolise Tiananmen. Of stocky build, he has thick black hair, heavy dark spectacles and a signal lack of charisma. Li Peng, Prime Minister of the People's Republic until 1998, was generally believed to have been the man who executed Deng Xiaoping's orders to suppress the 1989 protest. That made him a hate figure among Hong Kong democrats. The feeling was mutual. Li Peng made his first visit to Hong Kong for the handover. While he sat in the shiny new Convention Centre on the waterfront, shouting demonstrators outside waved banners denouncing 'the Butcher of Tiananmen'. But the Premier heard nothing, thanks to a policeman called Dick Lee, and a pragmatic decision he made that night.

A history graduate, Lee spoke twice to Jonathan Dimbleby for his book on the Patten years, *The Last Governor*. In 1992, he said that after the handover, 'we are afraid that we will be ordered to do things that we don't want to do'. He added that he would 'stand up and say no'. Four years later, he defined his job as 'enforcing the laws of Hong Kong. Whatever the law says, we carry out.' Even if the law was unjust? 'If the new government changes the law, then the police have to enforce it.' As 30 June turned into 1 July the Deputy Commissioner responsible for Security Affairs had a problem not with unjust laws but with a matter of immediate practicality.

The protestors in the street were within their rights, but if Li Peng heard them he might take umbrage, which would not be the best birth gift for the SAR. So Lee decided that loud music should be played to alleviate the strain for his men of watching over the protest. What better than a spot of Beethoven? As the protest chants rose, the Fifth Symphony came over the loudspeakers at high volume, drowning out their noise. Questioned about the incident later, Lee got into a spot of trouble for insisting on his cultural cover story. A document showing his real motivation came to light, and he was criticised for not telling the truth. Some thought this bore out Dimbleby's fears of back-sliding. For myself, I saw it as a pretty good example of the way Hong Kong can square the circle.

In 1997, such pragmatism seemed to ensure that everything would sail along in the SAR more smoothly than anybody had the right to expect. But nothing can be set in stone, particularly not in a place as exposed to the currents of the world as Hong Kong. Those who had forecast trouble after 1 July had concentrated on politics, freedom of expression and media. There were scary predictions of tanks in the streets, democrats under house arrest, censors in newspaper offices. But the first challenge came from a very different direction, when the East Asian economic crisis broke, starting with the devaluation of the currency in Thailand. At first, Hong Kong showed remarkable insouciance. As the crisis toppled currencies and economies throughout South-East Asia, the Financial Secretary even advised that it was time to start buying shares, and thought that a crash on Wall Street might help the SAR by sending funds in its direction.

Ignoring his advice, the market plunged. So did property prices, with all that entailed. As 1998 drew on, the golden goose of Hong Kong turned into a squawking turkey. A sure-fire bet for speculators was to take a short position in the market by betting on a fall and contracting to buy shares at a future date below their prevailing price. Then sell large amounts of Hong Kong dollars. Given the currency peg, this automatically forces up interest rates. That drags down share prices. So all you have to do is to clean up on your short positions, and you're in the money. It was done time and again in the summer of 1998, not just by cowboy outfits but by well-established international banks. Officials feared that the index could be brought down to a third of its existing value. To prevent that, Joseph Yam, the head of the Monetary Authority, Hong Kong's *de facto* central bank, proposed going into the market. It was something he had been thinking of since huge rises in overnight interest rates at the start of the Asian crisis showed how vulnerable Hong Kong could be to outside pressure. Yam worked on the plan for two weeks with Donald Tsang, the Financial Secretary. It was presented to the Chief Executive, who gave the go-ahead. A trial run was done with trusted brokers. The next day the government of free-market Hong Kong plunged in massively to buy leading stocks, followed by some overdue tightening of regulations a little later. The index shot up, the speculators were defeated, and the world was left wondering what had happened to Hong Kong's hallowed non-interventionist principles.

It was hardly what Deng, who died four months before China regained Hong Kong, had been expecting from the freewheeling capitalist icon that was meant to be a model for China's march to market economics. But after a pause following the handover, the course of events in the SAR had begun to take on its own momentum, played out against the imposing backdrop of China's meeting with the world and the mainland's engagement with the greatest economic and social challenge on earth. The two processes – Hong Kong and China, China and the world – are symbiotically linked. The SAR is both a part of the emerging nation to the north, and its bridge to the rest of the planet, as well as being a vital place which has to retain its own identity as a region of a monolithic power preaching an outdated political ideology that runs counter to everything that has made Hong Kong what it is. How one of the world's most extraordinary places deals with its vast dragon sovereign in the last year of the century says much about how men and women, institutions and society react when they become a testing ground for a unique experiment.

JANUARY

1–14 January

Eighteen months after Hong Kong returned to Chinese sovereignty, the wife of the chairman of one of the old British companies, the Swire Group, fires the traditional midnight gun in Causeway Bay to welcome in 1999. It is as if nothing had changed in 1997. Immediately afterwards, the other great colonial hong, Jardine's, holds its New Year party in the penthouse of its headquarters overlooking the harbour, with the host attired in a clan tartan kilt. It may be New Year but, this being Hong Kong, business is never too far away. At the Jardine's party, the boss of a big financial group comes up to ask me about the prospects of one of his clients buying into the *South China Morning Post*, the newspaper I edit.

Three babies are born on the stroke of midnight. There is a 600-metre swimming race on the south side of the island, and thousands gather in Victoria Park for a 'Family Fun Carnival'. The ballroom of the Grand Hyatt Hotel is turned into Camelot, with papier-mâché medieval décor, attendants in armour and champagne to wash down the caviar and lobster.

A New Year opinion poll reports that the number of people who are pessimistic about the future has fallen to 34.6 per cent from 42 per cent a year ago. Still, concern about the economy remains strong amid continuing recession. On the radio, the Chief Executive advises the unemployed to take jobs even if it means accepting a wage cut. 'My own experience shows the most important thing is maintaining confidence and to keep strengthening yourself,' adds Tung Chee-hwa.

The Hong Kong Special Administrative Region is about to face a year of truth. It will not take the form of the drama foretold so loudly by journalists and some politicians in 1997. It will be much more subtle, largely escaping scrutiny from abroad, a process with profound implications for the experiment being conducted here. The advance signs are there to be picked up, but most people are too busy welcoming 1999 and getting on with their lives to pay much notice. After all, a report from the European Union tells us that our basic rights and freedoms have been upheld since the handover.

Politically, the gulf between the government and the most popular political party grows greater by the day. To mark the end of 1998, the chairman of the Democrats calls Tung Chee-hwa 'a benign dictator', and his party gives the administration a 30 per cent rating. The Secretary for Constitutional Affairs tells a visiting American delegation that the people of Hong Kong are not really interested in democracy and that the Democrats are in an extreme minority. The linchpin of the administration, Anson Chan, warns of the destabilising effect of speculation about her own future.

In his New Year radio appearance, the Chief Executive advises people that 'destiny is in your hands'. That is going to become a major issue for the year ahead, with a long-running legal and political controversy which will bring a key element in the foundations of the SAR into question. The first tremors are already apparent as the government makes it known that it is going to ask the territory's supreme court to consider referring a human rights case involving mainland migrants to the Chinese parliament. The issue of the relationship with Beijing takes on another form during the New Year holiday when a nineteen-year-old demonstrator is arrested for defacing the Chinese national flag; two other men have already been charged for a similar offence. Given the central government's sensitivities over anything involving national sovereignty, how the courts will handle these incidents has a particular significance.

Up in the capital, President Jiang Zemin and Prime Minister Zhu

Rongji attend a New Year performance of Beijing opera and shake hands with the stars in their ornate ceremonial costumes afterwards. Zhu's future – and that of one-fifth of humanity – is riding on his ability to push through the biggest economic reform programme on earth. If he had a free hand, his task would be great enough. But much more is at stake than increasing industrial efficiency, expanding services and cutting down the bloated state sector. The politics of mainland economics provide an obstacle course that are bound to produce some extreme variations of fortune in the coming twelve months. Zhu's deeply entrenched opponents warn that the very foundations of the regime are at stake. They see the drive to modernise and open up the economy, including agreeing to abide by the rules of the World Trade Organisation, as deeply subversive for the maintenance of the Communist power which celebrates its fiftieth anniversary this year. Above all, Zhu has to convince his master that China can take the pain without cracking apart. President Jiang is a cautious, calculating man. Whether he is committed to thorough economic change is an open question. But his first priority is to retain power for himself and for the party which has cocooned his adult life. If that is threatened, Zhu can expect little support, however high his international star rises.

In his New Year address, Jiang pledges to 'continue to deepen reform and expand our opening to the outside world'. But reports by the *South China Morning Post*'s well-informed China editor, Willy Lo-Lap Lam, do not provide much comfort for reformers. At a meeting of the Central Economic Work Committee, Jiang is said to have sounded a familiar theme – the need to preserve social calm above all else. Every worker must have rice in his bowl, the President insisted. The authorities are particularly concerned about the appearance of underground trade unions. The performance of officials at national and local levels is to be judged by their ability to maintain stability.

Jiang's concern not to rock the boat any more than is absolutely necessary leads to a series of emollient decisions. Factories which had been due to be shut down at the Lunar New Year in February have been given a grace period. The move away from subsidised state housing and free medical care has been postponed. The jobless will get a special New Year payment to help tide them over. There is a

stick to go with these carrots: the full force of the state security apparatus is to be deployed to prevent trouble. One source says the public
security budget is being doubled this year because of the number of
potentially troublesome occasions over the next twelve months,
including the tenth anniversary of the Tiananmen massacre.

A poet called Ma Zhe has just been jailed for seven years for subversion after setting up a movement called 'Cultural Renaissance' to
press for political reform and literary freedom. In Shanghai, two members of the China Democracy Party are sent to prison for nine months
for allegedly visiting prostitutes. One says he was dining with a business
partner in a hotel room when two women came in and took their
clothes off; the police arrived immediately afterwards. The other says
he went drinking with a friend one night and woke up in custody.

In the city of Chongqing above the Yangtze Gorges, a bridge collapses on 4 January killing forty people. A senior official in the local
Communist Party is arrested and accused of taking a bribe to steer the
construction contract to a former school classmate, who then subcontracted to builders ready to pay the highest amount. The Chinese
news agency says that nearly every building regulation had been violated. The official wanted the bribe to pay for his children to go to a
good school.

In the Portuguese enclave of Macau across the Pearl River estuary
from Hong Kong, a crime wave gathers force. A suspected Triad
who ran a private casino gambling room is killed in a New Year
shooting at an aquarium shop. The deputy chief of the main jail is hit
by bullets in the face and shoulder; a little while ago, one of his
warders was shot dead in a café. In December, Macau will follow
Hong Kong to become a region of China. The gangsters are carving
out turf before the handover.

Further up the Pearl River, the family of a Hong Kong man hacked
to death in Guangdong province says the local morgue is demanding
payment of 12,000 yuan to hand over the body. This is a lot more than
mainlanders would pay, but the morgue insists that there is a special rate
for bodies of SAR people. The family takes the matter to the Hong
Kong government. It says the response is that 'because of one country,
two systems, it is not proper for us to interfere in mainland affairs'.

Divisions between an appointed government and a popularly elected opposition; the economy; the Chief Executive's pleas for people to look on the bright side; a looming challenge to the rule of law and the autonomy of the SAR; mainland migrants and flag desecration; the travails of Hong Kong residents on the mainland; Triad crime in Macau; China's balancing act between change and stability. A series of patterns is being set for the coming twelve months as the former colony moves towards its real handover in a year of its greatest change and challenge – and the mainland decides if there is to be such a thing as a truly new China.

15 January

A couple of the kind of incidents that so worry President Jiang are reported today. Outside Changsha city in Hunan province, 1,500 troops and police had to be called in to deal with thousands of villagers protesting against taxes and corruption. One demonstrator bled to death after being hit by a tear-gas canister. Reports from the area tell of a flood of incidents involving farmers, including attempts to break into banks and post offices. In Beijing, meanwhile, angry investors who lost money in the default of a brokerage affiliated with the army have been out demonstrating on the streets.

To counter such discontent, Jiang is shown on television announcing new moves against corruption, including banning officials from holding meetings in well-known tourist spots. As a sign that nobody is safe, a Vice-Minister of Public Security with the rank of lieutenant-general has been arrested for graft. 'The party faces some of the most serious challenges in history,' the President warns. The Prime Minister, who has forbidden his relatives to get involved in financial or property deals, repeats a mantra at a meeting of senior officials: 'We will kill, kill, kill.'

16 January

The SAR may be insulated from the mainland by a high and heavily guarded fence on the border at Shenzhen and by the promise of one country, two systems, but when it comes to the economy, the two are umbilically linked, for good or ill. Figures from the Hong Kong Monetary Authority today show that bad debts held by banks tripled last year. Most of that is because of mainland borrowers who cannot meet their obligations. Exposure of the local banks to Chinese firms has reached the equivalent of US$36 billion.

One particularly jarring piece of bad news from the mainland is the sudden collapse of a big investment vehicle called Gitic in Guangdong province. Investors from Hong Kong and abroad had thought that their loans to Gitic were guaranteed by the Chinese state. This turns out not to be the case. Though the books still have to be combed through, it is evident that billions of dollars have vanished.

17 January

Unemployment in Hong Kong has reached its highest total ever, at 5.8 per cent. Two years ago it was 2.5 per cent. Worst-affected sectors are building, manufacturing, import–export and retail. Companies are laying people off as never before. The government talks of creating 100,000 new jobs. But inflation is hovering around negative territory, shops are empty and everybody worries about their bonus at Chinese New Year in a month's time. There is little retraining for many of those losing their jobs. Manufacturing is unlikely to pick up even if the economy improves because factories have moved across the border to the mainland.

The Chief Executive keeps urging people to remain confident and to strengthen themselves. But as a unionist legislator says today, 'I ask Mr Tung: if you were out of work for three months, then for four months and then for six months, I would like to see if you wouldn't lose hope of getting a job.' This is a new experience for many people, who grew up in the boom years. It is altering the psychology of the place. Hong Kong will, undoubtedly, recover. It is, after all, a city of survivors; as one top businessman puts it: 'This place is like bamboo; it bends with the storm, but it never snaps – and always bounces back.' But the experience of the current recession has made its mark, which will not evaporate for a long time.

19 January

First-world infrastructure, third-world environment: the story of a city that grew so fast it didn't have time to worry about the air and water around it. Pollution readings hit record levels in the New Territories today. A foul yellow mist spreads across the city. Ships are on alert as visibility closes in.

There is a meteorological explanation: low winds and a temperature inversion which traps the air. But the truth is that nobody with the power to act cares enough about the environment to stop it being steadily degraded. Sometimes the atmosphere is so filthy that people with breathing problems are advised to stay at home. The incidence of bronchitis has more than doubled in five years. The cost of pollution-related illnesses is estimated at US$420 million a year. One day last September, air quality fell to the level of Mexico City, the most polluted metropolis on earth.

The causes are well known: pollution blown across the frontier from Guangdong, buses and cars that keep their engines idling for the air-conditioning even on cool winter days, and diesel taxis using illegal high-sulphur industrial fuel, much of it smuggled in from the mainland or diverted from construction sites and sold by the roadside under Triad control.

It is not only the air that gets filthy. Picnic sites end the weekends deep in litter. Debris is strewn across beaches. Household appliances are discarded at random: the government once produced a television commercial to advise people not to throw their old sets out of the windows of their flats. The harbour that first attracted the British is awash with rubbish, industrial debris and the outpourings of ships' engines. Levels of chemical and metal waste flushed out into the water reach danger levels. Some 1.75 million tonnes of partially treated sewage are pumped into the sea every day; a proper system will not go into service until 2001, four years behind schedule. A few old fishermen cast their lines from sampans by the shore just down from my office, and you can still take a boat to see pink dolphins playing in the sea. But marine life is dying, and if you are unlucky enough to fall into the harbour, it's best to have a quick jab.

20 January

Three executives of the *Hong Kong Standard* newspaper are jailed for a fraud involving the inflation of sales figures. There is a saying about 'statistics, lies – and newspaper circulation figures', but this is much more than an everyday story of press folk as it sets off the first of a series of politico-legal storms that will blow through Hong Kong during the year, involving senior officials and leading figures of the SAR establishment.

Two and a half years ago, a fax arrived in the management offices of the *South China Morning Post*. 'You may be interested to learn how the *Hong Kong Standard* is cheating advertisers and the ABC Audit system by creating phoney circulation figures,' it began. The method was to supply 15,000 copies a day to a distributor, who delivered the papers to a warehouse from which they were shipped off for recycling without ever having been offered to the public. The *Standard* charged the distributor the normal wholesale price, and so could include them in its sales figure. Approved by the Audit Bureau of Circulation, this formed the basis for advertising charges. What the ABC did not know was that the distributor submitted an invoice to the paper for 'Promotional Activities' amounting to precisely the sum it was paying for the unsold copies.

We were not the only ones to get the tip-off. The Independent Commission Against Corruption – the much-feared ICAC – was also on the case. Our management did not want to run the story, fearing that we would be seen as bullying a much weaker rival and opening a can of worms about newspaper circulation practices. I thought we should publish, but before I could argue the toss, the ICAC swooped on the *Standard*, questioned managers and the owner, and charged three people, making the story *sub judice*. The raid caused sharp intakes of breath in the Hong Kong establishment if only because of the identity of one of the people interrogated.

This was Sally Aw Sian, proprietor of the *Standard* and of a Chinese-language newspaper group. She was a *grande dame* of Hong Kong and the international press world. Her father, Aw Boon Haw, had made a fortune out of a widely used camphor-and-menthol ointment called Tiger Balm. Originally from Burma, he drove a car with the bonnet styled like a tiger's head, branched out into the press, and built Tiger Balm Gardens in Hong Kong and Singapore full of fearsome Chinese mythical figures. In 1931, he and the second of his four wives adopted the five-year-old daughter of a distant relative, changing her name from She Moi to Sian, or Goddess.

In 1951, Aw Boon Haw's eldest son was killed in a plane crash. Two years later, the patriarch himself died. Sally Aw Sian inherited the Hong Kong newspapers. She established a Chinese-language press chain in North America and Europe. Her main paper, *Sing Tao*, grew rich on property advertising. She became prominent in the world of international publishers, inviting famous foreign figures to join her advisory boards and sitting on committees of the great and the good. A local shipping magnate called Tung Chee-hwa was one of her non-executive directors, and she was appointed to Beijing's rubber-stamp Chinese People's Political Consultative Committee.

Rich as she was, the stout, bespectacled Sally Aw was famous for watching the pennies. She signed company cheques personally and checked reporters' expenses herself, returning them when she saw a taxi fare for a journey she felt could have been made by public transport. Unusually for a person in her position in Hong Kong, she rarely went out to social occasions. Unmarried, her main confidante appeared to be her adoptive mother, who had the next door office at *Sing Tao*. The two women lived in a gloomy, dark house in Tiger Balm Garden. By one account, when they flew abroad, they would drive by Rolls-Royce to the airport and then sit in economy-class seats or haggle for an upgrade. 'I go straight home after work and seldom go out,' Sally Aw once said. 'Sometimes I make a short trip by chauffeur-driven car accompanied by my mother. But otherwise, most nights I am working on my administration.' When I met her for the first time in Hong Kong, it was in a conference room with a wooden frieze of her father's heroic days on one wall and a huge Mickey Mouse doll on a side table.

After her initial successes, business became less promising. A mercurial manager, Sally Aw worked with faithful underlings who never queried her decisions, even when they made no sense. 'She will say yes to a project in the morning and no in the afternoon,' one former executive told *Asiaweek* magazine. Her empire was highly extended, ranging from property to dental clinics. She also ran into problems with the Hong Kong financial regulators.

A combination of bad investments and the 1997 economic crash forced Aw to sell off assets, including the Tiger Balm Garden, which went to the tycoon, Li Ka-shing. In 1998, she relinquished control of her big Chinese-language Canadian operations to the *Toronto Star*. By the following year, she was being sued over a HK$300 million debt as she negotiated to cede a minority stake in *Sing Tao* while trying to hang on to power and the chairmanship. It was an impossible dream, and she finally sold out to the investment bank, Lazard Asia. Not that Sally Aw did too badly out of the deal. She was taken on as an adviser at HK$9 million a year for six years, and given a loan of HK$58 million – exactly half of the group's annual loss.

It was no secret that, after questioning Sally Aw about the fraud, the ICAC was anxious for her to be charged, along with the *Standard*'s general manager, finance manager and a former circulation director. She was mentioned as a co-conspirator in the charge sheet for the other three, but was not brought to court. Some well-informed observers think that the Chief Executive, who had previously sat on her board, felt sorry for Aw, and that the Secretary for Justice would have picked up the vibes from her boss. 'She was old, her business was doing badly so he would have taken pity on her,' as one former member of the Executive Council puts it to me later in the year. 'There's a Cantonese saying: "Take pity on her this time." It would have been enough for Tung to have said that.'

For its part, the Justice Department, as is usual in such cases, refuses to give any details of why it did not charge Sally Aw, beyond saying that there were insufficient grounds to do so. That explanation runs into an immediate problem when the *South China Morning Post* prints a page-one story reporting what Aw said during her ICAC questioning. One of our excellent court reporters had seen a copy of the transcript. We held the story until the case had finished, and then ran it on the front page beside the report of the sentences handed down to the three *Standard* managers.

'I just wanted to raise the circulation figures,' Sally Aw is quoted as saying. 'This was a commercial decision, that is to get more advertisers.' She denied knowing that what was being done could be fraud or deception, and said she had left the detailed implementation to her staff. 'I agree [sic] to it, but I did not do it,' she added, 'because it was done by them.'

21 January

One of the most closely watched Chinese women in the world is in town. Wendy Deng, a 31-year-old vice-president of the STAR satellite television station, is staying in a HK$8,000-a-night suite at the Shangri-La Hotel. There has been much speculation in the international press about the tall, young woman, and whether she has significant connections with the mainland. Nobody has come up with much on her except that she was educated in the United States, and is hard-working, upwardly mobile and perhaps on the verge of marriage. The Hong Kong press shows more interest in her clothes than her political connections as she steps out in a burgundy jacket and black trousers with a grey bag slung over her left shoulder and a slightly shy smile on her face. A fashion designer sniffs that she looks 'very common, like a housewife'. Another leaps to her defence saying there is no reason she can't wear the same clothes as an ordinary woman. 'She isn't using the way she dresses as a statement about herself – she doesn't need to,' he adds.

In the evening, Deng returns to her hotel suite to change into a smart black dress with diaphanous sleeves and accompanies her smiling partner in a limousine with white-draped seats to a dinner with the Chief Executive. At sixty-seven, he is more than twice her age. His name is Rupert Murdoch.

The media magnate is in Hong Kong as part of a panel of international bigwigs who have been asked by Tung Chee-hwa to advise on how the SAR can improve its position as a world-class commercial and financial centre. Others on the team are from the USA, Europe and Japan. After six hours of deliberations, they tell us Hong Kong is too expensive, that the air is too dirty and that we need better education, good financial services and more tourists. One does not wish to be inhospitable, but I think we knew this already. Their prediction that Hong Kong's main markets in the US and Europe will remain restrained in 1999 raises some doubts about their powers as crystal-ball-gazers, given the robustness of the American economy and the resurgence of European growth. They will return at the end of the year at the taxpayers' expense with more sage counsel. The general opinion is that this is window-dressing which is not going to do much to help the SAR, and that Mrs Murdoch-to-be could do with some fashion advice.

24 January

Albert Ho Chun-yan, a tubby, determined solicitor, is elected vice-chairman of Hong Kong's biggest political party, the Democrats. He replaces an academic who was forced to resign last month for being too moderate. The change reflects a big problem facing the party which is going to have a major effect on the political landscape of Hong Kong.

Like the old Labour Party in Britain, the Democratic Party is a coalition between the working-class rank-and-file, middle-class professionals and deeply motivated intellectuals. It draws strength from long-time campaigners such as the intense veteran, Szeto Wah, who heads the post-Tiananmen movement, the Hong Kong Alliance in Support for Patriotic Democratic Movements in China. Its voting numbers come from the grass roots, but the leadership is mainly middle-class, symbolised by Martin Lee Chu-ming, its lawyer chairman with his cut-glass English.

The party grew out of a union of pro-democratic groups for whom the massacre in Tiananmen Square was a great spur to action. In the pre-handover period, its main platform was the defence of Hong Kong against oppression from the mainland. That proved a winning plank at the 1995 election. At the time of the handover, the Democrats were flavour of the month with the international media as speculation mounted as to whether its chairman would end up as 'Martyr Lee'. He announced that, whatever happened, he would not leave Hong Kong, and liked to stress that he was not anti-China, just against the regime in Beijing. The grim picture he painted of the future provoked the incoming administration to deplore those who 'poor-mouthed' Hong Kong to international audiences.

After the interregnum of the appointed provisional legislature, which sat for a year after the handover, the Democrats did well again in the limited number of popularly elected seats contested in the legislative election of 1998. But there were warning signs. Though they easily maintained their position as Hong Kong's most popular political movement, they stood more or less still in terms of their share of the vote, whereas the pro-Beijing populist party, the DAB, increased its slice significantly, and the indomitable Emily Lau racked up a huge plurality with her hard rhetoric and street-cred flair. The danger for the Democrats is that if fear of the mainland decreases, their appeal as the party which will stand up to Beijing will diminish while other groups attract voters who want a more radical approach or who feel that the DAB represents a pragmatic choice for the future.

It is not surprising, therefore, that the Young Turks among the Democrats are getting fed up. They see the proceedings at the Legislative Council as a charade into which their chiefs have been sucked. What is the point of winning half the popular vote if the government ignores you? The leadership is seen as being unrepresentative, too middle class and too male. Some of the most prominent and forceful pro-democracy politicians are women, but they do not belong to Lee's party.

The Young Turks dismiss the comfortable chairs and parliamentary rules of LegCo. They want to go out on the streets instead. Some would like to provoke a real confrontation. This leaves Martin Lee with a distinct problem. As a man who burned the Basic Law after Tiananmen and has never wavered in standing up for Hong Kong's rights, he has the weight of democracy on his side. But it is no longer sufficient to say, as his former vice-chairman did in a private discussion last year, that all the Democrats need to do is to tell voters they stand for democracy. After almost a decade of political debate in Hong Kong, Lee and partners have to explain the benefits of democracy and the practical disadvantages caused by its absence. The eight months since the 1998 election having shown scant evidence of the concrete effects of a dose of democracy, how much easier it may seem to the more radical party members to stage demonstrations, pick up single issues and keep the pot boiling against an administration prone to being wrong-footed.

But Hong Kong is not a radical place. An ideologically led protest compaign would scare off much of the middle class which votes Democrat and pays the bills. So it is not surprising if Lee says he still prefers a broad movement for democracy, and insists that he will not abandon the middle class, while carefully adding that support for the party derives principally from its willingness to speak up for the deprived. His new deputy is less academic than his predecessor, with stronger grass-roots links and a combative style. Taking up the job, Albert Ho talks about how healthy it is for different members to have different views. His appointment is acceptable to both sides in the party, but the Democrats face a big test in defining their own identity. Simply being on the side of the angels is no longer enough.

25 January

Just how cheap the mainland can be for Hong Kong manufacturers is shown by the Four Seas Handbag Company, owned by a couple from the SAR. Attention has focused on the firm's 200-worker factory in the boom city of Shenzhen after a packager and loader called Xu Zhangshu died in his sleep. Aged twenty-seven, Xu had tuberculosis, but colleagues say he was killed by exhaustion after working fourteen-hour shifts with only half a day off each week.

The daily rate for such workers is HK$10, roughly equivalent to US$1.27. The minimum monthly wage in Shenzhen is meant to be HK$430; Xu would had to have put in forty-three days to meet that. Sewing workers at the factory earn HK$1.50 (19 US cents) an hour. Four of Xu's fellow workers told Cindy Sui of the *South China Morning Post* that they couldn't quit because they had to wait twenty-five days to be paid each month. They say the managers have a quota of how many people they want to quit: 'Once they meet that quota, they won't give you your money so you can't leave.'

Many of the women workers in Shenzhen have arrived in the past couple of years from inland provinces. They put in fourteen- or fifteen-hour shifts and are closely supervised. At one plant with SAR owners, the girls are searched when they leave for the day. They pay 100 yuan a month to sleep in locked quarters patrolled by guards with electric batons. A Hong Kong academic who spent six months working with them reckons that there are 6 million such women in the Pearl River region. They get no health care and are often overcharged by local shops. They are resented for taking jobs from longer-established workers, and face problems when they go home to their rural villages with their urban way of life.

The hardships they face can become lethal. A couple of years ago, eighty-seven workers died in an inferno at a Hong Kong-owned toy plant where the windows were sealed and escape routes blocked. In another fire at a Taiwanese-owned factory making electric fans, thick smoke killed sixteen workers because the windows were covered by metal screens to prevent theft. Sixty-eight died in an earlier blaze in nearby Dongguan. 'There was this girl who was only fifteen,' the Hong Kong academic recalls. 'Every part of her body was charred except for her cherubic face.'

Ironically – for me at least – the story about the Four Seas Handbag Company appears in the *Post* on the same day as an investigation I had launched into conditions in the Pacific island of Saipan. This little-known place has a unique status as part of an American-administered territory called the Commonwealth of the Northern Mariana Islands. That means it escapes textile import quotas and can label goods 'Made in USA'. But it is not bound by American labour laws. So garment manufacturers have set up there using workers flown in from China who get around half the US minimum wage to turn out goods for celebrated brand names and retail chains. Many of the manufacturing firms are from Hong Kong. One SAR company, headed by a businessman called Willie Tan Wai-li, is the biggest manufacturer on Saipan, as well as owning cinemas, freighters, hotels, ice-cream distribution and slot machines. The *Post's* Glenn Schloss, who went down to Saipan to investigate, found that the workers had to promise to pay up to HK$33,500 to mainland officials and middlemen before leaving China. As a result, they were often deeply in debt to money-lenders. Having been told they would be working in the United States, they found themselves in sweatshop conditions in the middle of the Pacific, sleeping in rudimentary dormitories, charged high prices for their food and, according to one lawyer working for them, treated like indentured labourers.

But bad as conditions are in Saipan, what goes on there doesn't look quite so awful when you compare it with what is happening just across the frontier from Hong Kong. The money in Willie Tan's plants may be less than on the US mainland, but it is far above anything the women could make back home. In Saipan, garment workers get US$3.05 an hour. At the Four Seas factory, a seamstress would have to work fifteen hours to earn as much.

29 January

If you stand in the main square in the middle of Hong Kong and look up the narrow street between the metal and glass headquarters of the Hongkong Shanghai Bank and the old stone premises of the Bank of China, you see, neatly framed by the two high buildings, a red-brick edifice on a promontory. Once, this was the French mission. Since 1 July 1997, it has housed Hong Kong's top judicial body, the Court of Final Appeal (CFA). Sitting up there above Central, with the Anglican cathedral to its left and the main government offices behind it, the building looks almost like a fortress. As things are turning out, that is exactly what it is becoming, a stronghold where the fate of one of the vital elements of one country, two systems will be decided.

Up the wooden stairs inside, behind the green shutters, all is peace and solemnity. It lacks the scale and echoing corridors of the law courts in London, but in this small chamber under a white dome, history is being made, or unmade. The judges, who arrive in official white cars, are august figures. The Chief Justice is a member of a major Hong Kong family with relatives scattered through banking, academia, the Bar and politics. One sits on the board of my newspaper; another will appear in his court to plead against the government; a third was a candidate for Chief Executive. Another of the justices behind the wide wooden desk on a raised platform in the CFA chamber takes a lively interest in promoting French literature and culture; one evening, I find myself sitting beside him as we read passages from books about *l'Hexagone* at the Alliance Française.

The court proceedings are irredeemably old-fashioned, with the barristers' wigs and black court dress, references to obscure legal points and orotund speeches. What, one wonders, can the people whose case is being heard make of it all? They are would-be migrants from the mainland who want to come to live in Hong Kong. For them, the issue is simple. But the government's determination to keep them out is setting in train a process that goes far beyond the straightforward matter of their fate.

The Court of Final Appeal was born from controversy. It was needed after the handover to replace the Privy Council in London, which acted as the ultimate court in colonial days. Those who feared that it might not be fully independent pressed for a majority of common-law judges to come from outside Hong Kong. That always seemed a pretty far-fetched demand: which sovereign country would accept a majority of foreign judges on the top court in one of its regions? China initially refused any idea of foreigners. There was deadlock with London. Then business made its voice heard. At a meeting with a senior mainland official, a group of tycoons stressed the need for a supreme court to ensure the rule of law and the continuation of the common law for commerce and finance. Soon afterwards, Beijing agreed to one foreign judge sitting on the court's bench at any one time alongside four local justices. That clinched a compromise, but enraged the Chairman of the Democratic Party.

I met Martin Lee for the first time soon after the agreement had been announced. Over lunch in the placid surroundings of the Hong Kong Club, he put down his chopsticks, stared at me across the table and said: 'Mr Fenby, you are an Englishman. Can you explain to me how that man can sleep at night?' Which man? I asked. The Governor, he replied. Lee told me that he had been leaving a reception at Government House when Chris Patten had buttonholed him and said that if the Chinese thought he had been a tough opponent in the past, 'they ain't seen nothing yet' over the composition of the Court of Final

Appeal. A few days later came the compromise. 'That man betrayed me,' Lee said over our lunch. Better no court at all, he went on, than a flawed court. I had to disagree. If, for instance, the *Post* was accused of subversion, I would prefer to have my day in court than being subject to an administrative decision in a closed tribunal.

It was said that Patten confided to aides that the compromise had caused him a sleepless night. But his administration showed no hesitations about throwing its weight behind the deal. The Governor's press spokesman called me on the afternoon of the agreement to 'discuss' some lines I might like to consider for the next day's editorial. Somewhat annoyingly, most of what he suggested was already in the leader up on my screen.

For the first eighteen months of its existence, the court attracted little attention, but now it is at the very centre of things because it has found for the mainlanders and against the government. The case concerns children of Hong Kong residents born on the mainland. The court gives them the unrestricted right to come to live in the SAR. It extends this to all offspring of Hong Kong residents whenever they were born, including illegitimate children. The judgement rests on its interpretation of the Basic Law, Hong Kong's mini-constitution since the handover. That is likely to prove a red rag to the Beijing bull, which insists that the power of interpretation lies with its parliament, the National People's Congress (NPC).

The government argued for a far more restrictive approach, wanting to limit the right of abode to children born after their parents had become Hong Kong citizens. One of the judges tells me later that the administration's case was so badly put together that the court had no alternative but to find as it did: 'As judges we can only go on what is presented to us.' Not that the Department of Justice is too worried. One of its top British legal officers says: 'We have ways of dealing with this.'

FEBRUARY

2 February

A senior government chemist, Dr Ting Ti-lun, has a disagreeable surprise when he gets home to his fifth-floor government flat. The rod from which a valued Chinese painting had hung is broken. The Indonesian maid, Rukiyah, says his wife, Maria Mui Yuk-ming, is responsible. At that, Mui goes for the maid, hitting her over the head with the rolled-up painting. Dr Ting intervenes to take the painting from his wife. But she then slaps Rukiyah on the face. Finally, she grabs a broom and hits the maid in the stomach. 'It sounded like someone was getting a damn good hiding,' says a neighbour.

Charged with assault, Mui is fined HK$500 (US$65). The case has special resonance because of recurrent complaints of mistreatment of maids, of whom there are some 184,000 in Hong Kong. After the court hearing, Rukiyah says her daily diet consisted of an egg, a bowl of rice and two slices of bread – 'Sometimes I got a chicken wing.' She was not allowed hot water, and had to wash from a bucket. She adds that she was slapped regularly, given no holidays and told she would have to pay HK$5 a day if she wanted a light bulb in her room.

Some 135,000 of the maids are from the Philippines. They are generally referred to as 'domestic helpers', which is considered more polite than 'maids', or by the old Indian term of 'amah'. Filipinas are popular because they speak English to the children of the house, though some of their charges also grow up with a smattering of Tagalog, their national language.

On Sunday, they have their day off and flock to the streets, open spaces and walkways, particularly in the Central District of Hong Kong Island. The space under the Hongkong Bank sounds like an aviary as it is filled with their voices. Chater Road running through Central is shut to traffic every Sunday as the Filipinas take over. They play cards, write to their families, eat, have their pictures taken, show one another snaps, sing, play Scrabble, listen to tape machines, read, sit under sunshades, sell cheap clothes, buy towels and enormous teddy bears from Indian hawkers, practise line dancing, do one another's hair, compare lipsticks, send money home, read the tabloids flown in from Manila, and attend revivalist religious meetings.

A stranger to Hong Kong might wonder what all this was about. Indeed, one visiting British newspaper editor asked me where all the Filipinas' husbands and children were. The answer is that if the amahs have husbands and offspring, they are back in the Philippines, living on the remittances from Hong Kong and all the other places where Filipinas do domestic work. In the SAR, they can earn more as maids than professionals make in Manila. Some are content with one job; others work for several employers. Some people think their monthly minimum wage of HK$3,860 (US$500) is too generous. A local councillor suggests that a 20 per cent cut would be in order, and that the working day should be set at sixteen hours. She says she gets 'complaints from several employers saying their domestic helpers start around 8 a.m. and are going to their room at 9 p.m. and will not do any more work'. A letter-writer to the *South China Morning Post* laments that Filipinas are 'so well-organised and so well-educated about their numerous rights that employers are often at a disadvantage'. A legislator proposes that they should pay a special tax for the use they make of government services, and for the cost of cleaning up after their Sundays in town.

Discrimination comes from other sources, too. When Hongkong Telecom advertised a service enabling subscribers to block calls from certain numbers automatically, it helpfully listed those you might want to shut off as ex-lovers, loan sharks and your amah's friends. Employers are sent the results of health checks on maids and can choose whether to pass them on to the women: last year, one amah only learned that she was HIV-positive when her employer gave her the news.

The foreign workers have replaced Cantonese maids, known as 'black and white' from their black trousers and white Chinese blouses, and *ma-jeh*, or 'mother-sister'. At the time of the handover, there was speculation about a return of the 'black and whites' in the form of mainland women coming in from the Pearl River delta to take over from the foreign amahs. This has not happened, though a few locals have taken a government training course for domestic workers. Most of the maids probably have as happy a life as one can have as an economic refugee living apart from family and friends. But there are plenty of horror stories like Rukiyah's around. Welfare groups reported sixty-seven cases of beatings of maids in a year, thirty-four cases of more serious assault, including attacks with hot irons, and nearly 400 complaints of being overworked. There is an urban myth about the employer who says yes, of course her amah has a shower, that's where she sleeps. Indonesians seem to be particularly badly done by, probably because they speak little English and do not have the self-help networks set up by the Filipinas over the past decade. One twenty-year-old told of being slapped and shouted at during her nineteen-hour day, which began at 5.30 a.m., and of being bilked of her pay by an employment agency.

Indians and Nepalese have joined the hunt for domestic jobs, and also suffer from exploitation. A 44-year-old woman from Bombay is seeking compensation, saying she was paid HK$200 (US$25) a month for a year by her Indian employer here. She worked fourteen hours a day and slept on the floor of the room occupied by the family's grandmother, whom she had to take to the toilet several times a night. Not that all the complaints are to be believed, or all the tales of petty thieving are to be dismissed. One amah faked the kidnapping of herself and her four-year-old charge to try to get a HK$200,000 ransom. An Indonesian was filmed by a secret camera in the home where she worked punching the two-year-old son of the house on the face and thigh, throwing him on to a sofa and leaving him alone crying.

A letter-writer to the *South China Morning Post* told of a Filipina who got a wage 30 per cent above the minimum and other perks for agreeing to accompany her employer to England, but reneged on the bargain at the last moment. 'I find myself paying for out-of-season strawberries (which I hate), cosmetics (which I don't use), French mineral water (which I never drink) and anything else my helper thinks she is entitled to bully me for,' the letter went on. 'If the living is so bad here, why bellyache? Go home! I would certainly not hesitate to employ a legal mainlander if that option were available to me rather than put up with all the lies and deceit.'

Today, the maids learn that they are going to have to join in the financial pain of recession. The administration decrees that their fixed wage will be cut by 5 per cent. If they get their money at all, that is. It emerges that Rukiyah was receiving only a fraction of the stipulated HK$3,860 a month. The rest was kept by the recruitment agency that placed her with the Tings.

4 *February*

The Sally Aw case comes back with a vengeance, moving from the legal to the political arena. Leaving a meeting of the Executive Council, the Secretary for Justice repeats that there was not enough evidence to charge the newspaper owner. Then, despite having been warned by aides not to say this, the Secretary adds: 'At the time, the *Sing Tao* group was facing financial difficulties and was negotiating restructuring with banks. If Aw Sian had been prosecuted, it would have been a serious obstacle for restructuring. If the group should collapse, its newspapers would be compelled to cease operations. Apart from losing employment, the failure of a well-established important media group at that time could send a very bad message to the international community.'

This raises a couple of questions: can company bosses expect to escape prosecution if this might endanger their plans to rescue their firms from commercial decline – and are media groups immune to laws that apply to others? If so, that seems calculated to send a 'bad message to the international community' about double standards before the law.

The woman who delivers the message will figure prominently in the events of the year to come. Elsie Leung is even less of a natural political animal than the Chief Executive. A demure woman in her early sixties, the Secretary for Justice could have stepped out of the pages of a Victorian novel, with her conservative clothes and neatly parted black hair. She won public sympathy last year when she was the victim of a medical leak: after she had gone into hospital supposedly with a minor stomach complaint, an employee at the hospital sent a newspaper a copy of her medical records showing that she was in fact being treated for cancer. An invasion of privacy, no doubt, though, as a leading television executive pointed out, should the government have been allowed to get away with lying about the health of one of its leading members?

A specialist in Chinese family law, Leung is among those who are particularly anxious for us to understand China better. On one occasion, she said that if anti-subversion legislation was introduced in Hong Kong, it should take account of mainland norms. Asked why she came in for so much press criticism, she responded by pointing to the support she received from a paper called *Wen Wei Po*, which is financed by Beijing. Everybody insists that Elsie Leung is 'really very nice'. With her shy smile and gracious manner, she does not seem like somebody who would say boo to a goose, but she rarely engages in real discussion about what she is doing in the vital area of the law, backed by two British law officers who use their skills to press the government case.

The Chairman of the Bar Association calls her last statement inconceivable. 'If you are a rich man and you run a lot of companies, you are immune, but if you are poor you are fair game,' comments a law professor at Hong Kong University. Even the pro-business Liberal Party has to reject the notion of one law for employees and another for bosses. Margaret Ng, the representative of the legal constituency in the Legislative Council, tables a motion of no confidence in the Secretary. A big political drama is about to unfold, all because a newspaper played around with its sales figures.

8 *February*

The first major challenge to the supremacy of the courts in Hong Kong starts to take shape. A group of mainland legal experts warns that the Court of Final Appeal's verdict last month in favour of mainland migrants violates the Basic Law, and amounts to an attempt to turn Hong Kong into an independent political entity. The final word, the experts insist, must lie with the National People's Congress in Beijing, whose legislation and decisions are not subject to challenge or refutation. The experts say that the judgement was 'in direct opposition to the interests of Hong Kong residents and has hindered efforts to maintain stability and prosperity'. Their views are made known by the official Xinhua news agency.

The Chairman of the Hong Kong Bar Association, Ronny Tony, warns that 'it will be a great disaster if the rule of law turns out to be the rule of man'. Martin Lee, himself a lawyer, warns of a constitutional crisis if the NPC overrules the court. There is irony in the mainland position; in closed-door talks with the British, Beijing repeatedly promoted the idea of the reunion of Chinese people on both sides of the border. But that was then, and this is now. At a reception in the capital, a State Council official sounds the same tune as the experts, and wonders why the Tung administration doesn't simply change the law. Instead, the SAR government plays for time, saying it will study what the experts have said.

15 *February*

A 55-year-old woman called Gao Yu is freed from prison on the mainland today. She was arrested in 1993, two days before she had been due to leave China to become a visiting scholar at the Columbia School of Journalism in New York. After being held for a year, she was sentenced to six years for 'divulging state secrets overseas' by writing for a magazine and a newspaper in Hong Kong. Gao was no stranger to jails, having spent fourteen months in prison after the Tiananmen Square demonstration in 1989.

Now she has been freed on medical parole and is allowed to rejoin her family for the Lunar New Year starting tomorrow. Her son says she is suffering from high blood pressure, heart disease and kidney problems. A dozen other mainland journalists are in jail for reporting material that would provoke no official action in Hong Kong. The press freedom group, Reporters Sans Frontières, ranks China second only to Ethiopia in the number of journalists behind bars. Some have been imprisoned since the early 1990s.

One condition of Gao's release is that she must not talk to the press. This is a familiar stipulation. Xi Yang, a mainland reporter for a Hong Kong newspaper who spent three years in detention for writing about official economic statistics, has not been heard from since being sent off to a new life by his employers after he was freed, probably in Canada. The US Secretary of State, Madeleine Albright, will be in Beijing in ten days, and President Jiang Zemin is due to go to Europe shortly. The central government has a way of releasing a prominent dissident or two just before such visits, hoping to blunt attacks on its awful human rights record.

The freeing of Gao Yu does not signal any loosening of control of the media. Some mainland publications have grown slick and glossy. An increasing number have been able to undertake investigative reporting, but usually only in spheres where the authorities want to show up wrong doing, like corruption. A daily in Guangzhou, the *New Express*, has pioneered a mix of sensational crime coverage and political debate, seeking readers with 'youth, knowledge and wealth'. But experiments are tightly controlled, and as a general rule, the contradiction between the desire to raise revenue from advertising and the dead hand of politics is as heavy as was evident at a dinner which a group from the *South China Morning Post* had in Beijing last year.

The setting for the meal was quite an honour: the hallowed sanctum of the Great Hall of the People on Tiananmen Square. After our credentials were checked at the door of the huge, dimly lit mausoleum-like building, we were escorted to a lift which rose automatically to the first floor. There, young ladies wearing white gloves brought us tea, and I visited the lavatory, its door marked 'Gents' in English over the outline of a European head. After a suitable delay, we were escorted into a big square room with chandeliers hanging at each corner and an even larger one in the middle. We sat in a semi-circle of brown armchairs round our host, Ding Guan'gen, a squat, bespectacled man with no evident charisma who is said to have owed his rise up the ladder of power to having been Deng Xiaoping's bridge partner. After running the railways, he became head of China's Propaganda Department, though that evening he was introduced as Director of the Publicity Department.

Whatever his title, Ding is the chief propagator of the thoughts of President Jiang Zemin. He tells cadres that they should 'sing praises to the motherland, socialism and reform loudly, encourage further reform and maintain social stability, satisfy the spiritual needs of the people, and adopt the right attitude about the world, life and values'. In a homily worthy of Eric Idle, he exhorts them to 'do more to channel the opinion of the public to the bright side, persuade them patiently, clear their doubts, heighten their awareness and unify people's thoughts'.

When the women attendants had poured boiling water from thermos flasks on to the tea leaves in cups on tables beside our armchairs, Ding gave us the party line about the development of the economy, and asked us what lessons we drew from the South-East Asian crisis. He mentioned the film *Titanic* several times. Jiang is particularly keen on the movie, and would like China to be able to undertake productions of similar scope.

Dinner followed in the Beijing Hall. There were twelve courses, including lobster and duck, accompanied by tea and orange juice served from a plastic bottle. I can't tell you what it all tasted like. I had contracted a bout of dysentery from bad seafood at lunch, and had no appetite. My stomach rumbled ominously as I shifted the food on my plate in a vain effort to pretend to be eating. Each time I could feel a major explosion coming on, I moved my chair noisily, drawing surprised looks from our host across the table. I had to hurry off to the lavatory several times. I can't imagine what those who would write the report on the dinner made of my behaviour.

One of the participants on Ding's side of the table steered the conversation to the prospects for expanding advertising in the mainland media, for which he could see limitless possibilities if publications could become more attractive to readers. Later, we were told that he had been a minor press photographer in southern China a couple of years ago, but now had official backing to turn a group of newspapers there into money-makers. Ding listened quietly. All this talk of advertising and colour printing and popular journalism sat ill with his definition of the media's role as being to 'resolutely develop the leitmotif of patriotism, collectivism and socialism; and to combat the influence of corrupt and decadent thoughts'.

Before long, our host swung the conversation up the table to an elderly man who turned out to have been a former military officer but was now a senior editor of *People's Daily*. Commercialism was forgotten as this venerable figure mouthed platitudes about the role of the media in building socialism, and the need for 'objectivity', a phrase much used to mean that the official viewpoint should be amply represented. Ding suggested to me that I might like to have a discussion of professional topics with the fellow editor. Apart from the anxiety caused by my stomach, I must admit that I did not quite see the two of us conducting a debate on the merits of eight-column photographs, or putting sport on the back page. The ex-general nodded politely at me. I half smiled back. Ding said how pleased he was to have brought us together, and we trooped out into the evening air.

The sharper mainland editors know that the stilted diet of political news they are allowed to serve up has scant public appeal. Before the handover, the boss of one big mainland daily in Guangdong showed me the different sections of his paper. Here was sport, he said, and here were the entertainment pages; here was local news, here was foreign news. And what's that at the bottom of the pile? I asked. Oh, that's political news. What do you put there? I enquired. What the government tells us to, he replied, just as you print what the Governor tells you to. A Cantonese colleague explained that this was not quite the Hong Kong way.

So, extremely welcome as Gao Yu's release is, she is only one of a number of proverbial pawns. The international climate has certainly softened towards Beijing. After inveighing against George Bush for cosying up to the butchers of Beijing in his first presidential campaign, Bill Clinton has 'de-linked' human rights and trade. The Europeans tut-tut about the treatment of people like Gao Yu while getting on with winning contracts and exchanging high-level visits. Still, human rights will not go away, in large part because of Beijing's obduracy. The dissidents may be pitifully few and far between but the central government cannot give up suppressing any sign of discord which might threaten its authority in any way. So long as that remains the case and orthodox ideologues like Ding stay on top of the power structure, China cannot expect to be fully accepted into an international community that professes to regard the exercise of individual rights as an integral part of modern civilisation.

16–17 *February*

KUNG HEI FAT CHOY: Get Rich. That's the greeting for the Lunar New Year as we say goodbye to the Year of the Tiger and hello to the Year of the Rabbit. Forget the worst recession the territory has known. This is a time for celebration and fireworks. Julio Iglesias performs at the main indoor venue for an audience that includes the Chief Secretary, Anson Chan, and her retired police commander husband. 'Go back and make love like rabbits . . . and if you have a baby, call it Julio,' the crooner tells the crowd.

Elsewhere in town, the Chief Executive's matronly wife comes under flak for having 'abused' a goldfish while playing a game at a carnival which involved transferring the fish from one blue plastic bowl to another. The Society for the Prevention of Cruelty to Animals says the game might give the impression that people in Hong Kong do not respect animals. Betty Tung expresses her deep regret at the incident, and her unease at the suffering she has caused. Presumably the SPCA does not spend too much time in the markets, where fish are scooped out of tanks to be taken off wriggling in plastic bags and chickens have their necks slashed to make sure customers get fresh meat. But our First Lady has her sensitive side. Once, she telephoned me at home after a mildly embarrassing story about her appeared in the *Post*. She asked how she could avoid such awkwardness. It comes with the territory, I replied. She said she took the point, but she still sent me a letter and documentation to try to show that she was being badly treated.

The Lunar New Year is when you are meant to clear the decks, pay off debts, clean the dust from homes and give bank notes in paper packets to unmarried young people: the packets are red, the colour of prosperity. It is a time for family gatherings, prayers, feasts and everything that sounds lucky. At a lunch at the Chinese Chamber of Commerce, oysters and fungus are on the menu: the name of the dish in Cantonese sounds like *Kung Hei Fat Choy*. 'I'm not superstitious, of course,' says a banker sitting beside me, 'but I like to eat it all the same at this time of the year.'

Having been born under the sign of the horse in the twelve-animal Chinese zodiac, I am told that this is going to be a good year for me as regards work, family and money. I will be lucky with investments between April and November, but should keep an eye out for gastric problems. Those born under the sign of the monkey will have a bad time with off-shore investments; roosters and oxen should keep clear of meeting the sick and the bereaved; tigers may undergo law suits as a result of betrayal by friends. As for rabbits, it is to be a year of self-destruction, bloodshed and financial loss.

The Lunar New Year would be nothing without fireworks. The Chinese invented them, after all. On the mainland, however, individual firecrackers are banned in many major cities for safety reasons. But the Cantonese go on celebrating. Ten thousand fireworks are let off in Guangzhou up the Pearl River. Hong Kong easily outdoes that, with 31,388 being fired in a 23-minute display in the harbour. Great arcs of colour criss-cross the sky under the moon amid the rat-tat-tat of explosions. Each burst, each fountain of falling stars draws an appreciative 'Wah!' from the crowd. Barges sprout sparkling cascades of light. Rings of fire appear in the heavens, followed by cascades of silver rain. And then, as suddenly as it started, the show is over.

What remains is the blaze of lighting on the tall buildings along the harbour, decked out with displays to welcome the Year of the Rabbit. But even here, recession is making itself felt. Two years ago, the lighting king of Hong Kong, Terence Wong, put 60,044 bulbs on one office block in the Wanchai district at Christmas. Now, his business is down by 35 per cent. Some companies have gone in for the ultimate cost-cutting step of simply replacing December's Santa Claus with February's Chinese God of Money, taking out the reindeer and putting in rabbit outlines instead.

On the mainland, a New Year television programme called *Spring*

Festival Evening Party is said to have attracted a 93 per cent audience for five hours of singing, dancing and comedy. Guangzhou has chosen the occasion to inaugurate its 18.5 kilometre-long underground railway: unfortunately, cracks appeared in the tunnels just before the opening, and a local newspaper reports that passengers left 10 tonnes of rubbish a day in the trains, on the platform and in ticket lobbies; later in the year, its manager will be arrested for alleged corruption. In Guangxi province in the south-west, the authorities begin the Year of the Rabbit by setting up anti-pornography 'training centres' in major cities, destroying 78,000 videotapes and 80,000 compact discs. In Hebei province, south of Beijing, 100,000 laid-off workers are given free food.

18 *February*

Hidden away behind the buildings which the lighting king Mr Wong has illuminated so brightly for the Christmas and Lunar New Year periods in Hong Kong, 350 mainlanders camp out on the paving stones of the courtyard of the principal government building. They are 'overstayers': that is to say, they remained in the SAR after the expiry of permits issued for them to visit their families. Some 50,000 mainlanders settle legally in Hong Kong each year. In addition, an average of 2,000 mainlanders cross the border daily on two-way per-mits. Around 100 are estimated to overstay at any one time. The government wants this group of 350 to go back over the border to join the queue of others waiting to come across legally. They have refused to leave, and squat in front of the Central Government Office demanding to be allowed to remain.

By any definition, they are illegal immigrants. Most Hong Kong people would undoubtedly like to see the back of them; one local Chinese newspaper calls them 'repulsive'. For all the official talk about the need for Hong Kong to draw closer to the mainland, migrants are not popular. A poll by Hong Kong's Chinese University shows that between 60 and 80 per cent of those who replied regard them as un-educated, unhygienic welfare scroungers out to take jobs from locals. After lunch with a government official one day which included a lecture on how Hong Kong people should not feel so superior towards their fellow Chinese, my host glanced at a group of men in boxy suits getting out of the lift and murmured: 'Mainlanders. You can tell from the way they dress.' Many immigrants are from poor rural areas, country bumpkins who do menial jobs and find it hard to integrate into an advanced society. A recurrent jibe involves their supposed unfamiliarity with Western toilets. How do you know a mainlander has been there before you? By the footprints on the seat.

The presence of the overstayers in the courtyard of the main government offices is a testament to the strength of the rule of law. As long as their case is going through the courts, they will not be deported. Eighteen have even got what are called 'walkabout permits', allowing them to leave their camp and move about freely pending the outcome of the legal process.

Their authorisation to protest outside government headquarters on Lower Albert Road was obtained by two unlikely figures: a silver-haired Italian Catholic priest and a doughty Scottish grandmother. Born in Milan, Franco Mella came to Hong Kong in 1974, the year of his ordination. He was soon involved in defending the rights of squatters. For a time, he worked in a garment factory. A veteran of arrests and hunger strikes, he tells reporters: 'I am blessed by the Lord to be able to help give a voice to the poor, to the weak and to those who are fighting for basic human rights. In the Kingdom of God all people are equal, men, women, rich, poor, and this is how it should be on earth.' Although he crossed to work on the mainland in 1991, he remains a familiar figure at protests in Hong Kong and became the subject of a film called *Ordinary Heroes*. He wears faded clothes, has his hair in a headband, beds down with the protestors, and goes to the house of the Foreign Religious Missions every few days for a shower.

The mainlanders' other friend and protector is a lawyer from Britain who is pushing seventy and was previously best known for her defence of the Vietnamese boat people washed up in Hong Kong. Pam Baker, a wartime evacuee to South Africa who doesn't count the cigarettes she smokes each day and was divorced after twenty-seven years of marriage, came to Hong Kong in 1982. She worked for the Legal Aid Department for nine years. Then came the Vietnamese. With them largely gone, she decided she had had enough and closed her law office, intending to write, be a grandmother and relax. But then the overstayers' case emerged, and she rushed to the barricades. Baker is a woman who relishes a fight on behalf of idealism and human rights. Her tenacity drives the authorities crazy. Mother of six children, she has been a Nonconformist, an Anglican and a Catholic. Now she counts herself as an agnostic. As she explained in an interview with my colleague, Fionnuala McHugh, this came about after she visited one of her daughters, who had joined the Moonies. 'I used to be allowed to visit – they *smiled* all the time and, of course, there was no drinking and no smoking, I had to go into the woods with my hip flask and fags. I started reading everything I could on organised religion, and I realised they were *all the same*. So that's when I became an agnostic.' Adrenalin, she adds, is a great cure for Alzheimer's.

Protected by their permit, the protestors sit on the cobbles watched by two bored policemen. On one side are tall black railings erected after the handover. On the other are waist-high crush barriers hung with the demonstrators' red, white and yellow banners adorned with slogans in Chinese characters. Some of the overstayers sleep on mats or cardboard. Others listen to Walkmans, or talk on mobile phones. Three young women share a meal from plastic boxes. One has bundled up her belongings in a big bag labelled 'Tough City, Tough Jeans'. Two smart young men in dark suits circulate. A few yards away, a cashier takes money from motorists leaving an underground parking garage. A throng gathers when a television reporter arrives with a cameraman to check out the situation. A child walks daintily out of the crowd and puts a plastic bag of rubbish into a wicker refuse basket by the railings.

In their way, these people are the heirs of the millions who have come to Hong Kong from China ever since it began to look like a more attractive place in which to live than the mainland. Since China's border opened up, there has also been movement the other way, though in more temporary form. During this month's Lunar New Year holiday, hundreds of thousands of people from Hong Kong cross through the checkpoint at Lo Wu. Among the few who cannot cross the frontier to see their families, buy bargains or get cheap sex are democrats on the mainland's black-list: Martin Lee joked at breakfast the other day that Hong Kong women were happy for their husbands to join his party because they knew that this would prevent them setting up with a mistress in Guangdong.

20 *February*

An anniversary to remember, but one recalled by few people in Hong Kong.

Two years ago today, I had just gone to bed when the telephone rang. Our night crime reporter had received a call from a contact at a Beijing-funded Chinese-language newspaper which had been told to put a black border round the front page. That could mean only one thing. Deng Xiaoping, the veteran of the Long March and the Communist triumph, who then launched China on its course of economic liberalisation, conjured up the one country, two systems concept for Hong Kong and presided over the crushing of the Tiananmen demonstration, had been allowed to die after being kept alive on a life-support machine for months. The official report from the Xinhua news agency at 2.41 a.m. said he had died from Parkinson's disease, lung infection and the failure of his respiratory-circulatory functions at 9.08 p.m. the previous night. One could only wonder what went through the doctor's mind as he switched off the life support, after getting the word from on high.

We ran four pages on Deng wrapped round the main section of the paper. A huge black and white photograph of the patriarch covered most of the front. We followed that with a special lunchtime edition, and ten pages in the following day's paper. I later learned that our use of a black and white picture was seen in Beijing as a suitable sign of respect; as far as I was concerned, it was simply much more striking than a colour shot. I was also told that the propaganda chief, Ding Guan'gen, had waved these editions at mainland editors demanding to know why they couldn't do as well. It was not a recommendation I planned to make too much of. Later that year, a mainland journalist asked me how our editorial board had been able to decide so quickly on the coverage on the night. I told him that we did not have an editorial board, and that it wouldn't have had time to meet if it had existed. One country, two media systems.

That afternoon in 1997, everybody who was anybody in the Chinese community went to the bleak building opposite the main racecourse in Happy Valley which housed the office of Xinhua, the mainland's *de facto* embassy in Hong Kong. With less than five months to go until the handover, everybody who wished to be on good terms with the new sovereign turned up, among them the cinema tycoon Sir Run Run Shaw, Macau casino boss Stanley Ho Hung-sun, old China friend Henry Fok Ying-tung, and tycoons Li Ka-shing, Peter Woo Kwong-ching and my newspaper's chairman, Robert Kuok. The Chief Executive-designate went to pay tribute, wearing a black armband. Outside the building, a clutch of demonstrators shouted their 'grief-stricken mourning for the butcher of democracy'. Chris Patten drove to Happy Valley to join the throng, bowing three times before the altar set up for the occasion and shaking hands with the hardline Xinhua chief.

Deng had as much influence on as many people as anybody except Mao. He never visited Hong Kong (though his widow attended the handover), but as the prophet of economic modernisation, he could only be fascinated by the contrast between what his fellow Chinese had done here and their failure to achieve anything equivalent at home. It was under his aegis that the village of Shenzhen on the border grew into a money-chasing city of several million inhabitants. The patriarch who told the Chinese that it didn't matter what colour a cat was so long as it caught the mice made his last public appearance there in January 1992, and a huge colour picture of him posed against a blue sky still stands on its main street.

On the first anniversary of his death, the man who had introduced market forces to the mainland was honoured as the nation's 'symbol, banner and soul'. Jiang Zemin assured the editor-in-chief of the *Time* magazine empire that Deng had taught China the need to 'open its doors and establish economic links with the capitalist, developed world'. The National People's Congress is to enshrine Deng Xiaoping Theory in the constitution. The role of the private sector will be affirmed. In Shenzhen, a local newspaper says people have been visiting the giant poster to 'cherish the memory and take pictures'. But in a country where the size of photographs and the placing of stories still has a

Kremlinological importance, nobody can fail to notice that the main newspaper, the *People's Daily*, did not mention today's anniversary.

The way is being carefully prepared for Jiang Zemin to join the Mao–Deng pantheon. As well as the page-one photographs of the President opening industrial plants, giving his imprimatur to development projects, smiling at folklore groups and greeting visitors from overseas, the human side of Jiang is also being revealed to the waiting world. We know he is a dab-hand at karaoke, once singing along with Elvis's 'Love Me Tender' during an evening party at a Pacific region summit. He also likes to show off his knowledge of foreign languages, though what he said to Prince Charles in a brief one-to-one remark during the handover ceremony in Hong Kong remains unknown. The President is keen on quoting from Chinese poetry, and on letting visitors know about his familiarity with European classical music. To console himself for Deng's death, which he must have authorised, he is said to have read Tang Dynasty poems and listened to Mozart.

As he has grown into the job, Jiang has developed a taste for foreign travel. His vanity has bloomed, but he can also betray his insecurities. A stocky man with a pudgy face and heavy black spectacles, he was embarrassingly photographed giving his jet-black hair a last going-over with a comb before being ushered in to see the King of Spain. On a visit to the United States in 1998, he had a 'look-at-me-now' smile as he rang the bell at the New York Stock Exchange, donned a revolutionary-era tricorne and went through the publicity hoops. But he never matched the folksy appeal achieved by Deng when the pint-sized Long Marcher put on a ten-gallon hat at a rodeo or was dwarfed meeting the Harlem Globetrotters.

Protests that would not ruffle a Western leader can rouse Jiang to indignation. Visiting Switzerland, he warned the President of the Confederation that her country had 'lost a good friend' when pro-Tibetan demonstrators appeared in Berne. China's main official newspaper describes Jiang as a 'principal violinist', which leaves open the question of who holds the conductor's baton. He is the epitome of *feng-pai*, people who move with the prevailing breeze, mainland Vicars of Bray. The President is most at home with his cronies in the 'Shanghai faction' whom he has brought from that city to surround him in Beijing.

One biographer, Willy Lo-Lap Lam, describes him as possessing the *haipei* personality attributed to inhabitants of the city where he was mayor before moving to the capital. Their traits include 'an expansive, outward-going style bordering on the unctuous; an ability to handle one-self to good advantage in public arenas; a soft spot for lavish ceremonies and big feasts; and a concern for public relations rather than substance'.

Born in 1926 into a comfortably-off family in the Yangtze Valley city of Yangzhou, Jiang went through an orthodox classical education, but then joined the underground Communist Party in 1946 while studying engineering. He worked in a soap factory and for an American-owned firm that made popsicle sticks. In the 1950s, Jiang went to Moscow to the Stalin vehicle factory, where he learned the Russian he still uses on visitors from the former Soviet Union. Another trip took him on an engineering mission to Romania. Back in Beijing, he worked his way up the Ministry of Machine Building, keeping his head down in the Cultural Revolution.

The end of that upheaval and the fall in 1976 of the Gang of Four who had spearheaded it led to Jiang being sent to their former bastion of Shanghai, where he took charge of the city's industry and began to emerge as a political leader, involving himself in the development of the Special Economic Zones, or SEZs, which Deng Xiaoping launched to spearhead economic progress. Becoming head of the Ministry of Electronics in 1983, he forged ahead politically as a new member of the 200-strong Central Committee of the Communist Party. In 1985, Jiang rose to become Mayor of Shanghai, and went into the streets himself to argue with the first student protestors in 1986. His orthodoxy was not in doubt, but troops were not used in Shanghai as they were in Beijing to suppress the protests of 1989.

Twenty days after the Tiananmen massacre, Jiang was officially named General Secretary of the Chinese Communist Party. With the genius of a high-level survivor, he has confounded the sceptics who did not expect him to last long. Starting out by beating a neo-Maoist drum, he developed into a self-styled team-playing 'chief engineer'. Unlike Mao and Deng, Jiang does not give off a historic aura. Though his vanity is growing and he clearly revelled in the royal pomp of his visit to Britain in 1999, he has none of the imperial mystery which is meant to surround Chinese rulers. That does not mean that he is short of cleverness or great ambition. 'Behind the Buddy Holly glasses, Jiang is a very intelligent and shrewd politician,' remarks an American academic who used to play bridge with him in Shanghai.

The man is the system incarnate, ready to sacrifice everything to put off the day of reckoning between the party, the state and the economic demons unleashed by Deng. The contradictions would boggle the mind of anybody not steeped in the switchbacks of China's ideology. While his Prime Minister pushes on with plans to dismantle the state sector, the President instructs cadres to raise the level of their Marxist righteousness, and his protégé, Vice-President Hu Jintao, says they should 'check if they truly follow the mass direction as enshrined by Marxism'.

Obsessed with the paramount need to maintain stability, the 'chief engineer' may be as much the prisoner of the apparatus he heads as its master, a ruler who sits on top of the tree of party and state, but who cannot be sure of controlling the branches below him, a consummate trimmer who lacks final authority because of his care not to be caught out on a limb, a leaf that rose seamlessly in the wind as revolution gave way to administration.

The first direct sight Hong Kong had of the man in charge of the country it was about to rejoin came at the 1997 handover. Jiang walked stiffly like a man-sized doll; there was speculation that he was wearing a bulletproof corset. On the platform at the Convention Centre, it was the Chief Secretary, Anson Chan, who seemed to dominate, resplendent in red on a throne-like seat above the throng of dignitaries. On his second visit, a year later, the President was more at ease. He seemed to be positively enjoying himself as he surveyed China's newest region. He attended a gala performance that ranged from mask dancers to Cantopop stars and the soprano saxophone player Kenny G. He made an optimistic speech, and then presided over the opening of the new airport, leaving the administration of Tung Chee-hwa to deny that its haste to open the project in time for his visit was responsible for systems failures that began almost as soon as the President had left.

Jiang had every reason to be pleased as he headed home. It had been under his command that China had undone the shame of seeing Hong Kong under Western colonial rule. He had installed his trusted man in charge of the SAR, and if the economy there was not bounding along as it had done in the past, the transition had gone smoothly. That, Jiang well knew, had an importance stretching beyond Hong Kong. As he had told a pre-handover secret meeting across the border with tycoons from the territory, if things went wrong in Hong Kong, it would greatly complicate China's aim of recovering the island of Taiwan, the ultimate prize for his presidency. Though the Taiwanese reject any comparison with ex-colonial Hong Kong, Jiang sees a successful SAR as one of the keys to the full reunification of China. But can such a product of the system that has run China since 1949 understand how Hong Kong really works? It is the question the SAR has to live with as it watches the way the wind is blowing from the north.

21 *February*

The overstayers from the mainland are allowed to remain a while longer. In Immigration Tower in the Wanchai district, they are handed cards giving them temporary immunity from arrest and deportation.

At a meeting of the government's main think-tank, the Central Policy Unit, some members criticise the administration for the absence of a contingency plan to deal with legal decisions that could open the door to a flood of migrants. Officials reply that they hadn't planned on losing. That is part of their problem: they find it hard to imagine that they will make mistakes, and show an arrogance inherited from the Whitehall way of doing things. The civil service is sometimes referred to as a Rolls-Royce. Previously, they had a chauffeur on call by the Thames. Now it is self-drive.

Talking about the administration's performance one evening, a Hong Kong woman in her thirties says she does not think much of the Chief Executive. Who would do better? I ask. Well, she replies, Tung clearly isn't listening to his Chief Secretary, Anson Chan, and Anson seems resigned to that. As for the others, she doesn't think much of them either. So finally she concludes that maybe Chris

Patten would have handled it all much better. 'But that's not a good thing for me to say as a Chinese,' she adds with a smile and an intake of breath that whistles over her teeth.

26 February

As a first move over the Court of Final Appeal's verdict against it in the mainland migrants' case, the government is asking the judges for a 'clarification' – in particular, how they see their prerogatives *vis-à-vis* China's National People's Congress (NPC). The proceedings have had their lighter moments. When the government's lawyer asks the Chief Justice to clarify the verdict, the SAR's top judge replies, to chuckles from those in the courtroom, that this is exactly what has been done on page five of the judgement.

'It may be argued that this is what the judgement says anyway,' the lawyer blunders on. 'It may cause laughter . . .'

'We could do with a bit of light relief,' the Chief Justice remarks.

The court could have stood on its dignity and refused to give the requested clarification. That would have been politically provocative, and the judges are not by nature trouble-stirrers. So they come back with a carefully calibrated response. While saying that the court had not intended to challenge the NPC, their position does not basically shift. They acknowledge that they 'cannot question the authority of the National People's Congress . . . to do any act which is in accordance with the provisions of the Basic Law and the procedure therein'. But this does not mean they feel any need to alter their verdict. The ball is back in the government's court, and over cognac at a dinner, a senior official expresses deep concern at what lies in store. The government simply cannot accept the decision, he says. The court got the Basic Law wrong. The practical effects of its verdict would be horrendous in terms of immigrant numbers. If the court persists, the government will have to go to the NPC. There is no way of knowing what precedents may be set, opening the door to mainland interference in Hong Kong and giving the impression of an administration that needs Beijing to do its job for it. But if this is the price to be paid, so be it.

March

1 *March*

The annual Spring Reception at Government House, former home of British rulers of Hong Kong, for which a new name has not been found twenty months after the handover. The Chief Executive is smiling affably as he says he has so many problems to deal with, so many fronts calling for action. Not just the economy, but also tourism and the environment. He is keen on the idea of Hong Kong finding a new role for itself neither upstream nor downstream in high tech but in midstream, taking innovation by others and applying it to production. This sounds much like its traditional middleman role.

Tung says he was much impressed by what he saw in Israel on a recent visit on his way home from the World Economic Forum in Davos. After getting back, he took a couple of days off over the Lunar New Year to go walking. He enthuses over Hong Kong's country parks and trails. Recalling his days in Britain, he recalls the smog that meant you couldn't see more than an arm's length in front of you. Now it has been cleared up in Britain; the same should be done here. Indeed – and as Chief Executive, he is better placed than anybody else to get things done. But there are depressing precedents. Chris Patten promised a clean-up that never materialised. Officials say one has to be patient; the environment will certainly figure prominently in the

Chief Executive's annual Policy Address. That will be delivered in October. Meanwhile the air gets steadily worse.

2 March

Hong Kong may be special, but it is increasingly feeling the pressure from another small enclave built by refugees from China – Singapore. The Lion City, as it is known, has been busy attracting high-tech companies and getting its economy into leaner shape to meet the challenge of the recession. Eleven per cent of its GDP comes from electronics, and major international computer firms are being lured south by cheaper rents and tax breaks. The government there is decidedly interventionist in what it sees as the country's best interests in a way that would be impossible in Hong Kong. There are business links between the two – one of the big Hong Kong property firms is run by Singaporeans. But from time to time, SAR officials go public with their feelings about the other former British colony. The Trade and Industry Secretary, Chau Tak-hay, has just set off a row by telling a Legislative Council panel of Singapore's 'four great advantages'.

'First, the government has complete control of the legislature, which always supports it. Second, the media never criticise the government. Third, the government has complete control of the trade unions. Fourth, the people never dare openly criticise the government.' Singapore's highly active Consul-General calls those remarks inaccurate and misinformed. 'His assertion of compulsion and control shows a lack of understanding of how Singapore works,' he adds. Chau is unabashed. 'Of course we are different from Singapore,' he says. 'The opposition parties in Singapore do not raise opposition. If they do raise opposition, they might be arrested [but] our Legislative Council has sixty opposition members.'

Still, the attractions of the Lion City model are undeniable for some people here. Tung Chee-hwa is a warm admirer of its Senior Minister, Lee Kuan-yew. Sitting beside Lee on a platform at the World Economic Forum in Davos, the Chief Executive showed palpable deference to the older man. For his part, Lee lets it be known that he thinks the people running Hong Kong are good men and women, but lack experience.

Around the time of the handover, there was some speculation that Tung might try to impose a Singapore-style system, though that would be difficult under the Basic Law and would be strongly resisted. 'It's like a nice prison,' said one middle-class Hong Konger when I asked her what she thought of the other city. At a deeper level, the inventiveness and individuality that lie behind Hong Kong's success would die a lingering death in a society where dissent is frowned upon and consensus rules. Yet Tung clearly cannot get the lure of the Lion City out of his mind. At lunch with a group of editors, he reflects on the criticism he faces, and says he can't help being jealous of Singapore. 'But don't quote me on that,' he adds with a smile. 'Or else everybody will think I'm going to bring in their system here.'

3 *March*

The Financial Secretary, Donald Tsang, is driven to the Catholic cathedral this morning in his green BMW. Then he goes on to his office. The mainland migrants are camped just opposite. After lunch, Tsang goes down the hill to the Legislative Council chamber to deliver his fourth Budget. The spiritual preparation has become a habit. He also likes to invoke the titles of films in speeches: having spoken of *Godzilla* and *The Silence of the Lambs* in the past, he now likens Hong Kong's situation to *Saving Private Ryan*.

It is, most people agree, a good Budget. Tsang certainly shows a deft political touch. A year ago, he telephoned me from his car after delivering a more orthodox package to offer an assurance that he 'felt the people's pain' but could not divert from the tradition of balancing the books. Since then, things have changed. The government has left the strict path of non-intervention, and it is no secret that the Chief Executive wants a spot of reflation. So, Tsang's Budget is out to inject some optimism into the place.

There is to be a one-off 10 per cent income tax rebate; government fees and charges will not rise for six months after their last settlement; pay will be frozen for 330,000 civil servants and public sector staff; one of the jewels in Hong Kong's crown, the Mass Transit Railway Corporation, is to be partially privatised. Negotiations are going on to build a Disneyland on Lantau Island. This is a very popular idea, which was first publicly launched in an article in the *South China Morning Post* by the entrepreneur who developed the city's main restaurant and bar area in an old warehouse section of town. Some people wonder why, if Disneyland is such a good idea, the project is not being done in traditional fashion as a purely private-sector deal. Others fear that the government's public enthusiasm may put it at a disadvantage in negotiations. But the Financial Secretary appears to have achieved his aim of lifting people's spirits.

In keeping with the vogue for high-tech development, the budget also contains a surprise announcement that a 'Cyberport' will be put up on a previously protected 26-hectare site by the sea on Hong Kong Island. It is not quite clear what this HK$13 billion project involves: it seems to be a cluster of 'intelligent buildings' equipped with all the latest technology, which will attract foreign companies, create a local technological seedbed and catapult the SAR into a high-tech future. The project has been agreed with a company called Pacific Century, headed by Richard Li Tzar-kai, son of the great tycoon, Li Ka-shing.

The younger Li has had an eventful career, setting up the Star satellite television station and subsequently selling out to Rupert Murdoch at a good profit, investing in real estate in Tokyo and always pursuing his dreams of becoming a king of advanced technology. Nobody can have anything against his ambitions, particularly when Cyberport is due to create 12,000 jobs on completion in eight years' time. But two things arouse concern.

One is that the project includes a luxury residential development attached to it on prime, and previously unavailable, land. It turns out that as well as three office buildings and a 'cybermall', there will be 30 blocks containing a total of 2,932 flats, plus a hotel and a tower of serviced apartments. So this is a big property play as well as a leap into the cyberfuture. But the real departure is that the development was not put out to tender as is customary. The government is not meant to seal deals like this in private. Other developers are soon up in arms. They get an audience with Anson Chan, but the Chief Secretary can only say they should trust the government and that clear guidelines will be drawn up for the future.

I can't help thinking back to a flight from Hong Kong to Zurich at the end of January. In the first-class Cathay Pacific cabin were the Chief Executive and a group of prominent Hong Kong figures, including Richard Li. They were on their way to the Davos Economic Forum. Li made the mistake of travelling on his SAR passport, and was held up at the Zurich immigration desk because it did not have a Swiss visa. After Davos, the party went on to Israel to study the high-tech industry there. Now Richard Li's company has got the Cyberport project without other firms having a chance to compete, much to their annoyance.

5 March

A jolly evening at the annual dinner of the Pacific Rim wine society. As always, the occasion is presided over by the Deputy Chief Justice, a very tall New Zealander who revels in auctioning choice bottles for charity at outrageous prices. The police band marches through the hotel dining room, dressed in white helmets, white coats and blue trousers as though they were on the parade ground rather than a parquet floor. They play 'John Peel' and 'Rule Britannia' and 'Land of Hope and Glory'. A visitor from Britain seated at our table says he didn't think that this kind of thing would be allowed now that Hong Kong was part of China. By then, the Deputy Chief Justice and an eminent wine merchant from Bristol are on their feet singing along to Elgar.

11 March

If we were worried about the way things are going with the rule of law and Cyberport, a third shoe has just fallen with the case of the non-prosecution of the newspaper owner, Sally Aw Sian, which reaches its political conclusion today. The no-confidence motion in the Secretary for Justice tabled by Margaret Ng, the representative of the legal constituency in the Legislative Council, speaks volumes about the way politics works when the chips are down. The story so far has taken us through the decision not to prosecute Sally Aw, the sentencing of three of her underlings and Elsie Leung's remark that one reason she was not charged was because of the effect that might have had on her business. But now the tale gets a fresh twist.

To explain how this happens, it is first necessary to describe the arcane nature of the voting procedure in the Legislative Council. To pass, the motion put forward by the terrier-like Ng not only has to get an absolute majority in the chamber, but also the support of a majority of the thirty functional constituency members. That would normally condemn any anti-government motion to defeat, since most functional constituency representatives can be counted on not to rock the governmental boat. But in this case, the pro-business Liberal Party, which has ten functional seats, has already expressed its opposition to the Secretary for Justice's statement. The pro-democracy camp can muster twenty votes, mainly in the popularly elected seats, but also including a few functionals. Then there are some independents who may back Ng. Even if she falls short among the functional con-stituencies, a 31–29 vote for her motion in the chamber as a whole would represent a huge moral defeat for the government in its biggest test in the legislature since the handover.

In today's four-and-a-half-hour debate, Anson Chan delivers a strong speech which implicitly acknowledges the scope of concern as she widens her defence to take in the Court of Final Appeal. The rule of law is the foundation for the community, the Chief Secretary says. 'I can assure members that we have acted out of principle, not ex-pediency; that we have acted not to undermine the rule of law but to observe it; that we have acted not to challenge the independence of the judiciary but out of respect for it. We know precisely what is the rule of law.' This does not explain why Sally Aw is free at her home in the Tiger Balm Garden while the manager to whom she gave the green light is in jail.

Knowing the impact a defeat would have, officials have gone to work on the businessmen who pull the strings of the functional constituencies represented by Liberal Party members. The business-men do their duty. It could be argued that they are only exercising their democratic rights, just as voters might petition their MP to back the government on a no-confidence motion in the Commons. But these are not ordinary constituents. They are a small group of men who enjoy political influence because of the business and financial muscle they are now flexing on behalf of the administration.

At the last minute, the Chairman of the Liberals announces that the party has decided to abstain, after all. 'If all civil servants were to resign for their mistakes then the whole top tier of government might go,' he remarks in what sounds like considerably less than a ringing endorse-ment. The decision is particularly embarrassing for a prominent Liberal who lobbied the main Chamber of Commerce to distance itself from the Secretary for Justice. One party member, Ronald Arculli, a well-known solicitor, prefers to walk out rather than remain in the chamber and abstain. He is in tears as he leaves. 'Whatever the result, there are no winners,' he says. 'The loser is Hong Kong.'

There are two ironies in this. Arculli is on the board of the *South China Morning Post*. At a lunch of the board in a seafood restaurant back before the handover, his impending appointment to the Tung administration was the subject of congratulations and toasts. The job he was supposed to have got was that of Secretary for Justice. A year later, the *Post* ran a story about how a property developer was using shelf companies to increase his influence in a functional constituency on behalf of his favoured candidate – who was none other than the man who walked out of the Legislative Council rather than follow the pressure to stay and abstain.

The volte-face by other Liberals means that Ng's motion goes down to a 29–21 defeat, with ten Liberal abstentions. If the abstainers had voted as originally planned, the outcome would have been a narrow victory for Ng in the chamber as a whole.

The computerised voting system breaks down, so the Liberals have to raise their hands to abstain rather than pressing the buttons on their desks. Elsie Leung's supporters are beaming. A senior official in her department, Greville Cross, says the SAR is fortunate to have such a dedicated public servant. Sounding a familiar theme, the Chief

Executive hails the result as a vote of confidence in the integrity of the legal system. One pro-China legislator says that Ng, not Leung, threatens the rule of law; another talks of terrorism and the danger of 'handing over the jewels to Hitler', whatever that means. Business has spoken in an unusually open manner, but there is also an intriguing suggestion in a remark by a legislator to a reporter some time later. 'Only once,' he says, 'was I lobbied by Chinese officials: not to vote for the motion of no confidence on Elsie Leung.'

20 *March*

Recession may still have us in its grip, but the rich aren't doing too badly. The wealth of Henderson Land's Lee Shau-kee is reckoned to have grown by US$1.9 billion in the past twelve months. 'The worst is behind us,' he tells *Forbes* magazine. 'But like a patient recovering from a serious illness, it will be a gradual process.' Although corporate profits are generally down, the Hang Seng stock market index is up by 22 per cent so far this year. Sentiment is clearly shifting, and money returning. Who needs to bother about politics?

Another big beneficiary of this is 'Superman' Li Ka-shing, now estimated to be worth some US$10 billion. At the end of last year, he caused a shock by letting it be known that he was worried about the 'unfavourable political environment' here, and was unlikely to go ahead with an unspecified big project as a result. It was hard to see what was causing such concern to K.S., as his fellow business-men call him. Even less so when shares in his main company have doubled from their low of last year. The archetypal poor-boy-made-tycoon is as much king of the big deal as ever, and is about to get the recognition of an honorary degree at Cambridge, to which he has donated tens of millions of pounds. Opinion polls regularly place the dapper Li as the man Hong Kong people most admire. Starting out as a manufacturer of plastic products, he rules an empire stretching from Britain via the most strategic waterway in the Americas to Beijing's biggest building site. Li was the first Chinese to take over a big British trading company, Hutchison Whampoa. His other main firm, which originated with the plastics business he set up in

1950, is called Cheung Kong after the Cantonese words for a long river.

In public, Li, who looks much younger than his seventy-one years, strikes a graceful, courteous pose in keeping with his status in the community. He makes a point of attending ceremonies and funerals and staying to the end. Though he has a garden and swimming pool outside his seventieth-floor office on top of a tower in Central, he is not ostentatious about his wealth. His sleek black and white boat, *Concordia A*, is relatively modest by the standards of the Hong Kong mega-rich, though the bodyguards are very much in evidence – for good reasons, as we will see. When the great and good of Hong Kong gather for an important national occasion, he lines up on the platform with Tung Chee-hwa, Anson Chan and the director of the Xinhua news agency. In private, he is intensely focused on the deal at hand, symbolised by his purchase of a controlling stake in Hongkong Electric back in 1985 in just seventeen hours, including eight for sleep.

I first met Li in the autumn of 1995 when the *South China Morning Post* opened its new printing plant in the New Territories. As he went to make his speech, the chairman of the newspaper, Robert Kuok, said: 'Look after my friend Mr Li, will you, Jonathan?' There stood a slim, immaculately dressed man with black-rimmed spectacles and a friendly smile.

He said he had to go to a meeting shortly, but wanted to do Kuok the courtesy of staying and listening to his speech. So we stood on a gallery and watched the proceedings. At one point, Li sidled through the crowd and tried to use a telephone: wasn't the owner of the Orange network carrying a mobile? He seemed to be having trouble, so I went over and pressed the button to get an outside call. Li smiled, dialled and spoke briefly.

As the speeches finished, Li walked off, waving to me to stay behind. But he was heading in the wrong direction, straight on for the press hall where printing was in full swing. I had a vision of Hong Kong's best-known businessman wandering out on to a gantry, toppling over the railings and being chewed up with the next day's front page. I went after him, and guided him down to the front entrance and into his Mercedes. Do you want to go back to Central? he asked.

No, I said, I am staying for dinner (which ended with another noted local property tycoon downing a glass full of Scotch in one go, thinking it was beer).

A while later, I found myself walking out of Government House with K. S. Li after a dinner for John Major in the dying days of colonialism. Again, he asked me if I wanted a lift in his limousine. My red Honda was waiting in the line down the drive, so I declined. I seem fated to become the man who always turns down a ride with Li Ka-shing. Other offers came after a couple of dinners, and once at the opening of the new airport in 1998. Maybe I have lodged in Li's mind as a carless journalist.

Despite his offers of a lift, the *Post* seems to have fallen foul of Li's empire, though we have not suffered in the same way as a press group which lost advertising from his companies after one of its magazines ran several pages of photographs of the tycoon with a homely-looking woman at the airport. One of Li's senior executives told me outright in the spring of 1999 that we would never get an interview with his boss because the *Post* was regarded as 'unfriendly'. A little later, Li himself spoke of critical remarks about him and his family's projects in the 'English-language press'. When a columnist criticised the group, the matter was taken up directly with the paper's chairman. Li's lieutenants say they cannot understand why anybody is concerned about his influence. 'If you ever want to get anything done in this town, you always make your dispositions in advance,' as one of them put it.

23 *March*

Anson Chan Fang On-sang's term as Chief Secretary of the SAR is renewed until 30 June 2002, when the Chief Executive's term also ends. This will take her two and a half years beyond the normal retirement age of sixty. She and Tung appear together to make the announcement today. It is all smiles and expressions of mutual esteem. Tung says he did not ask for Beijing's approval but 'informed' the Central Government of his decision. Answering questions, Chan tells reporters that there are occasions when she does not agree with Tung, as there were times when she didn't agree with Chris Patten. But their relationship is 'based on trust and frankness'.

Chan is a tough administrator with a flashing dimpled smile who is always impeccably dressed. Married to a former senior policeman, she was born into a distinguished Chinese family in January 1940. One of her forebears was a leading general. Her mother is a well-known painter. As she rose through the civil service, she ran into a major controversy over a five-year-old girl whom Chan, as Director of Social Welfare, ordered to be taken from her mother. Social workers broke down the door of their home and put the child into care. The mother was placed in a mental ward.

In 1993, Chan was appointed by Chris Patten as the first local Chief Secretary. Two years ago, Tung's decision to keep her in her job was a *sine qua non* for confidence in Hong Kong. She has been the most vital single element in the administration so far, regularly pushing the two systems button when the Chief Executive or the Secretary for Justice sounds off about how we should put the one country first. Although a natural conservative, she shows a real respect for democracy and diversity as key elements in Hong Kong's character. A ferociously hard worker, she tops popularity polls and is genuinely respected. But some wonder if the agreement to stay on means she will find herself following the Chief Executive's agenda willy-nilly. A couple of members of her coterie of female civil servants say she is finding life with Tung and his protégés increasingly difficult. 'We all know how the power is flowing,' says one. But there is talk that she harbours hopes of succeeding him, and so will grow less ready to make waves.

Chan would have been the best choice for Chief Executive in 1997. But she didn't get anywhere near the starting gate at the time, if only because of her links with the British and her loyalty to Patten. Beijing is said to think well of her as a firm manager who has the keys to the Rolls-Royce government machine. Loyalty, even if it was to the last Governor, is a quality much prized in China. Beside the slow-moving, indecisive Tung, she cuts a brisk and reassuringly businesslike figure. Or is this all just a story that is being spread in an attempt to fan her ambition and to ensure that she keeps in line in the hope of future advancement? As for her own approach to life, Chan says, 'The most important thing is that you keep an optimistic attitude and do not make a fuss about little things.' She has taken to exercising in her office, and relaxes with an occasional turn on the ballroom floor – her twin sister used to run a dancing school. But a week after the announcement that she was staying on, she collapses as she leaves the Legislative Council chamber after delivering her speech in the Budget debate. She has to be taken out of the building in a wheelchair, and driven to hospital where the Chief Executive and other government officials visit her. A doctor says she is suffering from Ménière's syndrome, an imbalance of fluid in the middle ear that causes dizziness, hearing loss and nausea. She will be up and back to work in a week's time. But it is a reminder of the mortality of the pillar of the administration, who looks pretty much irreplaceable.

28–29 March

Hong Kong is not the only European colony to return to China as the millennium looms. Today we cross to Macau for the night, a hover-craft ride past the islands in the bay, across the mouth of the Pearl River delta and under a huge bridge to the landing stage of Europe's oldest possession on the Asian mainland. Deng Xiaoping dreamed of all China being reunited by the end of the century. Taiwan is still far from returning to the fold. But on the night of 19–20 December, Beijing will recover the smallest of its lost lands, with 410,000 people in 19.3 square kilometres, as the Portuguese fly home for Christmas for the last time.

Macau used to be known as a haven from the modern world, a place dotted with casinos and Portuguese restaurants under a sleepy administration, set on a somewhat seedy course of decline. Errol Flynn tried to introduce cock-fighting in the 1930s, and Portugal's neutral status in the Second World War made the enclave a Casablanca-like refuge from the all-conquering Japanese. More recently, there have been recurrent rumours of money being funnelled back secretly from Macau to fund the Socialist Party in Portugal: a local newspaper is launching a signature campaign for an investigation into the allegations.

I first came here from Vietnam in 1965, and stayed at a dowdy, shabby hotel where I drank *vinho verde* on the balcony and was eaten alive by mosquitoes before spending the night playing blackjack at a floating casino: I seem to remember getting out just about even. In those days, the 64-kilometre crossing took several hours by ferry boat. Now, there is Cantopop on the screens above our heads in the jetfoil, and Macau is just forty-five minutes away from Hong Kong. There are tower blocks on the waterfront and on the adjoining island of Taipa. But the casinos and the decaying colonial atmosphere still give the place a special character.

When we first arrived in Hong Kong in 1995, we left our super-efficient hotel one weekend to spend a couple of days in one of Macau's superior establishments. In our room overlooking the harbour, the television didn't work; the wash basin was cracked; the headboard threatened to tip over on to us, and it took so long to check out that we missed the hovercraft back. Welcome to southern Europe, we said as we waited to zip back to modernity in Hong Kong. But the atmosphere was mellow, the food was excellent and I found my favourite barber's shop in Asia at the back of the main square. We walked among the once-grand ochre buildings, through the shaded parks and along Shrimp Paste Alley, Knife's Lane, Pig's Lane and Straw Street. We admired the façade of the burned-out cathedral and climbed to the Portuguese fort on the hill above the church with its old cannons pointing out to repel any invaders. We ate Portuguese pastries and bought anti-itching powder in an old pharmacy. 'A weed from Catholic Europe,' wrote Auden. 'Nothing serious can happen here.'

The Portuguese arrived in 1513, and formally took charge of the place in 1557. The Dutch tried to invade, but fled after a cannonball fired by a priest hit a barrel of gunpowder in their midst and caused havoc. The Jesuits established the first Western-style university in Asia, the College of the Mother of God, in 1594. Their great church of St Paul's, with its Chapel of the Eleven Thousand virgins, was consecrated in 1623. Francis Xavier died here, after failing to get into

China. The diocese of Macau stretched across China, Japan and Korea, and down to Timor and Malacca.

As a trading centre, Macau dealt in spices, silk, pepper, cloves, silver, sandalwood, tea, ginger, nutmeg and plates – the fine new museum up the hill from St Paul's contains a porcelain bidet from Canton, reminding one of where china got its name from. The Portuguese settlers also prospered from taking silks and porcelain to Japan and returning with silver which they sold to China at highly advantageous rates. A foundry set up in 1625 was so good that it received orders for cannons and bells from Europe. Later, Macau became famous for its fireworks, with names like Roaring Lion, Camel, Elephant, Polar Bear, Black Hawk Extra Loud Firecrackers – and the *ne plus ultra* Supercharged Flash Firecrackers Super Zoo Brand. Matches were also a big industry. But both had died out by the early 1960s, and the place became a backwater, with its pink and white government buildings, its decaying colonial houses, its Portuguese restaurants, its Buddhist monastery with a vegetarian canteen, and its many ornate churches.

For some, Macau means the annual Grand Prix motor race run through the winding city streets. For others, the magnet is Fernando's restaurant in a bare brick edifice behind the black sand beach on the island of Coloanne, where the prehistoric inhabitants of Macau lived. Fernando's serves enormous portions of grilled, garlicky food from Portugal and its other former possessions: the chicken comes from Brazil, the sardines from the home country. The other island, Taipa, has an ornate church on a hill, and a restored colonial residence below that reflects a strait-laced life many thousand miles from home. In the city on the mainland, the Club Militar has been given a facelift, and outsiders can rub elbows with the colonial elite in its stylish dining room. Reclamation and development have ruined the gracious old waterfront, but there are still the small *pastelaria* round the main square in the middle of the old town, and the beautiful lines of the churches and the nearby Senate building.

At the back of the square lies the Shanghai Barberia, with its revolving red, white and blue pole, old reclining chairs in faded imitation leather and equally aged attendants, one with a huge powder puff of white hair who cuts my thin topping strand by strand this afternoon with all the attention of a brain surgeon. Inexplicably, the bibs they put round customers' necks used to be printed with a map of the Arctic; equally inexplicably, they have been replaced with bibs bearing advertisements in French and Japanese for a café in Tokyo called Bananas, which offers 'a meeting of European and Japanese cakes'. On the television set installed on the wall above my chair, a noisy Hong Kong gangster film is showing a fight in a warehouse. A man with a blowtorch confronts a man with a revolver. The blowtorch melts the revolver barrel, which bends downwards. The gunman abandons the pistol on top of a packing case. Another man picks it up, not noticing the state of the barrel. A minute later he points the gun at an adversary and fires, literally shooting himself in the foot. I laugh. The puffball barber holds his scissors aloft for a moment and then goes on cutting my hairs one by one. The cost is one-fifth of what you'd pay in Hong Kong.

We are here this weekend for the closing of a Macau monument, the Bela Vista. Launched as a hotel by an English boat captain at the end of the nineteenth century, it has served many purposes over the years, but has recently been a small jewel of a place on a hill, run by a Hong Kong company, with its elegantly furnished bedrooms, its cool dining room, its terrace overlooking the harbour and its none too distinguished food. Now it is to close as a hotel in order to become the residence of the Portuguese consul to China's last reacquisition of the twentieth century. On this Saturday night, the superb bedrooms are thrown open as though the Bela Vista was just opening and soliciting guests. There is a sumptuous buffet and a big band that plays show tunes and a bit of swing before launching into a Latin American medley. As the strains of the tango and *paso doble* waft out towards the sea, a Chinese couple take the floor. They perform perfectly, each movement synchronised on best dance-school lines. They know how good they are, pausing to look at the spectators and elicit applause. They could have danced all night, for sure, but at 2 a.m. it is time to wander down the hill to the Mandarin hotel and casino, where the punters are heading for the VIP room and a couple of heavy-looking fellows are keeping watch outside.

For, despite all its legacies from a past that set Macau apart from the pace and prosperity of Hong Kong, one industry dominates. Gambling is the lifeblood of this place, and the bloodstream is far from pure.

Macau's gaming tradition reaches back for more than a century, boosted in 1872 by the ban on gambling in Hong Kong except for the horses and a few mahjong parlours (and, more recently, a weekly lottery). The Portuguese started taxing gambling in the 1850s. They used the money not only to cover local expenditure, but also to finance the colony of East Timor, which was administered from Macau. A monopoly casino franchise was instituted in 1937, and was held for many years by a Hong Kong Chinese family, some of whose members live in the same apartment block as us. In 1962, the family dropped out (one story has it that they netted US$350 million for giving up the franchise). They were succeeded by a company which may be regarded as the real master of present-day Macau.

The Sociedade de Turismo e Diversoes de Macau (STDM) is headed by the dapper Stanley Ho, a member of a celebrated family which rose to fame and fortune as *compradors*, or local go-betweens, for Jardine's, the Hongkong and Shanghai Bank and other big expatriate firms. There were five brothers Ho, and they speculated jointly in shares and went badly wrong when Jardine's stock slumped – two of the brothers committed suicide. Stanley, who likes to be referred to as 'Dr Ho' for his honorary doctorate from the Macau University of East Asia, is also head of the property-owners' association in Hong Kong, where his Shun Tak company owns three big sites. In Macau, he was originally associated with a tycoon called Yip Hon whom he described at his funeral as the 'God of Gambling'. Now it is Ho who is the gambling king of the enclave. Indeed, given the STDM's position in the place, you might say that he is the real governor of Macau.

The casino takings account for a quarter of the territory's gross domestic product, and provide billions of dollars in taxes, even if the government's revenue fell by 13 per cent in 1999 due to the Asian recession. Five per cent of the workforce is directly employed by the casinos; many more depend on the tourists gambling attracts. Dr Ho's company has its own bank and a fleet of thirty-two high-speed ferries. It built the garish Hotel Lisboa, with its golden cupolas, industrial gaming areas for the ordinary punters and carefully protected VIP rooms on the upper floors for the high rollers. It runs horse and greyhound racing. It recently completed a major development project of roads and new buildings round the main waterfront. The French may know Macau as '*l'enfer du jeu*', but, for the territory's people, the roulette, blackjack and fan-tan tables are more of a source of deliverance from an economy that would otherwise have even less to offer since trade and manufacture moved elsewhere.

The STDM has also tested the gambling waters in Vietnam and opened the first casino in the North Korean capital of Pyongyang. The minimum bet there is US$10, or half a week's earnings for a local worker. Not that locals are allowed into the establishment, which has cost some US$30 million. It is part of a wider attempt by Macau to forge links with Pyongyang. North Korea's airline is due to run a weekly service to the Portuguese colony. Unfortunately, the flights will only go once a month due to limited demand.

The company invited 100 guests from Macau and Hong Kong to the opening of the Pyongyang casino in 1999. Among them was a flamboyant figure from the SAR, Albert Yeung Sau-shing, chairman of a conglomerate called the Emperor Group. The President of the Legislative Council, Rita Fan, worked for two years as the group's general manager. Yeung was the man mentioned earlier who was freed after a string of witnesses lost their memories when called to give evidence against him. In the course of his career, he has been jailed for attempting to pervert the course of justice, banned from being a director of a listed company because of insider trading, and fined for illegal bookmaking. Now he is launching North Korea's second casino in a US$180 million hotel complex in a trade zone on the border with China and Russia.

The future of the casino franchise after Macau's return to China has not been settled, but the STDM holds it until 2001. The territory's Basic Law contains an explicit provision that its government may 'define its own policies on the tourism and amusement sector' – just in case any officials in Beijing were tempted to meddle with the principal source of amusement. Dr Ho is sure to play the game with all the skill bred from a lifetime of experience as a high-level go-between.

Born in 1921, he has a house in Hong Kong with James Bond-style protection gadgets. A big philanthropist, he is vice-president of the local Girl Guides. A pledge to contribute large sums of money to the Franklin Roosevelt Memorial campaign got him coffee with Bill Clinton at the White House. When a Hong Kong newspaper asked its readers who they would most like to be, Ho came second to the mega-tycoon Li Ka-shing. Ho's cash, women and good looks were seen as his most attractive qualities. With his slicked-back black hair and elegant frame, he looks the part of the superb ball-room dancer he is. A couple of years ago, he won two business-class return tickets to Paris in the lucky draw at a French Chamber of Commerce gala dinner. The other guests wondered what Stanley would want with mere business class when he has his own US$18 million private jet, named after his mother, Florinda, on which he likes to watch videos and catch up on sleep as he spends 400 hours a year in the air.

After the share slump in the 1930s and the suicide of two of his brothers, Ho's father fled to Saigon. 'I was so broke, dead broke,' Stanley recalls. He worked his way through a scholarship education at the University of Hong Kong, and then moved to Macau when the Japanese occupied the British colony. As a possession of Axis-friendly Portugal, Macau was left alone. Ho made his first small fortune dealing in rice, beans and kerosene. Back in Hong Kong after the end of hostilities, he earned a much bigger fortune from real estate and trading. A report commissioned by the government into a big takeover which was kept secret for years found that one of his close associates funded the purchase of three properties in New York with money borrowed from the STDM by cashing gambling chips from a room at the Lisboa casino.

In his home on the south side of Hong Kong Island, Ho has a collection of multi-carat jewelled objects bought from the best Western suppliers. On his office sideboard, there sits a golden beast studded with diamonds and emeralds for eyes. He buys a new animal each year. Last year, it was a tiger. A week ago it was reported that his fourth wife, Angela, was expecting his sixteenth child – she has already had three sons and a daughter. Asked about Viagra, Ho was reported to have replied, 'I have absolutely no need for such things.'

The good doctor holds a 20 per cent stake in STDM. Behind him stands the formidable figure of Henry Fok Ying-yung, a long-time China power-broker who has risen from a childhood on a junk to great wealth and a vice-chairmanship of the Chinese People's Political Consultative Congress. After the Second World War, Fok built up a shipping business, and smuggled embargoed goods into the mainland during the Korean War; the grateful Chinese government later granted him a sand monopoly. Known, as a result, as 'the Sandman', Fok found that his China connections earned him a bad name with the British authorities, which was one reason he turned his attentions to Macau and southern China.

Slight and small-eyed, with his skin drawn tightly over his skull, he built China's first luxury hotel, the White Swan in Guangzhou, which still hands guests postcards of Queen Elizabeth's stay there. He also organised the China-backed US$120 million loan that bailed out the family shipping firm of Tung Chee-hwa when it ran into financial difficulties. Long a critic of the British – 'I feel more free,' he said at the handover – Fok is believed to have played a role in the subsequent elevation of the Chief Executive. To be sure, when people speak of Stanley Ho, they do so with proper respect. But Henry Fok counts for even more, even if the degree of his current involvement in Macau is opaque.

Gambling is 'a very special kind of business', as Stanley Ho told Greg Torode of the *South China Morning Post* in an interview in 1998. 'It is not good publicity to tell the world how much money we make,' he added. 'It might scare away our big clients. My God, I have been a sucker contributing so much, they might say. You need confidentiality very much, so you really need your own people.'

Ho's 'own people' have been none too fortunate. His first wife, Clementina, was seriously injured in a road accident in Portugal in 1972, and now lives in seclusion in a house in Macau on the ridge overlooking the strip of water that separates the colony from the mainland. His eldest son, Robert, died with his wife in another car crash in 1981. His right-hand man, Thomas Chung Wah-tin, bled to death in minutes after being slashed on his arms and legs on his way to a tennis game in the Mid-Levels district of Hong Kong in 1986: the crime remains unsolved. In 1992 a US Senate Committee hearing alleged links with associates involved in organised crime. In 1993 police raided Ho's Hong Kong mansion during investigations into the empire of the Australian businessman, Alan Bond. 'As we say in Chinese, real gold is not afraid of the fire of the furnace,' Ho said. 'I have done nothing wrong. I am very happy with what I am . . . No regrets, no regrets.'

He says he is not worried about the Triads fighting and killing one another, even if it does give Macau a bad name. 'At most, there might be a few dozen people killed,' Ho told reporters on a visit to Beijing earlier this month. 'It's none of our business.' What really worries him and other big businessmen in Macau is the threat of being kidnapped. There has been a series of unreported abductions, he says, with the victims not informing the police for fear of reprisals. Ho insists he does not know a single Triad member. 'I don't need them and I don't like them.'

No doubt. But, as a Macau police cliché has it, as light attracts mosquitoes so casinos attract criminals. Elsewhere, it is the Mafia; in this part of the world it is the Triads. Ho's company says it keeps a firm grip on its own operations. As for corruption, he once remarked: 'The whole world is corrupt. It's only a matter of degree.'

The practice of leasing out rooms at the casinos where high-stakes games are played is an obvious magnet for the criminals, as is the traffic in gambling chips and the pickings from prostitution and protection rackets. There are also the high rollers who fly in and want to be entertained, and the losers who need to borrow money for that elusive big hit. Traditionally, the big gamblers have come from Hong Kong and Taiwan, but some are now arriving from the mainland, like the deputy mayor of a big city who has been accused of gambling away the equivalent of US$3.5 million from municipal funds when he was meant to be attending a study course at the Central Party School in Beijing.

Loan-sharking is a favoured Triad activity, and one that fits in neatly with gambling. Freelance dealers in casino chips offer them on credit at extortionate daily interest rates. In one terrible case, a Hong

Kong woman went across to Macau while her husband was away sweeping the graves of his ancestors on the mainland during the season of family mourning. She lost all their savings. She borrowed money from loan sharks. She lost that, too. She went home and tried to kill herself and her children with gas, rat poison and, eventually, by slitting their veins. The father returned to a scene of carnage. His wife was taken to court and sentenced to jail – she had to be put in a specially protected area of the prison because the Triad loan sharks were still after her for their money.

Prostitution is another underworld mainstay. Smart hotel lobbies have their contingent of elegantly turned-out Russian tarts. In less plush establishments, saunas, nightclubs and on the streets, the young women are from the mainland, several thousand of them. They turn tricks for a couple of hundred local dollars, and give most of their money to pimps who provide them with hotel rooms. Many send much of their remaining earnings to their families, telling their parents they have jobs as waitresses or shop assistants.

When times were good in Macau and there was enough loot to keep everybody happy, each Triad gang kept to its own turf. Now the Asian economic crisis means that less money is being spent on gambling, and the hoods are at one another's throats for what there is. In a series of gangland killings, underworld figures have been shot or chopped to death. The last Portuguese Governor describes the current violence as 'unprecedented'. Nobody seems safe. A senior gambling inspector was shot dead and one of his superiors wounded twice in the head. A government prosecutor involved in fighting the Triads and casino crime was shot and wounded in the chest by two men on a motorcycle who also hit his pregnant wife in the hip. Journalists have been warned that if they write about the main Triad gang, 'bullets will have no eyes and knives and bullets will have no feelings'. In one incident, three men in a green van tried to kidnap the grandson of Stanley Ho's late partner, the God of Gambling, shooting him in the stomach before he forced them to flee by returning fire. Though the numbers are, by their nature, unverifiable, Triads may outnumber the 4,300 members of the police and security forces.

They are used to moving with relative impunity across the border with Guangdong province, but now police have pulled in 622 alleged Triads in a three-day operation. Half the inmates of Macau jails come from outside the colony. A leading local gang boss celebrated for his crime wave on both sides of Macau's border with Guangdong hails from Hong Kong. Some of the other hoods come from Taiwan, or from the mainland.

The threat from foreign mobsters is such that four local Triad bosses are said to have hatched a plan to unite their gangs to fight the interlopers. Before that could happen, the most prominent of the locals, a 45-year-old known as Broken Tooth, was arrested in the Lisboa Hotel after a bomb was set off under the car of the head of the Judicial Police while he was out jogging. Broken Tooth, whose real name is Wan Kuok-koi, has not been accused of that bombing, but rather of being the head of the much-feared 14K Triad gang, commanding associates known as Smuggling Queen, Fat Woman, Big Sister, Terrible Ghost, Scarface and Fishmonger. The head of the Judicial Police says that 14K carried out a string of attacks on officials and underworld murders including the sensational killing of a Hong Kong Triad boss known as the 'Tiger of Wanchai' during the 1993 Macau Grand Prix motor race. In another incident, three of Wan's leading lieutenants were shot in the street in 1997.

Wan, who has been described as a psychopath, is thought to have believed that he could shoot and bomb his way to control of the Macau underworld. Starting out as a seller of chicken wings, he ended up with more than twenty bank accounts and a string of properties, including a nightclub called Heavy Di with a large swastika and a skull and cross-bones on its façade. A visitor recalls seeing a life-sized mannequin in a police uniform hanging from the ceiling at the end of a noose. Broken Tooth lost the use of two fingers in a chopper attack and has been shot twice. An inveterate high-stakes punter, he was once caught on security camera footage jumping on to a gambling table and flinging chairs round the room after he had suffered a bad streak.

In a crazy act of self-glorification, he produced a film called *Casino*, studded with incriminating depictions of violence and soft porn scenes. He was watching a documentary about himself when he was picked up. He denies being anything more than a businessman and high-stakes gambler, and says his fortune is based on a big win at the Lisboa casino. Still, Wan has been charged with weapons trafficking, illegal gambling, loan-sharking, blackmail, unlawful detention and possession of fake identity documents, as well as being a member of the illegal 14K Triad organisation. At his home, police found a scanner which could have been used to listen in to their radio wavelengths: Wan says it was a gift from 'a fat woman who died in a shipwreck in China'. A former Portuguese gambling inspector who was shot twice in the head by two motorcycle gunmen in 1996 says Wan told him the 14K was 'my group'. The gang is alleged to have gone to China and Vietnam to hire killers to carry out revenge murders in Macau in the mid-1990s. Police reports say Broken Tooth had planned to establish a weapons factory in Cambodia and to buy tanks, missiles and rockets from arms dealers.

The main prison where he was first held is described as being out of control. Although there is one guard for every three prisoners, Triads rule the roost behind the twenty-foot walls. Wan is said to have run his gang from inside the jail by mobile telephone, and to have held all-night parties with drink and drugs. When he and eight other men were moved to a special high-security unit nearby, 300 police guarded them. The Judicial Police director says Broken Tooth provided another prisoner with Ecstasy pills during his birthday party earlier in the year: the man overdosed and died. The judge who was originally to have heard his case has decided to take retirement. A substitute has been sent from Portugal; he is rarely seen without a bodyguard. New prison guards have also been drafted in from Europe. Their families have stayed behind – it's safer that way.

The Broken Tooth case apart, the future of Macau's legal system is murky. Very few Chinese understand it. Many judges are new appointments. Most of the senior policemen will be going back to Europe. No wonder that officials in Beijing roll their eyes when the matter of law and order in the Portuguese colony is raised. Stanley Ho once suggested that Hong Kong might take responsibility for such matters after the handover in December.

That will not happen. On the other hand, if the Triads keep up their present level of activity, the Chinese army garrison in Macau might find itself as the ultimate arbiter of public security. They may not be on the streets in Hong Kong, but what price a PLA detachment fighting crime in Macau? Would a savvy Triad then claim democratic credentials and become a political martyr? Stranger things have happened.

From 20 December, this will be a problem for the new Chief Executive of Macau, a well-connected banker called Edmund Ho who has adopted the hopeful slogan 'advancing from adversity to opportunity'. Ho should have a much smoother political passage than his counterpart in Hong Kong. Portugal was ready to hand back Macau after its own revolution in 1974, particularly when local leftists flexed their muscles during the Cultural Revolution. But Beijing had other things on its mind, and didn't want Macau just then. So the Portuguese took the line that Macau was Chinese territory being administered by Europeans for the time being.

This meant that though the Governor has formally ruled from his pink palace, virtually nothing was done that would not find favour with the mainland authorities. China's influence is felt throughout the community, from the meetings of the local legislature in the Senate building to the decision to remove an equestrian statue of a nineteenth century Portuguese governor from a square opposite Stanley Ho's main casino because it was regarded as a politically incorrect piece of colonial symbolism.

The veneer of Portuguese rule has become even thinner than that of the British in their last years in Hong Kong. The President of Portugal, who did not get on politically with the more right-wing Governor, was reported to have thought of appointing Edmund Ho to run the colony back in 1996. There are around 2,000 'continentals' in Macau. Only a few hundred will stay after the end of the year. Most civil service jobs have already been transferred to local people. Though there are some 10,000 Macanese born from unions between local Chinese and Portuguese, particularly soldiers from the garrison who used local marriages as a way of avoiding being posted to the awful colonial wars in Angola and Mozambique, this is a Chinese city. Macau has always felt strong identification with the mainland, be it under the Kuomintang regime or the Communists. In recent years, money has flowed into Macau from China, funding the building of empty tower blocks by the waterfront. The neighbouring city of Zhuhai has had its eye on the colony.

When the Portuguese go, they will leave their mark, but it seems unlikely to endure to any great extent. Nine months before it rejoins a motherland it never knew, Macau remains a fascinating, outlandish place, with its casino bosses and Graham Greenesque officials, its Russian prostitutes and its sardines from the Atlantic, but it seems destined to become a true backwater, with a name that people recognise but cannot quite place on the map any more. Still, Dr Ho is not giving up. He is opening a tenth casino on Taipa island, making sure that he schedules the ceremony for an auspicious date. He is also diversifying into the Philippines. The share price of an obscure company there soared when Ho's interest in it became known, and he had a floating restaurant towed in from Hong Kong: speculation that one floor would be turned into a casino was dampened down after the Cardinal Archbishop of Manila said that this would destroy families and bankrupt homes. He is also pushing a big property redevelopment scheme in Hong Kong – just in case things go wrong across the bay in the place where nothing is ever supposed to happen.

31 *March*

The tax rebates promised in the Budget have been sent out with cheques worth HK$8.5 billion. But all the evidence suggests that rather than rushing out to spend and giving the economy a kick-start, people are putting the money in the bank.

APRIL

1 *April*

Mobile telephone ownership in the SAR has passed three million, or nearly three-quarters of adults. This is the second highest penetration in the world after Finland. Today the system has been made easier to use: if you switch telephone companies, you no longer have to get a new number. Advertisements proclaim this to be 'Independence Day'. To encourage people to sign up with it, firms offer free noodles, a yoghurt drink, cash and discounts. Spending on advertising mobiles has jumped by 70 per cent in the first quarter of the year. A television station prudently decided not to show a documentary on the possible health dangers involved in using them.

On the mainland, the poor state of land lines makes the jump to mobiles a sensible, if expensive, step. In Guangzhou last year, I watched a young woman praying at a temple. Her mobile rang. She took it from her pocket and conducted a conversation without missing a single bow towards the altar. In Hong Kong, the fixed-line system is perfectly good and local calls are free, but mobiles have become an inherent part of everybody's life. Being a non-owner is roughly akin to not being interested in making money. Such people do exist, but they are rare. There are jokes not a million miles from reality about diners at adjoining restaurant tables conversing over their telephones, or ordering the next course on a mobile. When a plane lands in Hong Kong, passengers rush to get out the telephones and make a call. So that small children don't feel left out, toy shops sell rubber mobile phones. One woman says her daughter rejects the toy and is only content with the real thing. The other day, a workman balanced on top of a bamboo scaffolding outside our flat was talking busily into his mobile without any visible means of support hundreds of feet above the ground.

Last summer, I lunched with a major Hong Kong property developer in the dining room of his penthouse office. He insisted on accompanying me down to street level when I left. Did I need a lift back to my office? he asked. No, I said, I had an office car coming to pick me up. Why didn't I call the driver to make sure I didn't waste any time waiting? I said I didn't have a telephone with me. Shocked, he handed me his. Two hours later, he sent a mobile round to my office as a gift.

2 April

The *Yancheng Evening News* reports that 100 condom dispensers are to be installed in Guangzhou city, selling a box of two contraceptives for the equivalent of 22 cents. They will be made theft-proof with special 'drill-in screws'. This follows a bad experience in the city of Chengdu where similar machines had a habit of 'disappearing during the night', the newspaper says.

5 April

Today is Ching Ming, the Festival of Pure Brightness or the Festival of the Dead. Like Easter, with which it coincides, it is a time to contemplate death, resurrection and the afterlife, for which the Chinese ensure that the departed enjoy worldly comforts by burning fake paper money and models of cars, houses, boats and mobile telephones which are wafted aloft in the smoke. This is a time at which Hong Kong people flood to the mainland, to visit family graves there: 140,000 people went through the frontier today.

Some 400 fires started by people burning paper money or leaving smouldering incense sticks at graves are blazing on the hillsides of Hong Kong. Most are in the New Territories. Government helicopters are busy water-bombing the flames. Dozens of people have to be rescued. Almost 9 million square metres and 5,400 trees are affected. A photograph of a fire on the crest of Kowloon Peak makes such a dramatic front-page image that some readers mistake it for the latest picture from the war in Yugoslavia. On the mainland, newspapers report that more than 50 people were killed and 205 injured in similar fires this week.

6–7 April

Some crime and economic news from China.

A restaurant owner in Henan province has been sentenced to death for pouring nitric acid into a vat of donkey soup at a rival establishment. In all, 148 people received hospital treatment after drinking it.

On the border between Guangdong and Guanxi provinces, police with rocket cannons have finally got the better of a twenty-strong gang that has been indulging in murder, robbery and drug trafficking for five years. The police were initially outgunned, but their 400-strong force triumphed after an eight-hour battle.

And on the economic front, a television price war has broken out. Like many Chinese companies, manufacturers are suffering from excess production, low domestic demand and slumping exports. Last year the mainland made 35 million sets, double the 1994 figure. In the first quarter of 1999, output has shot up by another 46 per cent. Five new producers have entered the market. But sales are still sluggish.

The biggest producer, a former military factory in Sichuan province which makes 6.7 million sets a year, announces price cuts of between 10 and 33 per cent. Sounding for all the world like rival newspapers inveighing against Rupert Murdoch's pricing tactics, the general manager of another manufacturer calls on the government to 'act against this vicious cycle of competition and move against firms that sell below production cost to ensure a level playing field'. But within two weeks, the other companies follow the Sichuan approach. Still, the depth of consumer caution is such that few people rush out to buy. Many city-dwellers either own or have access to a set. And even at the knock-down prices, televisions are still too expensive for most people in country areas. When rural incomes average 2,160 yuan a year, even a cut-price set at 1,800 yuan is an unattainable luxury.

9 *April*

The need to give the mainland economy a serious kick-start forms the backdrop to the most important foreign visit ever undertaken by the Prime Minister, Zhu Rongji, who is in the United States. The cooling of relations since Bill Clinton's trip to China last summer, in which he spoke of a new strategic partnership with Beijing, means Zhu's journey is an on-off affair till the very last moment, when it is approved by an emergency meeting of the Politburo. 'President Jiang made me come,' Zhu says in Washington. 'He is China's Number One. Of course I obeyed his order.' Thus does the Prime Minister fix final responsibility with Jiang.

In Washington, Zhu unveils an extraordinary set of concessions aimed at getting the US to agree to admit China into the World Trade Organisation, thereby sealing its economic relationship with the rest of the world. Although the Europeans get a trifle shirty when WTO membership is seen as being a matter for Washington to decide, the Chinese know who matters most in this process. So Zhu offers to slash import duties on a big range of products, from food and chemicals to cars and mobile phones. He says China will allow foreign ownership in telecommunications, hotels and insurance companies, a significant expansion in the activities of foreign banks, and the elimination of tariffs on computers and agricultural products. A leading American China expert, Nicholas Lardy, calls the offer 'breathtaking'. *Business Week* magazine describes it as an 'amazing deal'. Zhu jokes that if the extent of the concessions is made public back home, he will face a revolt. Before long, the Clinton administration will turn the jest into reality.

Despite his pre-emptive remark about Jiang, Zhu is taking a considerable personal gamble, given the residual strength of Chinese conservatives who disagree with his policies. But Clinton lets him down. Some senior presidential aides, including the Secretary of State, the National Security Adviser and the US Chief Trade Negotiator, are for an immediate deal. Yet, bowing to a mixture of congressional anti-China pressure and arguments from Wall Street, which wants even more, the President refuses to respond. Then his administration makes things far worse by posting the Prime Minister's terms on the Internet where they can be read by his enemies back home. According to the *Wall Street Journal*, a new phrase is born: to be 'Zhu'd' means having the rug pulled from under you at the last moment.

The Sino-US climate has already been soured by allegations of Chinese political funding and by continuing arguments over human rights. Blaming the 'bad political atmosphere' in the United States for the breakdown, Zhu gamely insists that the differences do not amount to much. Clinton stresses that he still wants a deal by the end of the year, and is ready to send an emissary to Beijing to re-open talks. But can Zhu offer anything more?

In his post-Washington travels, the Premier dons a ten-gallon hat, pitches a football at the Denver Broncos training camp and gives commodity dealers a Chinese hand signal for good fortune. In Chicago he says, 'It's like I am in a department store and I want to buy everything I see. But I do not have enough money in my pocket.' He asks his American hosts how stock options work, and quotes from the free-market philosopher Friedrich von Hayek. But some remarks are more pointed. Zhu says China is seeking improvement in human rights every day 'but the US isn't working as quickly to improve theirs'. On occasion, he goes off the screen altogether, calling Lincoln's opposition to the Confederacy 'a model, an example' for Beijing's policy towards Taiwan.

11 *April*

For anybody unacquainted with Hong Kong's popular Chinese-language press, today provides a good introduction to what you may expect on page one. At the time of the handover, the independence of the media and their ability to criticise Beijing and the SAR government exercised politicians, press freedom bodies and foreign correspondents. Now, it is their ethics and standards that give cause for concern. This morning's front pages show why.

Readers of the main popular papers were greeted with photographs of the body of a twenty-year-old woman found in a cardboard box on the stairway of a public housing estate, her mouth bound with tape. The photographers, who monitor the police radio, arrived in time to snap close-up pictures before the corpse was taken away. These show the twisted body in the box, with the thick platform heels of black patent-leather shoes sticking up in the air. One newspaper, *Apple Daily*, also runs a close-up of the woman's disfigured face across half the top of the page. (For the record, my paper did a two-paragraph story at the foot of the front page, with no photograph.)

Dumbing down and page three in the *Sun* have nothing on what is happening in Hong Kong. The popular press here has never been noted for restraint, but the launch of *Apple* in 1995 set off a full-blooded press war, which is being fought with sensationalism, paparazzi pursuit of celebrities, intrusion, price-cutting, advertising deals and the occasional use of faked photographs. Polls show the credibility of the media at an all-time low, with magazines ranked as the worst products on the market in Hong Kong. One particular incident has stoked concern. It involves a man whose wife threw herself and their two children off the top of a building after finding he had mistresses in China. *Apple* subsequently paid for him to make a trip to the mainland that ended with him posing in bed with two young women for the paper's photographers. As the outrage mounted and a rival newspaper castigated the man as 'human scum', *Apple* devoted its front page to an apology for having been led astray by misguided zeal to serve its readers.

The paper's owner, Jimmy Lai Chee-ying, is one of those archetypal Hong Kong figures who rose from being a penniless refugee to great wealth. Born on the mainland in 1948, he was smuggled in at the age of twelve. After working in garment sweatshops, he made his first serious money by stock market speculation. Then he built up a successful rag trade business, copying European designs and manufacturing techniques. From there, it was a natural jump into retailing with a chain called Giordano, modelled on Benetton.

Moving into the media, Lai launched a successful glossy, gossipy magazine called *Next*, and brought new life to the daily press with *Apple* in 1995. Awash with colour, graphics, sensationalism, short news items and consumer service tests, the paper was an immediate hit. It quickly soared to a circulation of 400,000, within spitting distance of the market leader, the *Oriental Daily*. *Apple* reflected the street-smart attitude of a man who eats at three-star restaurants in Paris but is in his element wolfing down Chinese–Malaysian food in a bare walk-up in the back streets. The stocky, crew-cut, jeans-clad Lai, who likes to read the abridged thoughts of great philosophers, appeared in his paper's launch television commercials in person. He stood with an apple on his head in a circle of shadowy enemies firing arrows. The clip ended with him munching the fruit, unharmed.

Lai has been the target of mainland enmity ever since he wrote a celebrated article in *Next* magazine describing the then Premier, Li Peng, as a 'turtle's egg' who should drop dead. His journalists are banned from crossing the border. When Lai tried to float his group on the Hong Kong stock exchange around the time of the handover, established finance houses were strangely unwilling to take him on. One underwriter withdrew at the eleventh hour, and it was not until the autumn of 1999 that he finally obtained a listing with a reverse takeover of a printing group. 'Controversy has been my nature,' he says. That has helped to make him a democratic hero, even if he did run brothel reviews in his newspaper as a reader service.

Lai tells me that his publications are successful because he does not come from a press background. 'I don't see newspapers any differently from the T-shirts I was selling at Giordano,' he says. 'I just wanted to go against City Hall. We advocate freedom and democracy, and we also have the sex columns. I don't see any contradiction there.' Still, Lai's critics have a point when they see the launch of *Apple* as a moment when the popular Chinese-language press headed for the gutter in a vicious war for readers. In March 1999, the *Oriental Daily* brought out a sister paper called the *Sun* to undercut *Apple*. One of the new daily's senior executives describes it to me as 'a children's paper for childish adults'. It has a drawing of the chairman's son on the masthead: when the news is good he smiles; when it is bad he frowns.

The only thing uniting Lai and the owners of the *Oriental* is their insistence that they are just giving the public what it wants. Still, pressure is growing for a press council to rein in the excesses. There are two snags with this. First, any such body might try to extend its activities to put a gag on stories which need to be covered but which inconvenience people of influence. Secondly, to imagine *Apple* and the *Oriental* sitting on the same committee is about as feasible as Jimmy Lai interviewing President Jiang.

Anyway, *Apple*'s proprietor is already off pursuing another career with a direct sales firm called AdMart, which enables customers to order goods through his publications, the Internet, telephones and fax. The established supermarkets are being forced to follow suit. They are also withdrawing advertising from Lai's newspaper and magazine. As if this was not enough of a headache, AdMart runs into a spot of bother when it is found to be unwittingly selling poor-quality wine in bottles with the Mouton Cadet claret label.

13 *April*

In another part of the Hong Kong media forest, I have been reading on the Internet about a sad wreck of a journalist who shows how justified fears were about the way the media would go after the handover. A pitiable victim of guilt-ridden obsessions, this refugee from London has turned his newspaper into a biased, stuffy, misinformed, hypocritical pro-China propaganda rag in return for hush money from a Beijing bagman. Fat and greedy, he possesses the ethics of a Mafia lawyer and the selective memory of a Latin American dictator. His news agenda is decided by a censor from the mainland or by the government's information services as he reels back from lunch and sleeps off the gin and tonics. Even his private life is a ruin: Hong Kong's dullest man, he is so boring that his wife has left him.

I must meet this pathetic figure some day, particularly since his name is Jonathan Fenby.

The depiction of me is to be found on an Internet website run by a man called George Adams, who used to teach teachers at the Hong Kong Institute of Education, and whose offer to write a column in the *South China Morning Post* I declined. I have never encountered Adams in person, but he describes himself in lonely-hearts style on his website as being six foot in height, of 'muscular' build, interested in swimming, running, cinema, music and the Internet; he dislikes cats, lawyers and 1997. He styles himself 'Dr' for his academic achievements, and fancies his talents as a satirist. He says the board of the *Post* has ordered me not to reply to his attacks, as if the paper's directors have the slightest idea of his existence.

All this would be just another example of a wayward, ego-boosting mind let loose on the Internet, except that, in his outlandish way, Adams represents the *reductio ad absurdum* of a process that has been going on around me since I arrived in Hong Kong in May 1995. One of my early surprises was to discover how Western correspondents in Hong Kong, local democrats, media watchdog bodies and Government House all seemed to have made a point of poor-mouthing the *Post*.

If we ran a photograph of the President of China on page one, it was a sign of kowtowing to Beijing. If I decided to use a text from China's news agency as a matter of record on a meeting between Jiang Zemin and a group of Hong Kong tycoons, I was met with sarcastic speculation about whether the *Post* was going to print Xinhua reports as a matter of course from now on. Martin Lee told a big media lunch in the United States that the bridge column was the 'only independent and interesting thing' in the paper, which presumably ruled out our extensive political news coverage, the regular columns by three pro-democracy politicians and the op-ed article we commissioned for handover day, by none other than the Chairman of the Democrat Party. Emily Lau accused us of censoring her out of the paper, although I gave her statistics to show that she was the single most reported politician in the pages of the *Post*.

Then there was the Governor, a politician who had masterminded the Conservative general election campaign of 1992 with its 'Double

Whammy' assault on the Labour Party. In the past, British rulers had been able to count on the loyal support of the *Post* as a pillar of the colonial establishment. But the sale of the paper in 1993 by Rupert Murdoch to a Malaysian–Chinese tycoon with strong mainland links made it suspect. So officials looked with a kindly eye on plans by the Oriental Press Group to set up a rival daily which would be more dependably in tune with official thinking.

The new paper saw the light of day in 1994, before I arrived in Hong Kong. Called the *Eastern Express*, it set out to be the *Independent* of the South China Sea, with a bold design, big photographs, long foreign features and an excellent sports section. Its editor was a British journalist, Stephen Vines, who had been the Hong Kong stringer for the *Guardian* and the *Observer*. Unfortunately, its local news was patchy, and it led with an embarrassingly wrong 'scoop' in its first issue. Despite Martin Lee's jibe, the main pro-democracy columnists stayed with the *Post*. Before long, Vines was replaced, and called on me to give evidence to get him his pay-off. A succession of subsequent editors tried to find a vocation for the *Express*, but in the summer of 1996, the owners reserved a big space on the front page to announce its closure.

There was no doubt about the government's interest in the *Express*. The *Post*'s political editor was invited up to tea at Government House to be urged by one of Patten's civil servants to move to the new paper; she decided not to go. There were reports of official advice over other senior appointments. The Oriental group's boss made a number of visits to Government House. Patten went to the Oriental headquarters. One of his senior aides made enquiries about which British newspapers the Oriental group might buy, specifically mentioning the *Independent* and *Observer*.

The motivation for all this activity may have been purely and laudably pro-democratic, but the *Express* was a newspaper which sought to compete in the marketplace with the *Post* and the *Hong Kong Standard*. That could have led to some pointed questions had civil servants acted in a similar manner back in Britain, but this was Hong Kong, and back home, Patten walked on water, with many friends in the media who brushed aside such behaviour as being quite normal for a faraway place of which they knew little.

But that left the question of what the bosses of the Oriental may have expected in return for launching the *Eastern Express*. Two of the group's founding members had been forced to leave Hong Kong for Taiwan in the late 1970s to escape drug trafficking charges. Reports at the time said they were alleged to be at the head of the biggest narcotics ring the territory had known. One had subsequently died. But the family members remaining in Hong Kong, who were never the subject of any drug allegations, wanted the other to be allowed to come home to die in peace.

In the mid-1990s, the head of the group, C. K. Ma, a nephew of the founders, was reported to have donated hundreds of thousands of pounds to the British Conservatives, and to have bought a printing press to turn out posters and leaflets for the party. The *Sunday Times* reported that Ma was known at Central Office as 'Golden Boy'. To thank him for his generosity, John Major issued an invitation to tea at Downing Street. Ma established links with a number of Tory MPs, and acquired prestigious properties in London. He mused about getting a British honour and sending his sons to Eton. He hired the former Cabinet minister, David Mellor, as his consultant.

It was against this background that C. K. Ma launched the *Eastern Express*, with a strongly pro-Patten editorial line. When the British turned down an application for his uncle to be allowed to come home shortly before the handover, Ma revealed details of the collaboration over the *Express*, noting each of his visits to Government House and a trip by Patten across to the Oriental headquarters on the Kowloon side of the harbour. Some senior local civil servants took a decidedly dim view of the administration having anything to do with the Oriental group. Interestingly, there is no mention of the episode in Jonathan Dimbleby's otherwise exhaustive account of the last Governor's years in Hong Kong. In his own book about Hong Kong, the founding editor of the *Express* economically refers to his proprietors simply as 'controversial', without any elucidation for readers unfamiliar with the Ma family saga.

Whether it was because he felt he had to justify his backing for the

Express or simply that he needed a media punching bag, the Governor seemed unable to find a good word to say about the *Post*. The falling-out had begun under my predecessor, a leading Australian journalist, who had certainly not adopted a line of uncritical support and once ordered an editorial telling Patten to shut up. On the fundamental issues, the *Post* never budged while I was editor in its support for freedom, human rights, democracy and the rule of law. That did not stop Patten poor-mouthing us to guests from London even as we printed his speeches as op-ed pieces. When one of his leading critics, the former diplomat Sir Percy Cradock, became a non-executive director of the *Post* a year before the handover, Government House took this as proof that we were in the enemy camp. (Cradock contributed a couple of articles, but never tried to get involved in the paper's contents.)

Patten's friend and chronicler, Jonathan Dimbleby, told me that the Governor simply had 'a blind spot' as far as the paper was concerned. Appearing at the Legislative Council early in 1997, Patten attributed views to us which were the exact opposite of an editorial we had written a few days earlier. When I objected, I was told that the Governor was entitled to say whatever he wanted. On another occasion, his Information Co-ordinator gatecrashed a lunch with the Financial Secretary and, to the evident embarrassment of my guest, launched into a lengthy denunciation of my failure to stand up for press freedom – shortly after I had written a 1,200-word editorial explaining why press freedom was so important to Hong Kong. (The official in question went on to take a job with the information service of the new regime after the handover.)

Correspondents, commentators and press freedom bodies, some of whom never read the paper, picked up the tune. In an unexpected bout of imperial nostalgia, a British Labour MP, Denis MacShane, told the Commons that the *Post* was a mere shadow of what it had been in the 1980s, when it had faithfully carried the official colonial line. The Lonely Planet guide informed its readers that the paper was 'known as the *Pro China Morning Post*' and vaunted the merits of the *Hong Kong Standard*, which was pursuing a more patriotic line. The *Observer's* Peter Hillmore reported that we were well prepared for the kowtow when it came to reporting Chinese dissidents: this was after we had devoted the front of our Saturday Review section to letters smuggled out of prison by the leading dissident Wei Jingsheng. On handover day, a BBC television presenter opened an interview with me by saying: 'Now, your paper's gone pretty soft,' waving a feature supplement as if it was the front page. In another BBC programme, a well-known British journalist and the founder of Index on Censorship referred to our 'pre-emptive cringe'.

The bottom line, which did not speak too well about my trade, was that the story was too simple and too appealing to be resisted. After the handover, Hong Kong was bound to go down the drain. For that to be true, the media had to be headed for the plughole, with the *Post* in the vanguard. The way we reported, commented on and analysed events was taken as a barometer of how Hong Kong was moving. 'You are the canary in the coalmine for Hong Kong,' as a visiting American editor put it to me. And since the bad-news story was the one that would sell, the view had to be negative.

Even when the *Post* was named best English-language paper in Asia and Democrats publicly praised our record, some still stuck to their guns. Stephen Vines, stringing for the *Independent*, has declared that the *Post* had been 'neutralised', which was satisfactory enough for Beijing. Jonathan Mirsky, the former East Asia editor of *The Times*, told a meeting in London that it had been the 'drip, drip, drip' of criticism in the first eighteen months after Rupert Murdoch sold the paper which had pushed me back on to the high road. 'It's a very good example of shame directing an editor,' he added. This overlooked the fact that the editor in question had been at the *Observer* in London during those eighteen months.

All things considered, I preferred the copy of an election poster Martin Lee sent me in 1998 inscribed, 'Thank you for your defence of press freedom in Hong Kong! Yours democratically, Martin.'

16 *April*

The stock market powers on despite otherwise gloomy economic figures. Foreign investors have decided that they may have overdone the flight from Asia, and want to hedge their bets in case the Wall Street bubble bursts. The Hang Seng index soars through the 12,000-point level, ending the week at a seventeen-month high. Property prices have slumped, but the share prices for big developers have more than doubled. Traditional valuations have gone out of the window. The Asian Development Bank forecasts more pain for Hong Kong. But who cares about such predictions any more?

The Hong Kong dollar has stood firm against the tide of devaluations all around it, and the Government has done well out of its intervention in the market last August: the overall value of its holdings has increased by 61 per cent for a paper gain of US$9 billion in eight months. The Financial Secretary waves his hands in embarrassment when I refer to him at an awards ceremony as Hong Kong's biggest and most successful fund manager. But he still talks about the government's pile of cash in rather personal terms. 'I have over ninety billion US dollars in reserves and no debt,' he tells a meeting of pension fund gurus.

Donald Tsang, who has taken to describing the market move as 'an incursion', says he hates what has happened, and never wants to live through such an experience again. 'Faced with the prospect of a market set to implode through manipulative activities,' he adds, 'I decided it was better to have a market in which to invest than to have no market at all.' Now the question is how the government is going to get rid of the shares to prove that this was an incursion, not an invasion.

18 *April*

A day trip by train to Shenzhen. The half-hour journey is like any commuter shuttle. There is no sense of going anywhere special, even when the loudspeaker announces, 'Welcome to China', as the train pulls into the frontier station of Lo Wu. At the crossing point, there are duty-free shops, Chinese soldiers in olive-green uniforms, and a special channel for 'VIP Honorary Citizens The Elderly and Handicapped'. A health form asks if you suffer from 'rash, HIV, VD or psychosis': one wonders who would reply in the affirmative. As my entry form is being checked, a young woman in uniform at the immigration counter picks up a *New Yorker* from a bunch of magazines I brought along to read on the journey. She points out the fashion advertisements to a colleague.

The Shenzhen river which marks the border stinks: a boy from Hong Kong holds his nose demonstratively on the way across the bridge into the mainland. It is the weekend, and most of the other passengers on the Kowloon and Canton Railway Corporation train are seeking bargains – cheap Chinese-manufactured goods, low-price hairdos and massages, fake handbags and watches handed over in perfectly imitated Chanel and Cartier bags.

The retail competition from Shenzhen is causing problems for Hong Kong shops. So much so that there are suggestions of imposing a departure tax on the SAR side of the border to make bargain-hunting dearer as well as to raise revenue. Outside the station, an avenue of stalls and shops sells everything under the sun. Curtains made to measure are in particular demand. Big department stores and arcades stand on one side of the road; lines of massage parlours and beauty salons on the other. One group of masseuses is kitted out in blue dungarees and red T-shirts; those at the Mang Bing Massage service wear red dresses with yellow sashes and hand out leaflets assuring potential clients in English, 'You are Welcome'. In some establishments, you can be pummelled by the feet of women hanging above you from metal bars. Hairdressing shops are a well-known euphemism for brothels – the 'human scum' widower in the notorious story in *Apple Daily* picked up the two young ladies in one. But Hong Kong women genuinely come to Shenzhen to have their hair done: in a hairdresser's near the station this afternoon my wife spent a tenth of what she would have paid in Hong Kong.

Boosted by low tax rates for companies, Shenzhen's industrial and technology parks are forging ahead in electronics, computers and software at a speed that should give the SAR pause for thought about its own ambitions to become a hi-tech centre. It now accounts for 44 per cent of the mainland's high-tech output, with exports in the sector rising 60 per cent a year. While Hong Kong sank into recession in 1998, Shenzhen reported 15 per cent growth, though its economy is still only a fraction of the SAR's. Most of the technology enterprises are funded by private Chinese investors, or from Hong Kong and Taiwan; only 10 per cent of the finance has come from the Chinese government. Twelve overseas venture capital funds have put money into local start-ups. Shenzhen's container ports comfortably undercut the rates in Hong Kong, and have boosted business nearly fourfold in the past three years. If other mainland cities could expand as fast, Zhu Rongji remarked on a visit, China's economy might surpass the USA and Japan.

The buildings along the main avenues are high and gleaming, the streets crowded and busy. The suburbs and adjoining towns house some of China's largest companies. A flashing display board at the Agricultural Bank of China gives the latest rate for the euro. There is a New York, New York disco and a championship golf club in the hills outside town. But for all its progress from a country village to a metropolis that has attracted millions of workers from all over China, Shenzhen is still far, far behind Hong Kong.

The pavements are cracked; stinking rubbish is loaded into open trucks; there is a fetid smell in the air. The weekend store promotions are flashily tacky, with young women in bright bathing suits teetering about uneasily on high heels outside the Shenzhen International Arcade. The big household appliance stores are yawningly deserted. Girls as young as six from poor provinces sing in the streets and restaurants, handing over their takings to employers who dole them out a small salary at the end of each month. Later, some become hostesses, and boost their money sleeping with clients.

The area is notorious as a sexual playground for Hong Kong men, who keep 'second wives' there or simply play the field of prostitutes and karaoke girls. It is also becoming a magnet for Hong Kong drug-users, who find law enforcement less of a problem than at home, despite the higher penalties if they are caught and convicted. A couple of SAR politicians were forced to resign recently after being spotted up to high jinks with bar girls over the frontier. A local newspaper reports that Zhu Rongji has ordered that the law be changed to face men from the SAR patronising prostitutes with the threat of six months in a labour camp. It sounds highly unlikely. Whatever the Premier's moral feelings, why would Shenzhen cut off the flow of money? This is, after all, a country where visitors to Mao Tse-tung's home village are offered sex as soon as they check in at the guest house.

If the queue of mainlanders who want to move to Hong Kong is as big as ever, Shenzhen women seem to be cooling on the idea of marrying Hong Kong men: cross-border marriages are running at half the peak of 1,069 a year at the start of the decade. A 24-year-old shop assistant told Cindy Siu of the *South China Morning Post* earlier in the year: 'My mum wants me to marry a Hong Kong man because she thinks they are rich. But to me their standard of living is not very high. My home seems better than a lot of Hong Kong homes.' 'You can't trust Hong Kong men,' says another. 'One of my friends has just found out that her father, a Hong Kong man, has a separate family in Hong Kong.'

For lunch today, we take a taxi driven by a migrant from northern China to a Muslim Chinese restaurant in a back street. The menu has the usual quaint translations of the dishes: 'insensitive slices of meat' and 'strongly fried sheep's heart'. We have neither. Nor do we taste the steamed sheep's head or the 'snow mountain camel's feet', having tried that last delicacy on a trip to the Muslim north-west of China last year and decided that it wasn't up to much. Instead we eat dumplings, kebabs, chapatis and aubergines. The head waitress recognises Monica Lewinsky on the cover of *Time* in the pile of magazines I am carrying. The bill for two comes to a little over three dollars. Outside, we buy three big bunches of asparagus for the equivalent of US$2.41; it's a rip-off by local standards, but at those prices, who cares?

Later in the day, we have a couple of cups of coffee in the Shangri-La Hotel near the station where the rich people gather on a weekend afternoon. A woman with her black hair in a perfect 1940s perm toys with an iced cappuccino. The band plays 'Just the Way You Are'. In the driveway, a Mercedes festooned with pink ribbons and carnations waits for the bride and groom. Our two coffees cost four times as much as our lunch.

This is a place where local officials on minimal salaries turn up at the golf course in black limousines with all the clubs any professional could wish for, and where the sewing workers at the Four Seas Handbag Factory earn 19 cents an hour; where fortunes are being made and village girls sing for their supper. Hong Kong is not the only place where Deng Xiaoping has left a legacy of one country, two systems.

19 *April*

An unexpected visitor flies in to Hong Kong for an interview with CNN – Wan Azizah Ismail, wife of Anwar Ibrahim, the former Deputy Premier of Malaysia jailed for six years last week on corruption charges after one of the most dubious and sensational trials of a politician in Asia for a long time. That she comes here demonstrates another continuing special feature of Hong Kong; you can say just about whatever you like, whoever you are and wherever you hail from. Whether anybody takes notice is another matter.

There was no question of Dr Azizah doing the phone-in from the state-run studios back home in Kuala Lumpur: they have a habit there of interrupting transmission when politically sensitive material is being put out by foreign broadcasters. The Prime Minister, Dr Mahathir, does not like critical US television stations. This is the man who blames the Jews for the Asian economic crisis, and who thinks governments which do not curb the activities of currency traders should be overthrown. (When I asked him how he squared this with his own central bank's past speculative activities, he replied: 'But we lost.' I don't think it was a joke.)

In Singapore, the local broadcasting station refused to help with the interview. Bangkok and Jakarta also declined. So Dr Azizah, who has emerged as a strong political figure in her own right at the head of a new party, came to Hong Kong. 'We brought her here because we didn't have to ask anybody,' says a CNN source.

At lunchtime, a limousine takes Azizah to lunch with the leading Malaysian–Chinese inhabitant of Hong Kong, Robert Kuok. Kuok, the chairman of the *Post*, became close to Mahathir as he built up his fortune. But I am told that he has always admired Azizah, so it is natural for him to see her during her visit to Hong Kong, whatever might be read into the meeting. A couple of years ago, a tea party was held in a suite at Kuok's Shangri-La Hotel on Hong Kong Island for Anwar to set out his ideas to a small group of journalists, an exposition studded with quotations from Shakespeare and references to Western literature.

That was before the Mahathir–Anwar rift and at a time when the chairman of the *South China Morning Post* had been most anxious to look after the Prime Minister. Mahathir's crusade against the forces of international finance had earned him considerable derision, and when he came to the annual meeting of the World Bank and the International Monetary Fund in Hong Kong in September 1997, Kuok arranged an interview in which the Prime Minister could reply to his critics. I was a bit leery about the motivation behind this, but the opportunity of an exclusive interview with the man who was going to be a star turn at the conference could not be passed up. I planned to run it as the page-one splash in the paper on the opening day of the meeting, a Monday.

On the previous Saturday evening, I and another journalist drove up to Robert Kuok's house in the hills of Hong Kong. The chairman was not there, and we waited by the pool with members of his family for an hour or so, sipping iced water and making polite conversation. Then Kuok arrived with Mahathir. The Prime Minister, my colleague and I went into a side room. We set up a tape machine on a table. Is this on the record? I asked. Yes, said the Prime Minister, before launching into a denunciation of currency trading, which could not be allowed to go on 'because there is no benefit to us'. He spoke forcefully but without raising his voice. Regulations would be introduced in Malaysia on Monday to limit currency trading to financing trade, he said. Then he got up, smiled, and went through to join Robert Kuok, Anson Chan and the other guests for dinner. Time for the journalists to leave. The story was too strong to hold for Monday. It led the Sunday edition.

The next morning, Anwar Ibrahim was handed a copy of Sunday's *Post* as he arrived in Hong Kong a day ahead of the IMF–World Bank meeting. The lead story came as quite a shock to him. He had not expected such an outburst before Mahathir's speech to the conference. The clampdown on currency trading would cause havoc when markets opened on Monday.

The Malaysian consulate had already issued a denial. No interview had been on Mahathir's schedule. The *Post* must have made the whole thing up. The Malaysian Finance Ministry weighed in, saying that the Prime Minister had been misquoted. A press conference was arranged at the IMF conference hall at 3 p.m. to denounce this latest tissue of media lies. Anwar also issued a denial, and made it known that he would be at the press conference.

At lunchtime, I went along to the Convention Centre with our tape recording of the interview, and my colleague's shorthand notes. I sent word to the Malaysian delegation that if the briefing went ahead, I would be happy to play the tape of the Prime Minister's remarks. The press conference was cancelled.

By then, it appeared, Anwar had spoken to Mahathir. The Prime Minister told his deputy for the first time about the Saturday night interview, confirmed our story, and said he had no desire to retract what he had said. Anwar managed to get the currency measures put off, though they came into effect after his own downfall. I was told subsequently that his denial sharpened Mahathir's antagonism towards him. In a conversation two years later, Mahathir told me that Anwar 'brought it on himself by the way he behaved; he was in too much of a hurry and thought he knew it all'.

The interview caused problems for me, too. After our story was widely picked up by international news agencies and foreign media, I was told that Robert Kuok felt humiliated by the storm it set off. He appeared to feel that his hospitality had somehow been betrayed by me, that he had unwittingly led Mahathir into a trap. Much was made of the fact that we had originally planned to hold the story for the Monday paper, but had run it on Sunday. I couldn't see how that changed anything, but it was advanced as proof of my bad faith. Nor were matters improved when the *Post*'s main headline on the opening of the conference reported George Soros calling Mahathir a 'moron'.

Since the Prime Minister was quite happy with what he had said, the complaints were somewhat hard to follow. Robert Kuok's pain was only understandable if he himself was embarrassed by his guest's remarks. In our conversation in 1999, after he had imposed capital controls, Mahathir asked: 'I said what I thought, what's wrong with that?' Having rejected the IMF rescue package adopted by South Korea, Thailand and Indonesia, he went on to plough his own furrow in defiance of international conventional wisdom, and was able to report revived growth and an improved trade position within a year. He felt no reason to worry about what he had said that evening at Kuok's home. But that did not stop a management executive at the paper telling me that the chairman felt he could never trust me again.

20 *April*

Despite his new shoes and a suit, Li Yuhui has his hands tied as he appears in court in the mainland city of Shantou at 9.30 a.m. today. The rope is knotted over his heart as if it could be the target for a firing squad.

A former lorry-driver, Li is known in Hong Kong as the Telford Gardens Poisoner, after a block of flats where, posing as a feng shui master, he killed three women and two girls with 'holy water' laced with cyanide at a 'life-lengthening' ceremony. Neighbours recalled that the curtains were always closed, and that a wok with a pair of scissors and a brush tied to it had been hung outside the door as a cabalistic sign. After the women's deaths, Li walked away with HK$1.2 million of their money.

A mainlander, Li was caught across the border, and brought to court in his home city of Shantou. The trial began in a local dialect which one of the defence lawyers could not understand, not to mention the pack of reporters from Hong Kong. The judge switched the proceedings to the national language of Putonghua. But then it turned out that Li could not speak Putonghua too well, so he was allowed to revert to dialect. Since everybody knew what the outcome would be, this all seemed something of a nicety.

After Li was found guilty, his wife, a hairdresser, with whom he was not on the best of terms, came up with 2,000 yuan for an appeal. Li claims that the murders were carried out in a ritual Zen ceremony by a mysterious monk who subsequently disappeared. When his appeal is rejected this morning, Li frowns, and asks to see his elderly mother and two children. The request is refused. He is not allowed to see his wife, either. His lawyer enquires whether the condemned man may give his last wishes. The judge says the officers at the execution site will take them down. His property is confiscated; some of it will be given to the relatives of his victims. In a typical final mainland gesture, he is deprived of his political rights.

Following the usual procedure, Li is driven in a convoy of vehicles to the shooting field immediately after the verdict has been read out. The Shantou City Intermediate People's Court formal execution ground is regarded as too public, given the crowd of Hong Kong journalists waiting there. So three policemen wearing white gloves take Li to an open space nearby. Two hold him. The third shoots him twice, at 10.15 a.m., three-quarters of an hour after he entered the court to hear the result of his appeal. 'Three pairs of white gloves donned by security officers and another one worn by the pathologist were abandoned on the ground afterwards,' writes the *Post*'s reporter, Stella Lee. Blood stains the earth. The body is burned in the local crematorium. The ashes will be returned to his family.

Local people in Shantou cannot understand the interest the Hong Kong media is showing in the case. After all, China executes at least 2,000 people each year. The authorities say this 'satisfies popular demand'. But Li's case involves a wider concern in Hong Kong following another headline-grabbing case which aroused deeper worries about the relationship between the SAR and the mainland, and the conduct of some rich and famous people.

That case starred Hong Kong's best-known gangster, Cheung Tse-keung, also known as Big Spender. Cheung was a pretty spectacular criminal by any standards. An ardent gambler, he was surrounded by stories of wild jaunts that took him from Macau to Las Vegas, of nights when he staked HK$200 million and of debts that rose to three times that figure. He became a celebrity after being charged in connection with one of the world's biggest cash robberies, the haul of HK$167 million from a security van at the airport in 1991. He was convicted, and then acquitted on a technicality – and then re-acquitted at a retrial. Outside the court, he posed for photographers in a red and white spotted short-sleeved shirt and white trousers, grinning and punching the air, his mobile telephone hooked to his designer belt.

Cheung was at the centre of a web of gangs. One became infamous for armed raids on gold and jewel shops, spraying bullets from AK47 rifles as it went into action. Other associates kidnapped Hong Kong men visiting the mainland and demanded ransoms amounting to the equivalent of US$2.1 million. Another group, with assault rifles and in military uniforms, staged highway robberies on the mainland, killing eight truck drivers.

Cheung had all the trappings of a famous hood. He posed lying on top of his yellow V12 Lamborghini Diabolo with pop-up headlights that cost US$350,000 in the showroom. He also had a string of Mercedes limousines. Driving fast, he said, 'makes me orgasm'. In one of his many homes, he kept a life-sized metal bust of himself. At social occasions, he appeared as a Cantonese Godfather, a caring family man who was kind to his two young children, a well-spoken, non-smoking teetotaller, however much vintage brandy he bought for his guests. He had two sphinx statues made with the face of his common-law wife, who had been working in the control room of the security company at the time of the 1991 airport robbery. He filled his flat with golden religious images to bring him luck. True to the Hong Kong style, Cheung bought thirty-one residential and commercial sites. In the middle of 1996, he went into a new line of business, grabbing very rich people.

Hong Kong has always been the scene of some spectacular kidnappings. But Big Spender was in a different league. On 23 May 1996, one of his men posted outside the offices of the tycoon Li Ka-shing called Cheung on his mobile telephone to say that Li's son, Victor Li

Tzar-kuoi, had left for the day. Victor, an intense, bespectacled man, was a major figure in his own right; he was in the process of taking over the running of the family's property empire. As Victor drove up the narrow road towards his home on the south side of Hong Kong Island, Cheung and an associate came up on either side in separate cars, and pinned his limousine between them.

The two gangsters, wearing bulletproof vests and carrying AK47 assault rifles and pistols, bundled Li into a waiting van, taped his mouth, bound him and drove him off to a safe house in the New Territories. Cheung then went to the home of Victor's father, made his demands and spent two days waiting for the ransom to be paid. One report had it that he insisted on the money being stowed in designer bags. At one point, Cheung was said to have been asked if he wanted to count the money. He lifted the bag, weighed it in his hand and said it seemed to be about right. As to why he had kidnapped the son and not the father, he remarked that Li Ka-shing could come up with more cash than Victor – HK$1.3 billion or US$160 million Cheung kept a quarter, and left the gang to divide up the rest.

The Lis said nothing, but rumours spread. Sitting next to Victor at a business lunch, I ventured to ask him if there was anything in them. He stared at me impassively from behind his glasses and said flatly: 'There is no truth in such rumours.'

Sixteen months later, Walter Kwok Ping-sheung, chairman of another big property company called Sung Hung Kai, was picked up outside his office by the harbour. The gang had been following him for seven months. Kwok, a big, reserved man, is one of three brothers who were all raised in the real-estate business. Their father's idea of a Sunday outing was to take the three boys round his property developments; after his death, the brothers still showed their mother major sites for her approval.

Big Spender had forked out HK$1.4 million to set up the Victor Li kidnapping, including the purchase of weapons. For Kwok, his outlay rose to HK$2 million. Both victims were taken to an isolated hut up near the border with China and put into a wooden box with air holes punched in it. Their eyes were masked and they were given roast pork and rice to eat through the openings. Victor Li was said to have been kept overnight with his legs in chains and his mouth covered with bandages.

Walter Kwok was held for six days stripped to his underwear and with his hands tied. Then his ransom was paid: half that of Victor Li at a mere HK$600 million. Again the victim made no complaint to the police. Nor did the family raise the alarm when he was kidnapped. Cheung took half the ransom and told his gang to 'swim across the river like a Chinese bullfrog', which meant they should flee individually and not meet again. According to mainland police, they managed to buy more than fifty pieces of property in China, and a fleet of luxury cars.

Now we enter the realms of the generally believed probability which remains unprovable. Cheung and his gang, many of whom were mainlanders, had dodged back and forth across the border at will. They met in hotels in Shenzhen to plan their coups. There was speculation that their weapons had been bought from the People's Liberation Army in southern Yunan province, a region celebrated for its lawlessness. Cheung was also said to have purchased explosives in Guangdong province and to have smuggled them into Hong Kong by boat. But, in Li Ka-shing, he had bitten off even more than he could chew.

Hong Kong's 'Superman' has powerful contacts in Beijing. When Jiang Zemin came to the SAR for the first anniversary of the handover, his generally anodyne speech was punctuated by a single sharp sentence vowing that contempt for the law would not be permitted. At the time, people thought he was referring to the upsurge in gang violence in Macau. Later, it seemed he was talking about Cheung Tse-keung.

The President handed the Big Spender case to the Vice-Minister of Public Security in Beijing. According to a mainland newspaper, officers from Hong Kong and Guangdong met in the capital on 10 January 1998. Two days later, three Public Security Bureau officials flew south. In Guangdong, they found that police were already on Big Spender's trail, investigating whether he was linked with the death of a police informer from Hong Kong who had been shot dead in the street in Shenzhen.

While all this was going on across the border, Cheung and his associates were keeping busy in Hong Kong. On 8 January, police hiding in bushes near one of his safe havens in the New Territories filmed him unloading big white boxes from a van into a Mercedes. Dressed only in white underwear, and wearing gloves, the crime boss is seen on the video making three trips to move the boxes. After Cheung had left for the last time, police emerged from the shrubbery to take soil samples. These showed that the boxes contained 800 kilos of explosives which Cheung was said to have ordered from mainland contacts at a meeting in the Lisboa Hotel and casino in Macau. The cargo was smuggled into the SAR, transferred from the van to the Mercedes and buried under a deserted container parking lot. On a subsequent trip to the scene, police arrested three men, but Big Spender had gone across the border.

On 23 January, an underworld associate from Hong Kong known as 'Old Fox' flew into Guangzhou city from Thailand. Police followed him to a meeting with Big Spender. The two men drove off in a Mercedes . Apparently noticing the tail, they abandoned the car and hijacked a taxi. Two hundred police were alerted, and the pair were nabbed half an hour later.

Both Cheung and the white-haired Old Fox gave false names. Later, Big Spender told one of his lawyers that he never imagined he would face a mainland court. He 'believed he would have to return to Hong Kong to be tried', the lawyer added. 'If he had known the law, he would never have dared to step over the border.'

News of his capture was not made public until July, though his 36-year-old wife did receive an anonymous call at the time saying he was being held on the mainland. After holding out for some time, Big Spender cracked when he learned that other members of his gang had been caught, and that one had grassed. Police said he told them that he had had a premonition of trouble when a big jade pendant he was wearing broke shortly before his arrest.

Video footage showed Big Spender dressed in a white singlet and looking relaxed as he was presented with an arrest statement. 'What is my offence?' he asked. A police officer replied, 'Explosives.' 'Explosives? Not smuggling?' Cheung said, before signing the statement with a smile and putting his thumbprint on it. In a later interview shown in a mainland television documentary, he told police, 'You take the credit. I've lost.' The documentary said that he planned to use the 800 kilos of explosives which he had been filmed transporting in the New Territories for 'threatening the Hong Kong government, bombing Hong Kong prisons and continuing to kidnap Hong Kong tycoons'. Cheung was said to be particularly keen to spring an associate who had been crippled when shot by police and was serving a long jail term.

In fact, the charges were more wide-ranging, and included having planned the kidnappings of Victor Li and Walter Kwok while on the mainland. But there was still no evidence from the two high-profile victims; everything connected with those crimes rested on the alleged confessions of Cheung and his associates. In other words, there would not have been enough evidence for a case to have been brought under the law in Hong Kong, which may have been another reason for dealing with him across the border.

Aged forty-three, Cheung stood trial in a closed court in Guangzhou with three dozen alleged accomplices, seventeen of them from Hong Kong. As the hearing opened, the first of two hastily-made films about Big Spender went on show in Hong Kong. On the train to Guangzhou, you could buy a video on 'China's biggest criminal case in the twentieth century'. Armed paramilitaries surrounded the court. Snipers crouched on nearby roofs. A barber's shop opposite the court was suddenly closed down 'for renovations'. The corridor leading to the hall where the hearing was held was curtained off.

On 12 November 1998, all the defendants were found guilty. Cheung, in an open-necked white shirt, a mauve cardigan and tan trousers, stood impassively behind a metal barrier at the front of the crowded court. Policemen wearing white gloves held each of his arms. One of his lawyers flew to London to try to drum up support for an appeal, which was rejected by a Guangdong judge known by the nickname of 'Iron Fist'.

Big Spender was shot at an execution ground surrounded by hills and wild grass outside the city. The following day, ten police guarding the site turned away the pregnant widow of one of the gang members who had gone there to burn paper offerings to comfort her husband's soul in the beyond.

A reporter who visited the site wrote that it was littered with the shoes of dead men, used cartridges, gloves discarded by the firing squad and cardboard signs hung round the convicts' necks recording their names and crimes. The execution procedure is simple: one policeman fires a single shot from behind. If that does not prove fatal, a second shot follows. Inevitably, the story quickly spread that Big Spender had needed two bullets to finish him off. His body was wrapped in canvas and taken to a crematorium close by. The ashes were then placed in an urn, which was given to a member of his family. The urn had no lid, and the relative brought it back to Hong Kong with a baseball cap on top to keep the contents from flying away.

Apart from providing the Hong Kong media with a top story, the Big Spender case aroused a number of concerns. One was whether you had to be rich and powerful and well connected to get justice in China. Another was that the Lis and the Kwoks had not informed the legal authorities. When Anson Chan and other senior officials took them to task for not at least reporting the crimes, Li Ka-shing complained of 'something like harassment'.

The third, and greatest, concern was why Cheung had not been brought back to the SAR to stand trial. He might have planned his crimes while on the mainland, but the main offences – the actual kidnappings and the handling of explosives at the hide-out in the New Territories – had been committed in Hong Kong by Hong Kong criminals against Hong Kong residents. The Guangzhou court seemed to recognise the problem: in delivering its verdict, it stressed the explosives, which involved illegal purchase on the mainland and smuggling to Hong Kong.

Then there was the nagging question as to why the Hong Kong police who had videotaped him in January had not carried out an arrest on the spot, but waited until Cheung had flown the coop before nabbing three much less important gang members. The Hong Kong authorities insisted that they had not had enough evidence. But it was only a short speculative jump to imagining that somebody had decided to leave him to the mainland police. After all, execution on the shoe-littered killing field outside Guangzhou would provide a much more conclusive end than a lifetime jail sentence.

And if Cheung had been brought back, just imagine the circus which would have followed, with Big Spender using the ransom money to buy a top legal team to perform in open court. Much better for Cheung and his gang to be shot in China without any of the embarrassment of a trial in Hong Kong. But what does this mean at a deeper level for the rule of law, and the relationship with the mainland? Not that Beijing can be fingered as the prime mover in this breach of the autonomy of the SAR. As is proving to be the case rather too often, the initiative came from Hong Kong itself.

The SAR government insists that there is 'no question of the independence of our judicial system being eroded or the mainland interfering with Hong Kong's jurisdiction'. But, as the chairman of the Hong Kong Bar observes: 'The issue is whether, putting aside the possible kidnapping charges, the fact that the Hong Kong government made no attempt to seek the return of some of these defendants in relation to possible robbery or firearms charges may give people the false impression that the judiciary and the rule of Hong Kong is somehow subordinate to that of the rest of China, and thus indirectly cast a question mark over the concept of "one country, two systems".'

An epilogue to Cheung's days of fame and fortune comes when his yellow Lamborghini is put on sale. Far from attracting a buyer for the notoriety of its late owner, it fetches less than 30 per cent of the showroom cost. Hong Kong people like to latch on to the latest fashion, but buying dead people's effects is not for them. If it had been Li Ka-shing's limousine, that would have been a different story.

25–27 April

There are two sets of true believers in Beijing at the beginning of this week. The great proponents of globalisation, or globality as it is now known, are at the China World Hotel for a session of the World Economic Forum devoted to China. Up the avenue, a very different event is taking place on the edge of Tiananmen Square. Some 10,000 members of a mystical deep-breathing cult called Falun Gong have come out of nowhere on a Sunday evening to demonstrate silently outside the high walls of the Zhongnanhai leadership compound beside the old imperial Forbidden City. Many are middle-aged women. They want to speak to the government about better treatment for their movement. They do not get anywhere, and disperse peacefully. But there is no doubt about the shock they have caused.

It is amazing that so many people were able to assemble in one of the most heavily policed places in the world without the authorities being aware of what they were planning. The cult, whose members perform deep-breathing meditation, claims 70 million practitioners in China: if that sounds like a big overstatement, even a movement one-tenth that size would be a force to be reckoned with. Explaining how they mobilise, an English adherent explains: 'A network of communication forms organically through the fact that practitioners know so many other practitioners. The numbers are so great and the commitment to their beliefs so strong that word spreads very quickly and practitioners act very quickly.' That sounds rather like Mao's peasant army. No wonder it spooks leaders who never forget the Great Helmsman's warning about a spark being enough to set off a forest fire. For all their control mania, the men behind the walls of Zhongnanhai don't have any idea what to do about a movement that is difficult to tar with any of the usual brushes of splittism, democracy or anti-party activism – though the fact that the Falun Gong leader lives in the United States lends the sinister touch of foreign influence.

At the Economic Forum, meanwhile, participants are divided between their desire to see China develop and their worries about what is actually happening in the economy. The path ahead is strewn with uncertainty, bad debts, corruption, unreliable statistics and the awesome task of pulling China into the modern era, not just in the showplace cities but in the millions of towns and villages caught in rural backwardness where peasants say that they can't keep the size of their families down because, without electricity, there is nothing to do at night except have sex.

After a couple of days in the capital, the Forum moves to Shanghai. The director of that city's Economic Commission says industrial output has risen by 11.6 per cent in the first four months of 1999, and exports by 18 per cent. Another speaker predicts that Chinese membership of the World Trade Organisation will bring a boom on the scale of the expansion set off by Deng's initial market reforms. Nowhere will benefit more than Shanghai; hasn't Zhu Rongji said it will be China's New York?

On the great Bund waterfront avenue, the old buildings that once housed foreign banks and the British-administered customs service are being carefully restored. The garish nightlife, the opium dens and the powerful criminal gangs have given way to karaoke parlours, high-priced claret and party members on the make; but local residents say there is still plenty of vice to be found if you know where to look. Those nostalgic for the heyday of the Paris of the East can still find ornate buildings from the 1920s or visit the hotel from which the Green Gang ran the city. Across from the Bund, vertiginous towers sprout in the new business area of Pudong. Richard Branson is scheduling the first direct flight from London, and Hong Kong's Chief Executive notes that some Western companies may start to go directly to Shanghai instead of using the SAR as a staging post. An American lawyer who has worked in both places finds Shanghai more go-ahead than the SAR – 'like Hong Kong used to be'.

The city has a fine new opera house and a stunning museum. Pudong is getting its own airport. A branch of a smart Hong Kong restaurant high above the Bund seems to be packed every night. In what was the French concession of the city before the Communists took over, you can eat lemon peppered duck and lobster in citrus juice in the former church of St Nicholas, built by White Russians and dedicated to the memory of the last Tsar. Light streams in through the stained glass. There are icons under the majestic dome and paintings of naked Western women in classical poses on the walls. The proprietors are a Frenchman and a Swiss entrepreneur who serves wine from a South African vineyard he owns.

Back by the Bund, on the street outside the old Peace Hotel with its art deco friezes and antediluvian jazz band, a young man approaches me saying he wants to practise his English. Where are you from? he asks. Hong Kong. Ah, Victoria Peak, Kowloon, Central

District, he says. I nod. And then he launches into a tale of a family art collection which I can pick up at bargain prices if I will advance him some money to get it out of hock. I decline this once-in-a-life-time opportunity, and cross the road. Looking back, I see that he has already approached another Western passer-by.

As everywhere on the mainland, the crust of prosperity is perilously thin. More than half the new office space in Pudong is empty. Shanghai Volkswagen rolls out 235,000 cars annually, but the city had only 9,000 private cars at the end of last year. One-third of state sector workers are surplus to requirements. More than a million jobs have disappeared in the 'dragon head' of the Yangtze since 1990 as old industries contracted. The director of the city's Economic Commission says 200,000 more will have to go in the next two years. Forty per cent of displaced workers are not expected to find new jobs.

In such a world, the appeal of the Falun Gong and of other cults is all too evident. Many Gongists grew up in the cult of Mao, assured that the iron rice bowl would never crack, accustomed to following predictable orders from a great prophet. Decisions were made for them from cradle to grave. Now the old ways are vanishing, and everybody is for themselves, poverty take the hindmost. Chinese officials, naturally, react with horror to any comparison of the cult's appeal with old-style communism. 'How can anyone compare trash to a huge mountain?' asks the Director-General of State Administration of Religious Affairs. But an uncertain old age is looming for many of these people. Health care has to be paid for. Jobs are disappearing. The iron rice bowl is cracked.

In the World Economic Forum conference hall, the brittle, exciting vistas opened up by Deng Xiaoping and Zhu Rongji; out on the streets of Beijing, an older world seeking reassurance. One country, two faiths.

27 *April*

At the reception desk of the Shangri-La Hotel in Pudong last night, I ran into a member of Hong Kong's Executive Council, the Chief Executive's secretive advisory body. Anthony Leung Kam-chung, a banker who is the Exco member responsible for education, could hardly contain himself. The council, he said, had just made an important decision. He couldn't tell me what it was, but insisted several times that the public reaction would be vital. Then he picked up his electronic room key and headed off for the lift.

28 *April*

Now I know what Anthony Leung was talking about in Shanghai. Regina Ip, the Secretary for Security, gives the Legislative Council scary figures for how many mainland immigrants would be able to enter Hong Kong under the Court of Final Appeal's ruling – 1,675,000, or a quarter of the SAR's current population. That could push the number of people here to 10 million by the year 2011. The population pressure would be intolerable, as well as the strain on housing, health, education, transport and welfare.

It is enough to make any normal person agree that the judges were out of their minds to let those people in. A cartoon in the *Standard* shows a Japanese tidal wave labelled 'Mainlanders' arching over the harbour front. It's a bit reminiscent of the stories in Britain of a wave of black and brown migrants about to swamp the country, or, indeed, the fears of what would happen if the people of Hong Kong were all given British passports before the handover. Critics point out that the government figure for illegitimate children is three times the total in an earlier official estimate. It means Hong Kong men have fathered more children in China than at home. And then there is the question of how many of the 1.6 million would want to move to the SAR: the legislator Margaret Ng points to 'a great arrogance – and ignorance' in assuming that all mainlanders are longing to come here. And would the mainland authorities allow so many people to leave? All in all, this looks like a dodgy exercise. But it is politically savvy. Apart from painting the judges as men who do not put the community's interests first, it sets the government's political critics on the back foot.

New legislative elections are due next year. Which grass-roots politician would want to go to the voters arguing that the rule of law takes precedence over keeping 1.6 million people from crowding into

Hong Kong? The Democrats are caught while the pro-Beijing DAB will be able to combine its inclination to back the administration with a stance of saving Hong Kong from a human invasion. No wonder the man from Exco was smiling as he picked up his room key in Shanghai.

MAY

7 *May*

Nato bombs the Chinese embassy in Belgrade in its Kosovo campaign against President Slobodan Milosevic. The building, which formerly housed a local government body, is destroyed. Three people inside die. Many others are injured. Sino-US relations are already tense over the Nato attack on Yugoslavia, which Beijing sees as a major challenge to the cherished sanctity of national sovereignty. The Foreign Minister calls it an ominous precedent. If Washington can take it upon itself to interfere in the affairs of a nation in defence of an oppressed minority, might it be tempted to help the Tibetans or the Muslims in China's Far West? And what about Taiwan?

The embassy bombing has made things far worse. The Americans give various explanations – the embassy moved a couple of years ago; the map used in the attack was out of date; faulty aiming techniques were employed. Less officially, there is talk of electronic transmissions from the building which could have been taken for military signals, or even of Chinese help for the Milosevic regime. Beijing waves all this aside. Building on genuine popular anger, the authorities bus in well-orchestrated crowds to stone the US embassy; for a while, the ambassador is trapped inside. China demands the punishment of the guilty, and substantial compensation. Washington will pay some money, but it will take its own time to discipline any wrongdoers. Conservative critics of rapprochement with the United States are jubilant. In Hong Kong, Martin Lee calls the bombing a 'mistargeting' and regrets that mainlanders had not been told about the ethnic cleansing in Kosovo. A column in the *Oriental Daily* says that 'people who see this kind of traitor on the street should spit on him and throw eggs at him'.

As well as Kosovo and the bombing, there is another considerable shadow over Sino–US relations, in the shape of a report by Congressman Christopher Cox alleging Chinese spying of US nuclear secrets. The report veers on to the wild side. Much of what it says Beijing stole is available on the Internet or from American whistleblowers. Its suggestion that all Chinese who visit the United States should be regarded as potential spies mixes racism and paranoia. The journalist Lars-Erik Nelson writes in the *New York Review of Books* about speculation that Beijing might have provoked the whole affair to create a wave of anti-Chinese feeling which would lead its scientists in the United States to return home with the secrets in their heads. Still, for all its exaggerations, the Cox report chimes in with growing American suspicions of China, including accusations about lavish donations to political campaigns. Whatever happened to the relationship hymned by Clinton in China less than a year ago?

For the man in the White House, that may be a matter for concern – but he has many other concerns to deal with. For Zhu Rongji, facing the Sisyphean challenge of licking into shape an economy that has never marched to the modern beat, the cooling of relations holds an even deeper threat, particularly after the way he went out on a limb with the World Trade Organisation concessions he offered in April. In the intensely political context surrounding him, he cannot afford to see too many more things go wrong. The Prime Minister has admirers, but few acolytes in a system which thrives on such people. No wonder he sometimes cuts an eminently lonely figure as he follows his favoured pastime of walking in the wooded hills outside Beijing.

15 *May*

My contract as editor of the *South China Morning Post* expires today.

At the end of January, I was told that the owners had decided not to renew it. No reason was given. The paper is doing well. We have expanded and redesigned it year by year. Circulation is resisting the recession, and profits are moving up. The *Post* took nearly all the prizes available to it in the two Hong Kong press awards, and has just been named the best English-language newspaper in Asia by a regional publishers' association.

This might not seem a recipe for dropping the editor, but I have no chance to make my case. Neither Robert Kuok nor his son, Ean, who has succeeded him as chairman, has spoken to me. I am told that their decision is irrevocable. Still, I have been asked to stay on until the end of the year while a new editor is found, preferably a Chinese journalist who 'understands' China and the region. It was suggested that I might help in the search.

I had come to the *Post* in May 1995 after eighteen months editing the *Observer* in London. Inheriting a paper in a dire state, we had hoisted sales back above the half-million mark, cut the losses and won a dozen awards, including Newspaper of the Year. But Hugo Young, chairman of the Scott Trust, which owns the *Guardian* and *Observer*, told me that the decision had been made to grant Peter Preston, editor of the daily, his long-standing wish to become editor-in-chief of both papers, and to sack me. The manner of the parting was abrupt: Young ordered me to leave the building immediately without speaking to any of my colleagues.

The evening after Young told me to go, I received a telephone call from Andrew Knight, who edited *The Economist* when I worked for it in the 1980s. He knew the *South China Morning Post* and its chief executive from his days as a top executive of the Rupert Murdoch empire, which had then included the Hong Kong paper. Now he had been asked if he knew anybody suitable to edit the *Post*. The owners who had bought Murdoch's shares fourteen months earlier specifically wanted a British editor to succeed the Australian incumbent.

The next morning, my wife and I drove across London to go for a long walk in Richmond Park to discuss the idea. When we were furthest from our car, cold January rain came down. Sodden and shivering, we went to Soho and ate a bad Chinese meal. Let's go where the rain is soft and the Chinese food good, we decided. A month later, I flew to Hong Kong and was offered the job after a 45-minute conversation with the chairman, Kuok Huok Nien – more generally known as Robert Kuok. A neat and utterly polite man in his early seventies, he proffered chocolates from a large box and waved away my ignorance of Hong Kong and China. My predecessor was to leave when I was fully installed. In fact, he stayed on in Hong Kong for nearly a year, but I began editing almost as soon as I arrived.

The *Post* was one of the most lucrative papers in the world. The peak year of 1997–98 saw a pre-tax profit equivalent to US$100 million, with a profit-to-turnover ratio of over 40 per cent. On several occasions, it ran 200 pages of classified advertising in the Saturday edition. The main news section was awash with retail and fashion advertising, and the business pages with corporate announcements. When I was offered the job, the *Post* had two English-language rivals, but commanded around 80 per cent of the market; after the *Eastern Express* died a year later, the market share went to 90 per cent. Some readers talked of 'the paper' as if there was no other.

One factor in the *Post*'s financial health was its attention to costs. Still, there were not many publications with a circulation of just over 100,000 that had an editorial staff of 280, and four to five daily sections. The reassuring thing amid the blizzard of advertising was that the *Post* was a serious newspaper which had evolved out of its old status as a colonial gazette. The readership was split more or less equally between Chinese and non-Chinese, as were the editorial staff. It was the only Hong Kong newspaper with staff bureaux in mainland China. The China editor, Willy Lo-Lap Lam, was a leading China-watcher with an enviable record of scoops about the inner workings of the regime. Its Beijing bureau was the best in the business. The paper had comprehensive local political coverage, a strong raft of columnists and some fine original writers. An early user of editorial colour, it also launched on to the Internet in time for the 1997 hand-over.

The chairman and principal shareholder was a legendary figure in Asian and international business. In rankings of Asia's rich and powerful, Robert Kuok regularly figures well up in the top twenty. The American business magazine, *Forbes*, put him on its cover with the headline 'The world's shrewdest businessman'. Born in 1923 as the son of a Malaysian–Chinese businessman in the town of Johore Bahru just across from Singapore, he was educated at one of that city's best schools, where he was a classmate of the Asian elder statesman, Lee Kuan Yew. During the Second World War, he worked for a Japanese company, rising to head its rice department. That led him into commodities, in particular sugar. Trading from a room at the Grosvenor House Hotel in London, where he acquired a taste for fine claret, he was said to have controlled 10 per cent of the world's sugar stock at one point. 'I risked everything without realising it,' he told *Forbes*. 'It was all rhythm. Have you ever seen [the basketball ace] Michael Jordan play when he's on a rhythm run? It was exactly like that.'

While branching out into other commodities, Kuok also built up Asia's biggest luxury hotel chain, went into property and insurance, and bottled Coca-Cola in China. He was known equally for his discretion and his wealth, and for his impeccable business and political connections. Despite being Chinese in a country which was promoting its Malay citizens, he developed strong links with the government, and went into Indonesia, where the Chinese are the regular target of racial hostility. As a leading member of the Chinese diaspora, Kuok was one of the earliest and biggest investors on the mainland, moving from commodity deals to big hotel and property projects. One of his lieutenants told me that few of these actually turned a profit, but it was the presence and commitment that counted.

A long-term player wherever he goes, Kuok won many brownie points from the Central Government when he did not let the Tiananmen Square massacre affect his investment plans. He was, as he said, a businessman who went wherever he could see a promising opportunity. He took the ways of the region in his stride, not necessarily approving but accepting them as the way of life in this part of the globe. He was also well known for his highly developed sense of privacy. When he complained about a book written about him in

Malaysia which he said was full of lies, I asked him if he would issue a rebuttal. He laughed at the idea of revealing himself to the world in such a manner.

Kuok and a Malaysian business associate bought Murdoch's stake in the *Post* at the end of 1993. Kuok's Kerry Media company (it has nothing to do with Ireland, having simply been bought as a shelf company) had 34.9 per cent, the most you can own of a company in Hong Kong without making a general offer for the rest of the shares. His partner, a conglomerate called Malaysian United Industries, had 21 per cent. MUI subsequently sold 12 per cent of its stake to the US fund Templeton Franklin to raise money in the face of the Asian crisis and its losses in other investments, such as the Laura Ashley business. With 34.9 per cent and the chairmanship of the *Post*, Robert Kuok was seen everywhere as the proprietor of Hong Kong's dominant English-language newspaper.

The acquisition set plenty of alarm bells ringing. Because of Kuok's mainland investments and his friendship with the likes of Li Peng, it was natural for observers and officials round Chris Patten to jump to the conclusion that the *Post* would become a mainland mouthpiece. Hence their involvement in the launch of the *Eastern Express*. That paper's first editor, Stephen Vines, later reported that a senior mainland official told two visiting Hong Kong businessmen shortly after Kuok's purchase that China was pleased to have 'got the *Post* in the bag'. A British newspaper correspondent was assured by a source close to the Hong Kong government that the deal had been financed by the Bank of China, though Kuok was quite rich enough not to need any help.

Patten was right to see the *Post*'s new chairman as an opponent. He was a member of the Hong Kong business world, which also included a number of prominent British figures who disliked the political reforms brought in before decolonisation. For them, Patten's methods were bad enough; but they objected particularly to his aims. Hong Kong, they insisted, could only suffer from becoming a more politicised city, which would upset its position as a business centre and lead to social discord. 'These days, the mood in Hong Kong is regrettably neither harmonious nor happy,' Kuok said in a speech in

1995. 'The British government's decision suddenly to launch in
October 1992 a drive for much fuller democracy in Hong Kong,
without consultation with China, was in my opinion ill-timed and
misconceived. China's reaction to having her pitch queered in this
fashion has not been surprising.' He went on to lament the polarisation of society, the 'great and needless tensions', the effect on small
businessmen and entrepreneurs, and 'the unfortunate tendency of the
media to pounce upon and magnify any display of acrimony or hostility between the parties'.

Apart from their political differences, Kuok loathed what he
regarded as Patten's arrogance and colonial condescension. Whether
the fact that Kuok's brother was killed by the British as a rebel during
the insurgency in Malaya fuelled his dislike of somebody he saw as a
latter-day imperial representative is best left to the psychiatrists.
Patten's Westminster wit grated with the local grandees, who took it
for Western superiority. Irony is not a quality much in evidence
among the Hong Kong establishment. Even some democrats could
find the Governor patronising and self-centred. Though it was, presumably, none of his doing, the headline on the *Sunday Times*
serialisation of Jonathan Dimbleby's insider account of the Patten
years – 'THE LAST DEMOCRAT' – raised more than a few hackles among
those who would be fighting that fight in Hong Kong long after he
had left.

When I mentioned the apparent cultural gulf between the
Governor and the tycoons to one of Patten's aides, the response was
that people like Kuok were just trading on their supposed irritation as
an excuse to cover their opposition to democracy and their desire to
be left free to go on making as much money as possible. But watching a big local figure who was a major Conservative donor being left
to wander round a Government House reception for John Major, or
overhearing a bumbling Downing Street official asking the head of
another major conglomerate in Bertie Woosterish tones, 'Are you in
business, Mr Woo?' pointed either to a condescending lack of preparation or to yet another manifestation of the sense of superiority felt
by both the British and the Chinese which can make relations
between them so difficult.

Correct as he was to see Kuok as a stern critic, I was determined to draw a line between the chairman's views and the newspaper's editorial approach. The *Post* could not follow the model of British newspapers which the Governor had known in his previous incarnation, where a word from the owner was sufficient to dictate the editorial policy. This created a strange situation. In public, basing myself on what appeared in the paper, I strongly rejected allegations that the new ownership had made it sell out to Beijing or had turned it into a puppet of China. But that was exactly what I found myself fighting against. By its nature, this tussle had to remain private. A moment's fleeting glory as a champion of the freedom of the press would do no good for the thing that mattered: what was printed in the newspaper each day. There was also a question which involved a certain degree of ego on my part. If I walked out or made my disagreements with the owner and management so public that I was sacked or had to resign, who would take my place? Various names of more pliant or politically reliable successors were mentioned from time to time. I had to think that my departure would be a bad thing for the *Post*, and gamble that, when I threatened to go if the owners and managers insisted on doing things I felt would be wrong, I would win – and live to fight another day, even if this meant boxing in the shadows and side-stepping questions about proprietorial influence.

My first tussle came almost immediately after I arrived in Hong Kong, on a Tuesday. The following day, I was told that a decision had been taken the previous weekend to merge the editorial operations of the daily and Sunday papers, which had been run separately up to then. Twenty-five jobs would be cut. The board wanted to exert control over editorial spending now that the *Eastern Express* had proved no challenge to the *Post*.

As part of the changes, my predecessor set off a storm by dropping a cartoon strip called 'Lily Wong', which regularly lampooned the mainland and forecast the worst after the handover. The cartoonist, an American called Larry Feign, had just done a set of strips on allegations that Chinese officials were selling the organs of executed prisoners. Feign, who was not on the staff, was well paid, and an economic reason for dropping him was given. But, naturally, the charges of political censorship flared up. Not having been involved in the decision, I cannot deliver a definitive judgement. My own feeling was that finance certainly counted, but that my predecessor had fallen out of love with the strip and found the cartoonist highly irritating. Sometimes, editors simply decide they don't like something in their paper and drop it.

The list of the twenty-five staff journalists who were to go in the merger of the editorials was sent to the deputy chairman, Roberto Ongpin, a former member of the Marcos government in the Philippines who was a business associate of Robert Kuok. When it came back, on Friday afternoon, the name of a leading journalist at the paper, China editor Willy Lo-Lap Lam, had been added. He would have been a grievous loss. The only possible reason for dropping him would have been to curry favour with China, where the *Post* was involved in a project for a business paper.

On Saturday morning, I met the paper's chief executive, Lyn Holloway, for coffee in the deserted bar of the Hong Kong Club. I told him that if this individual sacking went through, I would pack my bags and return to London immediately. If this was how the paper was to be run, I would not take up the editorship. The decision was abandoned. The journalist worked for the *Post* throughout my time as editor though Ongpin, in particular, kept coming back to his supposedly negative effect.

This was the first of a series of such incidents over the following years as I received instructions which could only be refused. I was told that Kuok and his son, who succeeded him as chairman in 1998, were particularly annoyed by the way the paper described political figures who backed the mainland government as 'pro-China' or 'pro-Beijing'. One afternoon in 1998, at a weekly meeting with senior managers, I was asked how I was feeling. Fine, I said. You'd better be, they replied; the Kuoks had blown up yet again about the paper having called somebody 'pro-Beijing'. This practice must stop, they insisted. Wearily, I said that this was ridiculous, and I was surprised it was still being brought up. Did the Kuoks think there was something wrong with being pro-China or pro-Beijing? Did they regard friendship with the mainland as a badge of shame? There was no way I was going to ban the phrase from the *Post*. All right, said the managers equally wearily, we will tell them that is your view.

At one point, I was advised to submit editorials about Malaysia and the Philippines so that they could be vetted by Kuok and Ongpin – even if it had been acceptable, this was a highly impractical suggestion given the amount of travel they did. On half a dozen occasions, I was told to sack or move staff journalists whose writing displeased the owners. Sometimes I refused outright; on a couple of occasions, I tap-danced round the edge of a problem until the storm passed. On one occasion, I let myself be boxed into a corner.

In the spring of 1997, a Saturday morning telephone call from Robert Kuok as he drove to China ordered the dismissal of a columnist who had referred to the publisher Jimmy Lai having called the former Prime Minister, Li Peng, a 'turtle's egg'. I said no, as I had to previous suggestions that the man in question should be fired. But a few months later, urged on by senior colleagues, I decided to move the writer from his column because I felt it was not good enough, and was full of items that did not fit in its place in the business pages. Just before he was to be moved, he wrote a column containing two items which I thought were particularly silly, and fully justified shifting him. One linked the new SAR regime to the murderous military dictatorship in Nigeria; the other said that Tung Chee-hwa and his colleagues should go round with condoms on their heads because they acted like 'male appendages'. Sod's law dictated that Robert Kuok was having lunch that day with a visitor from Singapore. Kuok vaunted the merits of the *Post* compared to the other city's *Straits Times*. His visitor pointed to the 'male appendages' item and asked if that was what Kuok regarded as quality journalism. The lunch over, the chairman called the paper's chief executive and demanded that the columnist be fired from the paper immediately.

As in the past, I refused to do so. But there was a problem, since I was going to move him a week later in any case. So I told the chief executive that he would no longer be doing the column, but that I was planning to move him to a lighter column elsewhere in the paper.

He was duly replaced as previously planned, but I was then told that Kuok still insisted he was sacked. A new column was out of the question. After several weeks of stalemate, the journalist came to my office and said he had a solution: we should pay him six months' money, and he would leave the staff and write as a contributor on a monthly retainer. That was done – though he didn't get six months' pay. He wrote two columns at the weekend for eighteen months before leaving the paper, joining the opposition *Standard* and setting himself up as an avenging angel to denounce the evils of the *Post*. This seemed somewhat bizarre since he had taken management guidance on the contents of his column at a time when I was insisting on editorial independence, had sent me an unbidden and unwanted message assuring me that he would be a 'flexible friend' in sensitive matters, and had written to me congratulating me on our defence of press freedom and saying how 'superb' our front pages had been. Hell hath no fury like a columnist scorned.

The main battle at the time of the handover in 1997 involved a Monday political column written by the pro-democracy passionaria Emily Lau, a former journalist and popularly elected legislator who led a political group called The Frontier. Robert Kuok was adamant that she must go; I was equally adamant that she must stay. This had its ironic side, given her recurrent expressions of concern that the *Post* was exercising self-censorship and a bias against the democratic camp.

Although she had been a journalist, her columns were rarely pearls of editorial writing, and occasionally recycled her radio talks or speeches. Still, whatever my reservations about her writing, or her economy with the truth, I could not think of dropping Lau's column. The abolition of the elected legislature on 1 July meant that representatives of the democratic camp like her lost their main platform. They had not been defeated by the electorate, but had been arbitrarily deprived of their seats in favour of a provisional legislature selected by a committee chosen by another pro-Beijing body without the voters having a chance to express their views, and in defiance of the findings of every opinion poll. In my view, this rolling-back of democracy gave the press a special role to play, and made it essential to go on running columns by Lau and two other pro-democracy legislator-columnists, Christine Loh and Margaret Ng. We also approached the Democratic Party chairman, Martin Lee, to write for the paper regularly, but he said he preferred to reserve himself for big occasions.

Later, when a new legislature gave popularly chosen members a chance of getting back in, I changed our line-up of regular columnists to avoid giving electoral advantage to any of them. But in 1997–98, Emily Lau had to stay in defiance of the angry telephone calls from Robert Kuok to the paper's chief executive, which were duly passed on to me.

I was told that somebody was employed at Kerry Holdings to go through the paper for anything that the chairman might find objectionable. But Robert Kuok rarely spoke to me directly. Since his views were more often expressed through his subordinates, it was not always clear whether they represented his full and considered opinions or were the work of executives operating like Henry II's knights rushing off to do their master's bidding on Thomas à Becket.

On one occasion, the approach was considerably more direct. One evening in June 1997 when I was out of the office for a couple of hours, the chief executive, Lyn Holloway, called my deputy up to his office and told him to issue an instruction that the Tiananmen Square crackdown should no longer be described as a 'massacre'. When I got back to the paper and was told of this, I rescinded the order. Later that night, I faxed a letter saying I would resign if the instruction was allowed to stand. The next day, I was asked if I could keep the word out of headlines at least. No, I said. That was that, for the moment. I never knew if a call from Robert Kuok had been behind the whole thing or if this had been the initiative of an underling: I doubted, however, that it contravened the chairman's wishes. Some time later, the issue came up again, but was not pursued when I recalled what had happened in 1997.

That did not stop correspondents and press freedom bodies stating as a matter of fact that 'massacre' had been banned from the *Post*. In fact, as anybody reading the paper could see, the M word kept appearing – 168 times in one twelve-month period. But such things never go away. Some time later, I was presented with a list of do's and don'ts typed in a series of numbered points on one side of a sheet of A4 paper. They included the prohibition of 'massacre' and sanctions against out-of-favour staff. Once again, I declined to carry them out. Once again, the order was not pressed – and the pressure later eased after the appointment of a new senior manager who, though a loyal Kuok man, also knew the importance of democracy and the rule of law.

In the spring of 1997, Kuok appointed a man called Feng Xiliang as a consultant to the *Post*. White-haired and self-effacing, Feng was the offspring of a well-to-do family in Shanghai. Born in the 1920s, he attended that city's most famous school of the pre-communist era, St Joseph's. After the war, he went to the United States to study journalism at the University of Missouri. Returning to China, he worked on English-language propaganda magazines, and is said to have suffered badly during the Cultural Revolution.

Rehabilitated, he became the first editor of the mainland's English-language newspaper, *China Daily*, in the early 1980s. Later, he went back to the United States as its representative in New York. He was not in Beijing at the time of the Tiananmen demonstration, when a delegation from *China Daily* marched to the square wearing hats emblazoned with the newspaper's masthead. There are differing accounts of when he returned to Beijing and how he behaved when he got back. But in 1991, Feng went off again as a Mass Media Fellow at the East-West Center in Hawaii. He developed a liking for California, acquiring a house in ultra-right-wing Orange County. But he then came to Hong Kong to advise a pro-Beijing magazine called *Window*, set up by T. S. Lo, a sad-faced lawyer who wanted to become Chief Executive and nurtured a deep dislike for the *Post*.

Lo's feelings cannot have been warmed by the polls we were printing at the time. In the absence of a popular election, I felt they were the only way of letting opinion be articulated, even if the choice of candidates was severely limited. For T. S. Lo, they were a killer. He hardly managed to scrape up 1 per cent support, and duly dropped out, closing his magazine and depriving his adviser of a job.

Survivors don't stay unemployed for long, and Feng's name was mentioned as a deserving case to Robert Kuok, supposedly by Lu Ping, the head of China's Hong Kong and Macau Affairs Office, who had been a classmate in Shanghai. Kuok took Feng, now well into his seventies, under his wing, and decided that he was just what the *Post* needed. Like officials I met in Beijing, the chairman said that the paper should 'understand' China better. And who better to enable us to 'understand' the mainland than Feng Xiliang, a man who had earned himself a seat in the upper house of China's parliament?

I was told of Feng's appointment after it had been signed and sealed. As it happened, I was going to Thailand for a week's holiday the following day. I spent some time walking up and down the beach trying to decide if this was the break point. The timing was acute: there was less than three months to go to the handover. Somewhere along the sand, I decided to take Feng's position literally. He had been taken on as a consultant. So I wouldn't consult him.

News of the appointment hit the headlines in London, Paris and New York. I could insist till I was blue in the face that a consultant is a consultant is a consultant, and that I was still the editor. To no avail. 'BIG BROTHER KEEPS AN EYE ON THE MEDIA UNDERLINGS' warned the *Independent*. In France, *Libération* called Feng 'the man parachuted in by Beijing'. The *International Herald Tribune* ran the story on the front page under the banner 'NEW HONG KONG EDITOR: HE EDITS WHAT, EXACTLY?'. When I telephoned the *Herald Tribune* to ask why it had promoted Feng to an editor's job, the reply was that 'consultant isn't a headline word'. Going a step further, the *New York Times* described Feng as 'senior editor'. The *Asian Wall Street Journal* noted that 'suspicion that the 76-year-old Mr Feng is a real-life political commissar is sending shivers up the spines of journalists all over Hong Kong, who are asking themselves: what if this is only the thin end of the wedge?'. In London, *The Times* linked fears about Feng with 'concerns from Hong Kong's pro-democracy faction that the *Post* is shying away from extensive coverage of the territory's political issues'. *The Times* correspondent could not have been reading the paper too closely: in the previous three days we had run twenty-four pieces, including three front-page splashes and two editorials, on proposed changes to civil rights legislation.

Feng's location became a particular cause for comment. I had installed him in a windowless room opposite my own office. I put him there precisely so that I could keep an eye on what he was doing. If he called in journalists to tell them how to 'understand' the mainland better, I wanted to know. But the foreign correspondents reported that Feng had been put in a 'specially built office' to keep watch on me. The *Financial Times* had him 'set to take a desk alongside Jonathan Fenby'. The *Guardian* went a step further: Feng was taking over my office as I was moved to new premises – presumably in a mainland thought-reform institute.

As if it makes a difference where anybody sits in this electronic age. Only one person, a journalist at the *Post*, asked me the key question: was Feng going to be logged on to the editorial computer system? The answer was no. Without that, he had no access to copy. There were some other relevant questions that were never asked. Would he attend editorial conferences? (No.) Would I talk to him about the contents of the paper? (No.) Would he be involved in discussions of coverage of mainland China or Hong Kong? (No.)

Of course there were fears about what the appointment meant. I felt them more keenly than anybody else. I had made it clear that if Feng did try to interfere, and was backed up by the chairman or the paper's management, I would go. Still, as a journalist with thirty-five years in the trade, I was hardly surprised if those fears took precedence in the reporting over my account, even if it was personally wounding that some correspondents now ranked me as an editor willing to work under a political Big Brother. Around this time, a leading British business figure in Hong Kong said after dinner at his house high on the Peak that I seemed to be having a hard time with the foreign press corps. Yes, I agreed: you told them the truth, but they wouldn't believe it. My host, who had sometimes taken issue with our coverage of his company, patted me on the knee and said with a smile: 'You see what it's like, Jonathan.'

If consultant Feng had been meant to whip us into line, he did a lousy job. Soon after his appointment, we devoted the front of our

Saturday Review section to the letters smuggled out of prison over the years by dissident Wei Jingsheng. Reporting and comment in the *Post* went on just as before. On handover day, my front-page editorial stressed the importance of democracy and freedom. The Beijing bureau continued to file hard-hitting reports from the mainland. Emily Lau wrote her columns, as did other pro-democracy politicians who lost their seats at the handover. *Post* correspondents visited Tibet and other sensitive areas of China, and filed straightforward reports of what they saw and were told by locals. In Hong Kong, the paper revealed how the government planned to put Chinese state bodies above the law, and reported on secret Chinese arms-dealing through the territory. We were regularly banned from distribution on the mainland when we ran photographs of dissidents, the Dalai Lama or President Lee Teng-hui of Taiwan. And Tiananmen was still a massacre.

But some people stuck to the party line, continuing to see Feng Xiliang as a censor and me as a man who dared not tell the tuth. Asked in a radio discussion about my insistence that the consultant was not influencing the contents of the paper, Jonathan Mirsky of *The Times* replied, 'He would say that, wouldn't he? If he said that this man is that kind of person, he'd be out of a job.'

Throughout all this, Feng padded discreetly in and out of his office, took trips to California, and made arrangements for occasional visits to Beijing by senior executives. The controversy stirred up by his appointment had clearly shaken him. 'There's so much talk,' he told an Australian journalist, Alan Knight. 'I begin to wonder why I am doing this.' Some of the hundred or so correspondents who came to interview me during the handover peered across the passage outside my office to catch a glimpse of Big Brother. His room was usually empty. When Feng was there, he sat alone reading newspapers and making telephone calls. To begin with, one or two members of the editorial staff dropped in to speak to him and to try to take the measure of the newcomer. Feng seemed grateful for the company, but the visits soon tailed off. I started to feel almost sorry for the small elderly man with well-combed white hair and a quietly courteous manner. I wondered

what he would do if, just once, I invited him to an editorial conference, or asked what he thought of a column criticising the
central leadership.

Feng's most useful role was in helping to set up a meeting shortly
before the handover with China's Foreign Minister, Qian Qichen,
who was overseeing Hong Kong policy. Before the interview in an
official guest house in a garden in Beijing, Qian greeted Feng as an
old friend. The Minister's answers to my questions came as if by rote
until I asked about some hard-line statements he had made on the
freedom of expression after the handover. How could they be
reconciled with the promise that the Hong Kong system would
continue unchanged after 1 July? I wondered. Oh, the Minister
replied, he had just been expressing a personal opinion. As a
member of the Chinese government, he naturally did not approve of
criticism. But so long as the law was not broken, people in Hong
Kong could say whatever they liked. Martin Lee called the interview
the most important statement by a mainland official before the
handover.

Eventually, in the autumn of 1998, Feng packed up his belongings
and left for the management floor above to pursue purposes unknown
to me. His departure from the editorial and his total lack of any effect
on the paper was not mentioned by any of the correspondents who
had reported his arrival so breathlessly. But the penny had dropped
with one man. 'You've sidelined Feng,' Robert Kuok remarked one
day with a notable lack of pleasure in his voice.

This was far from being the tycoon's first expression of disquiet.
When we met for the first time in 1995, he had said that the *Post*
should be independent, and could criticise the government in Beijing
by all means. But he did not want it to be anti-Chinese in the sense
of being against the Chinese as a people or a race. Over the following
years, it became clear that, for him, the Chinese people and the
Chinese authorities were increasingly lumped together. To begin
with, he objected to what he saw as our pro-Patten slant, which
might have amused the Governor. Given the passage of events, this
eventually faded into insignificance beside other concerns – the
paper's reporting and comment on mainland China, its attitude

towards the new administration and the business community in Hong Kong, and its support for democratic politicians. Even more fundamental, I believe, was Kuok's complaint that the paper was out of his control.

He did not keep his views to himself, asking why couldn't the *Post* toe the line? Why didn't it do what it was told? Why was it so anti-China? Why was this the only asset he owned which he could not control? His position was delicate. As a leading member of the Hong Kong-Beijing establishment, he had sat on the Preparatory Committee set up by China to map out the future of the former British colony. The head of the mainland's Hong Kong and Macau Affairs Office, Lu Ping, went golfing at a Kuok-owned country club across the border. When leading politicians from the north visited Hong Kong, they saw Kuok. But there was his newspaper criticising the Preparatory Committee, urging Lu to change his tune, laying in to the new administration in Hong Kong, and writing about problems on the mainland which Beijing denied existed. To people from a system where the media follow orders, this must have been distinctly puzzling.

The billionaire head of a major conglomerate of his own creation, Robert Kuok was used to having his way. As a non-executive director remarked to me one evening: 'The Kuoks have 34 per cent of the company but they act as though they own it. They don't. But who's going to remind them of that?' The problem was that the *Post* editorial had a life of its own, and this had to be maintained. If that was the case before the handover, it became even more so after 1 July, particularly when the democratically elected legislators were deprived of their seats and the rule of law was brought into question. Kuok insisted that he did not want the *Post* to become a party-lining organ, like the *Straits Times* in Singapore, which he regularly lambasted. But the instructions I received would have led it to go that way and would have undermined its spirit. Kuok liked the idea of a paper that was independent, but was uncomfortable with the prickliness which this inevitably aroused.

What is surprising is that I was not fired much earlier, as certainly would have happened under a Western press baron. But now the yellow light is flashing with the non-renewal of my contract. Given this, should I stay on till the end of the year as suggested, or leave immediately? I have no doubt. Apart from wanting to remain in Asia a while longer, this is turning out to be an extremely important time in the short history of the SAR. Two years on from the hand-over, the real game is beginning: not in the stark terms predicted in 1997 but on a more subtle plane. That is not attracting much attention outside Hong Kong: tanks in the streets are much easier to comprehend than the steady advance of weak-kneed consensus, the over-riding exercise of authority by the executive and the erosion of the rule of law. Western governments are anxious not to let problems in Hong Kong get in the way of a good relationship with Beijing. As was apparent from before the handover, the SAR is on its own in dealing with the dragon it joined in 1997. In these circumstances, editing the *Post* has taken on a special edge, and I want to go on for as long as I can.

18 *May*

A prime example of what is happening comes when the government of Hong Kong makes it known that it is going to ask the Standing Committee of China's parliament, the National People's Congress (NPC), to issue its interpretation of what the Basic Law says on the right of abode case which the SAR administration lost at the Court of Final Appeal. The government's argument is that the interpretation by the court was not in accordance with the 'legislative intent' of the framers of the Basic Law. Determining what that intent was nine years later is a tricky question, particularly since some sources say that the mainland was keen at the time for all Chinese to be treated equally, thus implying that it might well have wanted a wide defini-tion of who could come to Hong Kong.

One recalls a remark by Chris Patten about China's desire to have a mechanism for a 'post-remedial verdict' on Court of Final Appeal decisions: the Governor characterised this as 'if we don't like the result we've got to find some way to overturn it'. Now that is being done not by Beijing directly, but by the administration here.

19 *May*

There is a debate in the Legislative Council today about the government's decision to go to the NPC. The democratic camp tries to get
more time for discussion. It fails. So 19 members, headed by Martin
Lee, walk out of the chamber. They have dressed in black for the
occasion. Lee speaks of 'a dagger striking at the heart of the rule of
law'. Margaret Ng of the legal constituency warns of the beginning of
the end of the rule of law. But the pro-Beijing DAB party insists that
the rule of law will be strengthened, and Liberals say the government
has public support. After the walk-out, the motion backing the government is passed by 35 votes to 2.

I remember the time I asked Martin Lee what he would do if his
electoral victory brought him no more influence and he replied,
'Make noise.' That's the way it has become. But who is listening?

20 *May*

The *Post*'s strong criticism of the government for going to Beijing to
over-rule the Court of Final Appeal earns us a visit from Anson Chan.
The Chief Secretary's office calls in the late morning and says she has
to see me before the day is out. She argues that we must realise that
this is an exceptional case and must trust the administration. There has
been a thorough debate, with very strongly held views on both sides.
Some may see referral to the National People's Congress as an erosion
of the independence of the judiciary and the high degree of autonomy promised to Hong Kong. But the rule of law underpins
everything here and has not been undermined. Yes, there is legitimate
concern about the mechanism by which judicial decisions could be
referred, but the Central Government has made it clear it does not
wish to interfere. 'It would prefer for Hong Kong to sort it out but,
if we could not do that, they were ready to help,' as one official says.
Thank you very much.

When questioned, officials say no guarantee that this will be a
one-off event could be promised – 'just watch this space'. The
Chief Executive and his administration are not likely to act in an

arbitrary way, we are assured. And then comes a return to a familiar mantra of trust.

Trust us, but don't observe how we finessed last year's electoral arrangements to handicap the democrats, or how we treat the legislators or the Court of Final Appeal. Forget about the decision not to prosecute Sally Aw, and how we put the muscle on functional constituency members. Don't regard the award of the Cyberport project as anything untoward, and turn a blind eye to how hard we find it to defend Hong Kong people arrested on the mainland.

As I accompany Anson Chan to her green BMW, I ask her if this is the first of a series of visits to newspapers which have criticised the government. 'No,' she says with her trademark smile. 'You are the only one who matters.'

I do not write a recanting editorial. In fact, there is very little news on the whole reinterpretation issue. After having given it pages one, two and three for the last two days, the story goes inside tonight.

22 *May*

The paper which appears the day after Anson Chan's visit is, I am told, taken by the weekly meeting of senior brass as a sign that a sudden descent by a top official can shut the *Post* up. My informant, who is well versed in the ways of government and the media, chuckles as he tells me this at a lunchtime party for the departing head of the Swire conglomerate, Peter Sutch, a man who knows how to enjoy himself as a human being while rising at dawn to do his job, and who gave British business a good name after the handover.

It is a hot and steamy day, and some people drink too much out on the lawn of the Swire residence, Taikoo House, high on the Peak. Since I am working that day, I'm on mineral water. A society lady with a red face upbraids me for the paper's attention to the right of abode issue. Is anybody really interested in that, she asks. Face it, we don't want all those people from the mainland to come here, do we?

23 *May*

Civil servants take to the streets in the biggest labour demonstration seen in Hong Kong since the handover. Waving bright yellow banners and wearing yellow headbands, an estimated 10,000 of them – the organisers say 26,000 – march through the centre of Hong Kong Island to the Central Government offices.

In the courtyard where the mainland overstayers camped, they chant denunciations of plans to reform their working conditions and make them subject to efficiency criteria, with fixed-term contracts in place of lifetime employment and performance-related pay instead of automatic annual increases. 'Fake reform, real exploitation,' they cry.

There is talk of strikes if the government does not back off. Hong Kong's civil service may be admirable in many ways, but it has lived a protected life for much too long. Salaries, allowances and conditions are out of step with the times. Private sector companies have cut wages and bonuses and laid off staff. But the civil service has remained immune. Now the pressures are catching up with them. The recession is real, even for the men and women in the bureaucratic Rolls-Royce.

24 *May*

Dinner with a generally pro-government member of the Legislative Council. Surprisingly, our host lays into the administration. He is no radical, and voted to save Elsie Leung from the no-confidence motion. But tonight he unsparingly criticises the Chief Executive for lack of leadership, and backs the concern we have expressed in the *Post* about the rule of law. Foreign businessmen he meets are starting to wonder how solid Hong Kong is, he adds. Who would have thought that a test case for mainland migrants could have ended up having such an effect?

26 *May*

I am handed a letter setting out the company's plans for the *Post*. It has been decided that, after I leave, an editorial director will be appointed as well as a new editor. The new arrangement is to be announced next week. If I stay on as editor till the end of the year, as agreed earlier, I would be the longest lame duck in newspaper history. I have to go right away. Anyway, the new editorial director is sitting in the office opposite mine – an American former editor of the *Asian Wall Street Journal* in both Asia and Europe, who was hired by the Kuoks and the *Post*'s management as my deputy the previous summer, without my being consulted. When I had objected, I was informed that the management had the right to do as it liked in editorial appointments, and that the hiring of Robert Keatley was a no-go area. This meant there had been a Kuok laying-on of hands, with which nobody should presume to argue. Still, when I dug my heels in, my management colleagues 'implored' me to 'try to find a way of making this thing work'. I flew to Washington to see Keatley and we agreed that he would join the paper as senior associate editor, but would not replace my extremely effective deputy.

Keatley arrived in Hong Kong in October 1998, and moved into Feng Xiliang's old office. We got on well enough, but the Kuoks' back-channel contacts soon sprang into life. Robert Kuok's son, who had become chairman, discussed editorial matters with Keatley with no reference to me. At the instigation of the management, Keatley canvassed in New York for a new business editor without my being informed – the search ended in fiasco after the existing incumbent of the job was tipped off about the approach and I kicked up another stink. Throughout, Keatley assured me that he did not want my job, but now he is to become editorial director. Although he is not due to take up the post till the end of the year, the announcement has – for some inexplicable reason – to be made right away. Do the Kuoks want to nail things down this time, and make sure there is no slip-up in getting their man into the job? Anyway, I clearly have to resign as editor, though I will stay in the job until 31 July and then serve out the agreed six months' notice as a writer and consultant. There is a final ironic twist in September when I am asked to go back to edit the paper half a dozen times. More farewell performances than Frank Sinatra.

29 May

Arriving at the Shangri-La Hotel for a website competition ceremony at which he and I are to present the prizes, the Financial
Secretary looks at me and says: 'Jonathan, I don't want you to think
that I necessarily agree with my colleagues who think you have gone
bonkers.' Presumably he is referring to our criticism of the Tung
administration. But he also insists that he never reads the *Post* except
for one columnist whom he likes. His press secretary stands behind
him with a perspex folder filled with newspaper clippings, many of
which are from the *Post*.

At lunch, after the awards have been handed out, Tsang appears
rather more familiar with the contents of the newspaper as he takes
me to task over an editorial criticising the government's economic
forecasting. 'Nobody blames the Observatory if a typhoon hits' he
says: I bet they would if it predicted a calm and sunny day.

Tsang, who looks much younger than his fifty-four years, has had
an interesting political career since 1997. Before the handover, he
called in our political editor to give a brave interview defending the
Bills of Rights that the incoming regime was going to emasculate.
The general conclusion was that Hong Kong's first Chinese Financial
Secretary was about to lose his job. But he hung on, and spent the
early stages of the economic crisis insisting on the need to maintain
Hong Kong's traditional low-spending, budget-surplus policies, even
if the results caused him considerable personal anguish.

After that, Tsang seemed to be fighting an increasingly difficult
battle, since the Chief Executive and some of his advisers clearly
thought it was time to let out the fiscal belt. Now this has been done,
and he has used the crisis to introduce some significant changes which
he hopes will contribute to making Hong Kong the premier financial
centre in its time zone. Last year's stock market intervention followed
by this year's Disneyland deal – which he lists as a 'project of hope' –
gave a fresh fillip to Tsang, another of Hong Kong's excellent ballroom dancers who has taken to wearing a red lapel badge depicting
the Hong Kong and Chinese flags. He finds Beijing's sovereignty
'benign' and is one of those senior civil servants who likes to illustrate

the point by contrasting the colonial hours spent reading and drafting telegrams from and to London with the absence of any messages from the Central Government. For a short while there was speculation that his star was riding so high that Tung was toying with the idea of promoting him to succeed Anson Chan as Chief Secretary for Administration and number two in the government. But the story is that Beijing came down for Chan to continue driving the administration's Rolls-Royce.

Tsang's standing with the public is good, though he insists that he will always chose patriotism over popularity. But he has times when he tires of life at the top. And the combination of criticism from politicians with little grasp of economics and the need to play to the gallery cannot sit too easily with a man who finds it endearingly hard to hide his human side and whose skin can be reassuringly thin.

JUNE

2 June

Dinner at the official residence of the Chief Secretary on the Peak. It is one of a round of farewells for Peter Sutch, the gregarious chairman of the British Swire group, which owns Cathay Pacific Airlines. His departure coincides with a dispute with the pilots, who are resisting new working terms. As a negotiating tactic, they have hit on the device of calling in sick just before they are due to go on duty, using doctors' certificates saying the stress of the dispute makes them unfit to fly. The *Post* takes a dim view of this, provoking furious e-mails from anonymous pilots on their website.

The *Post* 'is no more a real paper than *Pravda* was in the eighties', says one. Its journalists have been bought by big business and 'must live with the shame of having sold out'. 'For them, money is more important than facts,' says another. A third warns that the editor's 'legacy will follow him wherever he goes (we will make sure of that), but maybe his upcoming job in Russia, Libya, Chile or Saudi Arabia will further increase his financial gain'. Could I find myself one day in a Cathay plane with a pilot who remembers my name ordering me to be ejected without a parachute?

3 *June*

Hong Kong may be deep in recession, but the rich are still spending. James Tien, leader of the Liberal Party, is a very wealthy man who moved at the right moment from the family business of making clothes to property and finance. Tonight he and his wife, Mary, throw another goodbye dinner for the Sutches at their new home just down the road from Anson Chan, with a spectacular view over Hong Kong harbour. The Tiens are proud of their plantation-style mansion with its huge wide-open rooms, wooden panels, mahogany, tiled floors with inlaid patterns, sofas and chairs scattered about, a terraced garden and an illuminated swimming pool. They have spent three years doing the house up, building a road down to it, having a US$1 million security system installed and setting up a wine cellar, which houses 2,000 bottles including some 1947 clarets.

A slim, sharp man who looks much younger than his sixty years, Tien is yet another offspring of Shanghai, whose parents made their money in the garment trade after moving down to Hong Kong. His mother watched the business like a hawk, going into the factory seven days a week to check on the work rate. In the early 1990s, Tien and his brother decided not to join the exodus to southern China. Instead they went into property, the export business, a big marina and other higher-margin avenues of profit. Tien became chairman of the General Chamber of Commerce and a legislator for its functional constituency. After the leader of the Liberals failed to win a popularly elected seat in the Legislative Council in 1998, he took over as leader of the party which has 10 members in the legislature, none of them chosen by a geographical constituency.

The *Post* has been steadily critical of the party over its lack of consistency, and regularly takes Tien to task. But he stays friendly, and asks nothing in return for his hospitality. We are far apart in our beliefs, not to mention our ways of life and the wine we drink. But it is still possible to have a civilised relationship even if he once said he believed Hong Kong should be run by a natural élite of a couple of hundred people.

4 June

'I just want her to know about history,' says a middle-class Hong Kong mother looking down at her three-year-old daughter. The child has no idea what is going on. But for the mother, and tens of thousands of other people, this is the day on which the difference between Hong Kong and the rest of China is most tangible, and most moving.

Today marks the tenth anniversary of the Tiananmen Square massacre, and the annual vigil is being held in Victoria Park amid the skyscrapers of Causeway Bay. Last year was a test occasion, the first commemoration since Hong Kong rejoined China. As such, it was an opportunity for people to assert themselves, but nobody really believed the claim by the organisers that 40,000 turned out (the police have refused for some time to give their estimate). The tenth anniversary gives the vigil a special significance. But maybe Hong Kongers are growing bored, and will heed the advice of the Chief Executive to relegate Tiananmen to the baggage of history.

Tung Chee-hwa is going to be disappointed. Seventy thousand people gather, sitting on concrete football pitches and holding candles in paper triangles to remember the dead. A statue of the Goddess of Liberty modelled on one which stood in Tiananmen Square rises from one section. In the middle of the crowd, Queen Victoria sits on her plinth.

Black flags with white inscriptions flutter in the air. On the stage at one end of the park, bands and singers perform in front of more banners and a giant video screen where images of 1989 play over and over again. Police mingle with the crowd, but there is no aggravation. Everybody gets to their feet as a flowered wreath with a black and white ribbon is carried through the throng. The veteran pro-democracy campaigner and legislator, Szeto Wah, walks beside it. With other leaders of the remembrance movement, the bespectacled, elderly Szeto mounts to the platform as a stringed lament arches through the warm air. A teenager carrying a burning torch moves to join them, and the torch is used to light a commemorative flame in a large urn. The line of men on the platform lead the singing of a dirge. Modern synthesiser music takes over. The dissident Wan Dan talks to his mother in Beijing on a hook-up from the USA through Hong Kong.

Tonight, this is the only place in China where the truth about 1989 is being told in public. But the vigil does not stop life going on around it. Trams rumble by, the passengers peering out at the scene. Tennis-players keep up their game on the courts in another part of the park. Shoppers pile into late-night stores on adjoining streets. There is a scuffle outside a night spot called STIX, and the usual rush for taxis.

'This is what China could be like, if only they would let it,' the mother says. The crowd is mourning for what might have been, for a brief spark of hope extinguished, as so often in China's history, by autocrats for whom life can only be lived on their terms. In Beijing, Hong Kong reporters ask Zhu Rongji about the anniversary. Mockingly, he thanks them for reminding him of the date: he says he had forgotten what day it was. Police arrest a lone man who tries to wave a banner in Tiananmen Square. The *People's Daily* says the army's action in 1989 had been very timely and very necessary, to protect China's independence, dignity, security and stability. The central authorities have ordered the Bank of China to freeze donations sent by Chinese students in Germany for the families of victims.

To jolly along mainland punters, a series of measures has been announced to pump up the stock market, which has duly risen by 40 per cent in two weeks. Such action might strike a bell with one of the leaders of the protest ten years ago. On the eve of the massacre, a young woman called Chai Ling was filmed telling a Western reporter that blood would have to be shed, though not hers. When the tanks rolled into the square, she was gone. After hiding in China, she was smuggled out through Hong Kong. Now established in Boston, she is launching an Internet software company called Jenzabar.com. A press release recalls how she led 'thousands of students against a Communist government more ruthless than Microsoft'. Chai Ling, it adds, is 'a dynamic personality who has found many similarities between running a revolution and an Internet start-up'. She has 'used the techniques and charisma of a true revolutionary to impress CEOs to back Jenzabar'.

Later, I hear that the Central Government was none too pleased with the way foreign and Hong Kong media remarked on the unique nature of the vigil in the park, and on the space given to it here. The *Post* ran the usual big photograph of the occasion on page one with a descriptive story, and I wrote an editorial and a column arguing that Tiananmen should not be relegated to the baggage of history whatever the Chief Executive might say.

5 June

The website 'Not The South China Morning Post' has a capitalised headline, 'LATEST POST EDITOR FENBY TO BE REPLACED BY WALL STREET JOURNAL MAN SAY SOURCES'. Maybe I have underrated Dr Adams.

10 June

The legal saga over the right of abode rolls on. The State Council in Beijing accepts Hong Kong's request for an interpretation from the National People's Congress. The Secretary for Justice makes it plain that local courts will have to abide with whatever the NPC decides. Whatever the 'trust us' officials may say, the dragon's breath is getting hotter.

11 June

Press matters.

At the annual gala of the Journalists' Association, Anson Chan does a karaoke song on stage in return for donations of tens of thousands of dollars to the organisation from the guests. The Association's chairperson delivers a lecture on falling press standards. 'Reading newspapers is no longer an enjoyable exercise,' he tells us. 'Bloody explicit pictures displayed prominently are challenging our level of tolerance every day. Sex and violence seem to be the only activities worth mentioning in Hong Kong. This undesirable trend poses a grave danger to the standard of professionalism of journalism.' The audience snickers in the knowledge that he has just left his job on the editorial page of the respectable *Economic Times* to join the sensational *Apple Daily*.

The next day, the *Post* wins eleven of thirteen English-language prizes in awards organised by Amnesty International, the Journalists' Association and the Foreign Correspondents' Club.

Two days later, the paper's directors are told that I am going. I had informed two of them whom I met socially in the last few weeks. They both expressed shock and regret. One tells me he understands the Kuoks were 'under a lot of pressure'. He does not say who from, but it isn't hard to guess.

17–21 *June*

The *South China Morning Post* enjoys a great advantage as the only Hong Kong newspaper, except for those funded by Beijing, allowed to have staff correspondents on the mainland. That is a relic of colonial days, when it was regarded as British and its reporters were put on a par with foreign correspondents in China. As a result, it comes under the Foreign Ministry, and the Ministry is regarded as being somewhat more flexible than the Hong Kong and Macau Affairs Office or the official Xinhua news agency which oversee the mainland access of other Hong Kong publications.

But now an official calls in one of our Beijing correspondents to say some people are unhappy with this state of affairs: not because of our coverage of the mainland but because of our attitude towards the Hong Kong government. Before the handover the *Post* had supported the Hong Kong government, she adds. But now it is an opposition paper. The mainland Hong Kong and Macau Affairs Office (HKMAO) and Xinhua are angry about this. They say the *Post* should not oppose what is being done in the SAR, and want to take it under their wing.

There is also word from Beijing that the paper's coverage of the 4 June vigil in Hong Kong came in for criticism in the capital. My column arguing that the history of Tiananmen Square must not be buried is seen as having 'gone too far'. When I bump into a mainland official in Hong Kong and he asks if I will still write for the paper after stepping down as editor, I wonder if it is an entirely innocent question.

24 June

The first thing most post-colonial governments do is to rename buildings that reek of imperial days. But not only has the SAR left Victoria Park and Queen's Road unchanged, it has also taken an eternity to decide what to call the former home of the British proconsuls. Finally it has been determined that the residence of twenty-five governors since 1855 will become Heung Kong Lai Bun Fu, meaning a place for greeting guests. The new name was chosen from more than 2,300 submissions. The legislator representing the travel industry says it is less attractive than the old name; he predicts that tour guides will still call it by the Chinese term for 'former Governor's house'.

The Chief Executive will not move into the white mansion, with its tower built by the Japanese during the Occupation, the grass tennis courts where Chris Patten used to play in the morning, and the kitchens which have recently undergone a US$1.3 million renovation. Tung Chee-hwa has occasional lunches there, and the house is used for receptions and formal gatherings. But the twenty-eight domestic staff have relatively little to do, and the heavy metal gates remain closed most of the time.

Government House was the scene of two memorably symbolic events at the end of colonial days. In the first, the Chief Executive-designate paid a visit to Chris Patten. After their meeting, the two men exchanged platitudes for the press outside. As Patten walked back inside, Tung stayed to talk more to the reporters. The photograph – of the Governor's back and Tung's face smiling to the cameras; of the old and the new – made the front page.

And then on the last afternoon of colonial rule, the mansion on Upper Albert Road was the backdrop for what I found the most moving single moment of the handover. Although his final speech in the rain that evening had a simple grandeur, it was Patten's departure from Government House which brought the tears to my eyes. As he stood in front of the building, the Union flag was hauled down, neatly folded and handed to him. The last Governor blinked back his emotion. Then he went inside to escort his family out to a big black car flying his standard. The Daimler had been due to make three turns round the driveway to signify an eventual return. It did not.

25 June

On the mainland, more than 100 people are executed to mark United Nations anti-drug day. Calls for the abolition of the death penalty cut no ice in Beijing. China sees a lot of bullets in the head as the best way to deal with its mushrooming narcotics problem. And it is quite a problem. Seizures of heroin on the mainland rose by one-third last year. Police reported arresting 34,200 drug suspects; 27,000 were found guilty. Drug-related crimes have soared. The number of registered addicts is almost 600,000. Seventy per cent of the 400,000 HIV carriers have been infected through needles.

26 June

The National People's Congress delivers its verdict on the migrants' case today. As expected, it reverses the decision of the Court of Final Appeal. This means that only mainlanders born after one of their parents became a permanent resident of Hong Kong will be eligible for the right of abode here. A senior NPC official takes the Court of Final Appeal to task for not having consulted the Chinese parliament in the first place.

The government exults. The Secretary for Justice castigates those who have expressed concern about the whole procedure as scaremongers out to 'destroy their own fortress'. Such critics should drop their 'arrogance' and 'open their eyes and learn more about the mainland systems', she adds. They must accept that there is now a new constitutional order. An NPC deputy from Hong Kong invites his friends to tea 'to celebrate as Hong Kong is about to rid itself of a disaster'. A senior British official from the Department of Justice says the administration can ask for an interpretation from the NPC whenever it wishes – before, during or after a court hearing.

By coincidence, a seminar on the common law is being held in the Shangri-La Hotel today with local lawyers and bigwigs from London. The Chief Justice, Andrew Li, makes a brief appearance, but is clearly anxious not to discuss anything to do with the NPC. A red-faced legal eagle from London says heartily during the tea break that he's happy to see how well everything is going. Reacting to the decision is a tricky matter for London and Washington. They know how sharply Beijing will object if they are seen to be interfering in SAR internal affairs. The US State Department worries about the potential of the NPC ruling 'to erode the independent authority of the Hong Kong judiciary'. The British statement is diplomatic, but clear that 'the principles of independent judicial power and of final adjudication are integral to Hong Kong's high degree of autonomy'.

Not being bound by the niceties of diplomacy, I write an editorial for the next day's paper headed 'Much more than interpretation at stake':

> What happened yesterday is as simple as it is important. If it means anything, the rule of law means the law is above politics. The law may be changed by politicians operating through a legislature. But those politicians cannot act as judges in interpreting it. Nor can they appeal to a political body for redress when the decision of the highest court goes against them.
>
> But that is what the Hong Kong government has done. The National People's Congress is a political body. The Hong Kong government has chosen not to seek to change the law, as would have been the normal common law process. Instead, it decided to ask the NPC to hand down an interpretation of the Basic Law in order to overturn a Court of Final Appeal verdict.
>
> The administration here will now invoke that interpretation to define the Hong Kong law on mainland migrants, clearly placing the supreme court in Hong Kong in a subservient position to the NPC. Equally, the ruling given in Beijing today will no doubt be challenged in a string of law suits. At the end of that process, the Court of Final Appeal will have to decide whether it accepts the reversal of its own judgment – and agrees that it was wrong not to seek prior interpretation. If it does accept that, it will have recognised the

supremacy of the NPC and invalidated its own arguments; if it does not, a further crisis will follow.

The air is full of assurances from the government that the rule of law remains inviolate. Naturally, officials will downplay the significance of what has happened. But nobody in the administration will rule out a similar procedure being followed in other cases. Indeed, a senior legal official has said the government may seek intervention on any provisions in the Basic Law it sees fit to raise before, during or after a trial.

So, two years after the handover, the major challenge to Hong Kong's system has come not in the political arena, as many had expected, but in the legal field. In a sense, this makes what has happened all the more serious.

Politics are a relatively recent phenomenon in Hong Kong, and the Basic Law lays down a timetable for moving towards democracy. The preservation of the legal system acted as a counterweight to that slow process, with the courts enjoying backing across the political spectrum – including, crucially, the business community, which may take a leery view of democracy but knows the importance of maintaining the status of the law in Hong Kong.

But now what had appeared to be a bedrock of Hong Kong's way of life as guaranteed under the Joint Declaration and the one country, two systems concept has become subject to an essentially political process. The NPC ruling was a stark statement of where power lies. By taking the court to task for not requesting an interpretation by the NPC before issuing its verdict, it laid down another benchmark which undermines the court's independence and authority.

Within Hong Kong itself, there is a very real danger that application of the rule of law is becoming a partisan issue. Being for or against the interpretation route will be seen as a gauge of being for or against the government. On Friday, the Secretary for Justice branded those who make a link between interpretation and the rule of law as scaremongers who were destroying their own fortress. That way lie witch hunts that would do Hong Kong great damage and add to the polarisation of society. As Elsie Leung Oi-sie rightly said, foreign investors believe that a sound legal system is a great advantage of

Hong Kong. But this does not mean everybody has to tamely accept whatever the government ordains. Indeed, the Chief Executive has spoken positively of the contribution that the 'noise' of debate makes to Hong Kong.

The legal arguments will continue for months, if not years. But the basic point cannot be evaded. At the time of the handover, there was an understandable tendency here to put the emphasis on the preservation of the Hong Kong system under Deng Xiaoping's celebrated formula. Now, the Secretary for Justice has made it plain that the one country comes first followed by the two systems. This has led the government to apply for legal interpretation to a 'one country' political body which is used to supervising the mainland courts in a completely different legal system from ours, and to humiliate the supreme judicial body in Hong Kong in the process.

The administration may deploy strong practical arguments for what it has done. It may bring out legal advice filled with learned references to sections of the Basic Law. But it cannot pretend that there has not been a major political shift with potentially far-reaching implications for the autonomy of Hong Kong and the relationship with the Central Government as the SAR enters its third year.

28 June

I am invited to join a *South China Morning Post* directors' lunch after a board meeting. It is held in a private room of an excellent Chinese restaurant on the harbour front. The chopsticks are gold-plated. Before the eating starts, the chairman says a single, short sentence of appreciation for my work as editor which is lost in the general chit-chat round the table. Then he leans forward, takes a dim sum dumpling from the dish in front of us and places it on my plate.

30 June

A successful surveyor and rising politician, C.Y. Leung, takes over the significant post of convenor of the secretive, thirteen-member

Executive Council which advises Tung Chee-hwa on policy issues. His predecessor, an elderly man with thick glasses, was a pillar of the old regime and received a knighthood before adapting to the new order in the seamless manner of so many members of the Hong Kong establishment.

Tall and self-assured, Leung is seen as a face of the future. His well-groomed head rising above the crowd of much shorter Cantonese reporters as he fends off their questions is a familiar sight at official occasions. He is thought to have ambitions to become Chief Executive. At forty-five, he can wait out two Tung terms. Leung has managed to balance making money with political correctness. Unlike his predecessor, he kept well clear of the British and concentrated on building up connections with the Central Government.

Though few people would bet against him being at the helm of the SAR in the next century, his performance so far has not been exactly impressive. In particular, he was the main force behind a government pledge to build 85,000 housing units a year which has had to be watered down. Given his involvement in property, some opposition politicians raised conflict of interest questions, but as one Liberal Party member remarked, any prominent figure chosen as Exco convenor by the present administration is likely to have business connections.

JULY

1 *July*

The second anniversary of the handover. Last year, Jiang Zemin came to mark the occasion and to open the new airport. He and his entourage occupied 141 rooms in one of Li Ka-shing's hotels, and were ferried around in six armour-plated Mercedes-Benz limousines. This year, Jiang contributes some verses to a commemorative pillar inscribed with Chinese poetry, but does not make the trip south himself. Instead, he sends a protégé, Vice-President Hu Jintao, who declares that 'The previous social and economic systems as well as the way of life in Hong Kong remain unchanged.' As usual, politics is left out of the list. There are some small protest demonstrations. When Hu takes a boat trip, he is shadowed by a group angry at having been bilked in a mainland property deal.

A poll by Hong Kong Chinese University shows the percentage of people happy with the government has fallen to 25 per cent. The proportion who are dissatisfied has risen from 12 per cent in 1997 to 20 per cent in 1998 and now to 46 per cent. Forty-three per cent say that the rule of law has deteriorated and democracy has been eroded, around double the figure of a year ago.

The head of the main pro-Beijing political party refuses to join other party leaders in contributing his thoughts on the anniversary to the *Post* because of the way we have handled the right of abode controversy. And on a social note, the editor has been dropped from the invitation list to the anniversary ceremonies. Last year, there was a card for them all, including the opening of the new airport. Today, nothing. My social acceptability seems to be about as low as in Patten's last days. Or maybe the fact that I am on my way out speaks sufficient volumes in this status-conscious town.

On page one, we run a photograph from an anniversary occasion showing the Secretary for Justice, Elsie Leung, who has been stressing the importance of the one country, and the Chief Secretary, Anson Chan, who insists on the two systems. The two women wear very similar blue suits, but look in opposite directions. My handover day editorial starts from there.

The evident differences of views between the Chief Secretary for Administration and Secretary for Justice about the balance between one country and two systems could not have come at a more apposite time. Their divergence may be awkward for the administration in which they both sit, but it points up more sharply than ever the crucial issue facing Hong Kong two years after the handover.

On July 1, 1997, this newspaper wrote in a front-page editorial that Tung Chee-hwa had to keep reminding Chinese leaders that they must respect the two systems. Now, two years on, the question is whether the Chief Executive himself and some of his senior colleagues are the ones who need reminding.

It was, after all, the administration which Mr Tung heads that decided to ask the National People's Congress to over-rule the Court of Final Appeal. The remarks by the Secretary for Justice before the NPC handed down its judgment underlined fears that it is senior figures here who will undermine the preservation of the system we were promised two years ago.

Having been on a visit to North and Central America at the time of the NPC decision and the rule of law controversy, Anson Chan Fang On-sang was particularly well placed to judge the extent of international concern at the erosion of Hong Kong's autonomy that is implicit in the administration's approach. The government may argue with all the force at its command that the rule of law remains unaffected; that is not the way many overseas observers see things. Some of them are businessmen for whom one great attraction of Hong Kong was that its legal system was not subject to vagaries of interpretation by a political body outside its control. As Mrs Chan noted, Hong Kong cannot take the goodwill which it has earned since the handover for granted.

The problem is compounded by the way in which the government has been ready to put expediency – or its own interests – ahead of some of the long-standing principles on which the Hong Kong system has been based. This is not to decry change. The SAR should not be a static society, and a process as unique as the one launched in 1997 is bound to bring diversions from the road map laid down in the Joint Declaration and the Basic Law. But those changes need to be spelled out clearly and to be connected to the broad thrust of policy to explain where the government is heading.

The present danger is one of drift interspersed with sudden shocks to the system. Two years on from the handover, there are some basic questions which need to be addressed. How is the economy to be diversified from its dependence on property and the stock market? Is more government intervention necessary in more complex times? Does the executive have any real desire to improve relations with the legislature? Is democracy just window dressing to keep Western opinion happy? Is all the talk about improving the environment just that – talk?

In a sense, the undemocratic administration which rules Hong Kong has shown itself much more responsive to public feelings than might be expected from such an essentially conservative executive. Measures such as the stock market intervention or the halting of a tide of mainland migrants have undoubtedly been popular.

What has been lacking has been a broad policy theme to make clear where the administration and the SAR are heading. The government spokesman gives the administration credit for taking difficult decisions, but the reality is that it has usually sought the pragmatic way out, almost as though it actually had to run for election.

This does not mean such decisions are necessarily wrong – pragmatism can be a valuable quality. Reliance on pragmatism does, however, mean that when the big tests come – notably over one country, two systems – the experience is that the administration finds it hard to stand on principle.

2 July

Three people from Hong Kong are in Inner Mongolia hoping to bring home a 63-year-old businessman from the SAR. Lok Yuk-sing has been held in prison without proper charges by the Public Security Bureau in the town of Dingsheng since 12 June last year. He was detained at gunpoint in a hotel restaurant in southern China because of debts to a mainland company owed by a cashmere firm for which he used to work. When he saw the armed men, he thought he was being kidnapped. In many ways, he was. Lok's former boss has disappeared. The ultimate owner of the firm, a big Hong Kong group called Lai Sun, washes its hands of him. So Lok remains locked up, suffering from ill health and extremes of climate, and subsisting on the mainland prison diet.

I became aware of the case when his son-in-law sent me an e-mail about Lok's plight. We led the Sunday edition with the story, and then sent a reporter, Cynthia Wan, to Inner Mongolia with Lok's relatives in the spring, when they were allowed only a brief meeting with him. Now the family has been told by its legal representative that Lok is going to be freed for the second anniversary of the handover. Two family members have gone to collect him. Cynthia Wan is with them.

Lok's former firm owed its mainland creditor HK$4 million. Two security officials tell his relatives that they will have to pay a HK$4.7 million bail to get him out of prison. You people in Hong Kong are rich, the officials explain. They also denounce the family for telling the press about the case, and produce clippings from the *Post*. Some have Cynthia's picture byline. Fortunately, the officials do not recognise her.

Cases like this obviously cause more concern than the fate of gangsters and murderers. A growing number of Hong Kong people are involved in cross-border business, and fear being locked up without trial because of commercial problems. Another man has been held since March in Guangzhou over a customs declaration for ten lifts. He has been denied bail. His company has paid legal fees of HK$100,000, but sacked him in May. His wife says their five-year-old son calls out in his sleep for his father.

Apart from cases involving Hong Kong people, an Australian-Chinese businessman, who was grabbed from Macau in a disagreement with a relative of Deng Xiaoping, has been held for more than five years. A city councillor from Taiwan and her boyfriend were kidnapped last year in northern China over a business row. After being kept for two days bound and sedated, the man escaped, but the woman died when she was overdosed with sleeping pills. Another Taiwanese who disappeared in Shenzhen is thought to have been murdered by business associates.

The SAR government is moving with extreme caution in Lok's case. This is in striking contrast to its attitude towards the boss of Lai Sun, the ultimate owner of the trading firm for which Lok had worked. When the 84-year-old chairman was accused of bribery in Taiwan, Hong Kong's Chief Executive used his influence to get the old man freed on bail to return home before sentence was passed. When it is a matter of the mainland and an ordinary Hong Konger, concern seems a lot less.

The government also seems to take what it is told by mainland police at face value. In Lok's case, the Secretary for Security says she has been assured by the Beijing authorities that no bail request was made, though Cynthia Wan witnessed the demand. On his return to Hong Kong, Lok's son-in-law, John Wong, sends me another e-mail, saying 'At least HK SAR government now treats it more seriously than before . . . We need media who are able to speak out and fight for justice for the HK citizen, particularly post-handover.'

3 July

In the city of Chengdu, a sperm bank has been set up which will accept only donors who have at least a master's degree. A philosophy professor called Yu Ping-zhe objects that sperm from well-educated people may not be any better than that of ignorant folk. Anyway, clever people are often ugly, so good looks should be a criterion, too. The bank responds that it can charge high prices for sperm from intellectuals who can provide 'intelligent and healthy sperm'. 'Our sperm is vintage,' a spokeswoman says.

5 July

Farewell reception for the departing US Consul-General and a one-day-late 4 July party at his residence on the Peak. The low level of attendance from the government is striking. Tung Chee-hwa has made it known that he is going to leave most foreign national-day celebrations to Anson Chan and Donald Tsang. He gave the Consul-General a dinner a few days ago, but he might also have turned out tonight, given the importance of the US for Hong Kong. Chan comes early, but does not stay to make the speech, which is delivered by the Secretary for Financial Services, hardly a top figure. Only a handful of other officials attend.

That is in interesting contrast to a seventh anniversary party for the pro-Beijing Democratic Alliance for the Betterment of Hong Kong (DAB) this week at a hotel in Central. The Chief Executive's presence is enough to ensure that a flock of top bureaucrats attend. Tung joins the party bigwigs in cutting an anniversary cake.

Led by an earnest, intelligent head teacher, Tsang Yok-sing, who says he gained his Chinese patriotism on a trip across the border as a teenager, the DAB aims to become the ruling party in Hong Kong. The party leader's brother, who was imprisoned by the British for involvement in anti-colonial protests and then edited a newspaper financed from the mainland, is joining the government's think-tank. Having done well at the legislative elections last year, the DAB is establishing itself as a populist rival to the Democrats. Like them it has internal strains, though of a very different nature. On the one hand, it wants to profit from increased democratisation, but it also owes loyalty to Beijing, which backs the drawn-out development of the political system laid down in the Basic Law. Equally, it is torn between the temptation to become the government's most potent ally in the legislature, and the benefits to be had from criticising an administration that is fast shedding its initial popularity.

There can, however, be little doubt that the DAB will strengthen its position as the year goes on. Membership of Hong Kong parties is tiny, so with 1,300 signed-up adherents, it can already claim to be the biggest political group in the SAR. It aims to boost its numbers to

30,000 by 2006, and to become the Labour Party of Hong Kong: whether old or new style is not yet clear.

7 July

In Los Angeles, Chinese football players face the might of the United States in the final of the women's World Cup.

China has done well, hitting home nineteen goals and crushing the reigning champions, Norway, 5–0 in the semi-final to face the home team for the title. Their goal-scoring knack evaporates in a nil–nil draw in the final. The United States win the penalty shoot-out 5–4. Some of the Chinese are in tears as they receive runners-up medals.

Vice Premier Li Lanqing telephones the team to tell them, 'I hope you can learn from the experience and make a new contribution to our country's sport.' The White House spokesman talks of a tradition of sport helping to build bridges stretching back to the ping-pong diplomacy before Richard Nixon recognised the mainland. China's propaganda department warns the media not to politicise the game for fear of sparking off anti-American demonstrations. But newspapers quickly show that suspicions about US skulduggery are not confined to the bombing of the embassy in Belgrade.

Indeed, one mainland press report draws a direct link between the two events. It notes that the Chinese team was put up in Los Angeles at the Ambassador Suite Hotel, whose name amounted to 'spiritual torture' for the players by reminding them of the bombing. A Beijing soccer fan is quoted as pointing out that the Chinese team was at a disadvantage because the final was held in the afternoon, and they had not played any afternoon games before.

Ignoring the pollution back home, the *Sports Daily* newspaper writes that the fumes from vehicles in Los Angeles would have tired the visitors. The *Beijing Morning Post* notes that the Chinese flew 20,400 kilometres, crossing from coast to coast four times, whereas the home team covered less than half that distance. When video film shows that the US goalkeeper moved off her line too early for a vital save during the shoot-out, China's sporting ire soars.

8 July

The Chief Executive says he is determined to do something about the worsening air pollution. Leaders of political parties say they will make it a big issue. We all know that exhaust fumes from diesel vehicles are a major cause of foul air. But today the Legislative Council votes by 47 to 7 to back a government proposal that will block attempts to increase the fine for smoky vehicles from the present paltry HK$450 (US$58), which is just one tenth of the fine for smoking inside a taxi.

The argument against boosting the fine is that it would be unfair at a time when other official fees and charges are frozen because of the recession. Fear of antagonising the powerful taxi and transport lobby is more germane to the way the Democrat and DAB parties line up with the administration.

9 July

For half a century, the island of Taiwan, to which Chiang Kai-shek fled as head of the Republic of China in 1949, has been a running sore for the mainland. Today, its President, Lee Teng-hui, makes himself even more of a 'criminal for a thousand years' in Beijing's eyes.

After the Kuomintang arrived across the Taiwan Strait and consolidated its power with a massacre of the local inhabitants, the island became a tightly controlled fortress that the mainland could not conquer, holder of China's seat in the United Nations, defended by Washington, shot through with corruption. Then, as the old KMT dictatorship crumbled, it grew into the most democratic part of greater China, and the home of a bustling high-tech economy. With 21 million inhabitants, it built a gross national product of US$271 billion, and foreign exchange reserves of US$100 billion. Its economy has been relatively less hard hit than others in the region by the Asian economic crisis, maintaining annual growth of 6 per cent and increasing exports by almost 10 per cent. Its political culture has grown increasingly vibrant. Money politics are still important, but locally born politicians have supplanted the ruling class that accompanied the Generalissimo across the Strait fifty years ago. Though Chiang's dreams of reconquering the mainland evaporated long ago, it is not surprising if many Taiwanese see their island as a model for China in the twenty-first century, or as a place that should simply be left to get on with its own life. One economist at a big Japanese research institute observes: 'If you asked the Taiwanese where they'd like to be located, they'd probably say off California.'

The irony is that as Taiwan has grown and prospered and become more democratic, so it has become more isolated as the world commits itself to a 'one China' policy ushered in by Richard Nixon's recognition of Beijing. Taipei is reduced to paying large amounts of money for recognition from small states, and staging gimmicky exercises to assert its existence which usually end up annoying the international community. As it made clear by sending its fleet to the Taiwan Strait in reaction to mainland war games in 1996, the US is not going to allow an invasion of the island. Nor, despite the fortune Taiwan spends on lobbying in Washington, does it want Taipei to upset the Sino-American relationship. Balancing those two objectives is a major problem. Clearly Taiwan is not going to give up what it has achieved. Equally clearly Beijing is not going to blink first. So all Washington can do is to pray that the two will not step over the brink.

That prayer is not aided by President Lee Teng-hui's habit of cutting through the fudge which the rest of the world would like to pour over his island. Having been brought up in the Japanese system during the occupation of the island, Lee is the subject of deep suspicion in Beijing. Officials there tell you, as proof of his perfidy, that when he dozes off at a dinner he sometimes comes round speaking Japanese. Not that Lee does much to exclude the idea that his real agenda is independence. His latest sally is to say that relations between Taiwan and the mainland should be on a 'special state-to-state basis'. In fact, the island does have all the attributes of a state except for international recognition. Inevitably, however, Lee's remark enrages China.

A Beijing-funded newspaper in Hong Kong reports that fighting against Taiwan's independence has been listed as the main task of the Chinese army, and quotes a mainland expert as saying that the PLA always undertakes military action once an objective has been set. 'A war will surely break out if Lee Teng-hui continues to act wilfully,' the

expert goes on. To which a member of the Chinese Academy of
Military Sciences adds his opinion that the Taiwanese President is 'an
abnormal test-tube baby bred by international anti-China forces in
their political lab'.

10 *July*

An Internet stock called China.com, which was listed on the Nasdaq
stock market in New York this week, has trebled its share price in a
single day. The company, whose owners include a Hong Kong property firm, China's official Xinhua news agency and America Online,
offers Internet access in China, Taiwan and Hong Kong. There is not
much there at present, and it only ranks as the seventeenth most popular website on the mainland. But put the words China and Internet
together and you have a goldmine.

14 *July*

The World Economic Forum places Hong Kong in third place in
world competitiveness, behind the United States and Singapore. But
when the report moves from government policy and the big picture
to the microeconomic ways in which firms actually work, the SAR
slips down to twenty-first place. The analysts have noticed aspects of
the economy which are usually concealed by the sheen of small government and low taxes, such as the array of non-competitive practices,
cartels and antiquated management.

    Then Standard and Poor's rating agency weighs in with a negative
verdict on Hong Kong's long-term outlook. It says the SAR is vulnerable to loss of confidence because of regional developments,
potential political mismanagement and the government's appeal to the
NPC.

16 *July*

A further sign of Beijing's view of the proper role of the Hong Kong
media. The Deputy Director of the Hong Kong and Macau Office,

Liu Mingqi, tells a visiting party of journalists from the SAR that the Tung government deserves support. There is, he notes, a suggestion that the Chief Executive's popularity has dropped. But 'public opinion has been misled. Over the past two years, Mr Tung has shown good leadership. Hong Kong people should feel lucky they have a good Chief Executive.'

In the past, mainland officials avoided commenting on the Hong Kong press in deference to one country, two systems. But now Liu Mingqi shows no inhibitions. Speaking about the right of abode issue, he says that 'Some people, including some newspapers, have fuelled the row and caused all the controversy.' He singles out the faithfully pro-Beijing newspapers, *Ta Kung Pao* and *Wen Wei Po*, as having done well. 'They helped explain government policies. News media should explain government policies . . . Some people have taken to the streets to say "Down with this or that." It's like the behaviour of some people during the Cultural Revolution.'

20–22 July

The authorities in Beijing have launched a major campaign against the Falung Gong sect. Thousands of practitioners are rounded up as they demonstrate for better treatment for their movement, or carry out their deep-breathing exercises in public. Most are released after short detention. Some undergo what one mainland newspaper calls 'persuasion tactics' by police.

Sects and secret societies have a long history in China. The two major figures of the Kuomintang regime, Sun Yat-sen and Chiang Kai-shek, were both associated with such shadowy movements, which often merged into the world of the Triads. There is no way the authoritarians in Beijing will allow the deeply suspect Falun Gong to continue.

One adherent who was detained for two weeks with ten others in the northern industrial city of Dalian reports that when they did their exercises in jail, 'the guards took our trousers down and gave each of us fifteen lashes with a leather whip. Our buttocks were covered in blood.' He says they were also hit in the face, beaten with rubber truncheons and handcuffed to window frames for hours. In Shandong province, a woman farmer arrested while working in the fields died in prison. The Falun Gong website says she was tortured with electric batons and rubber clubs and 'electrified with old-style rotary telephones'. The semi-official China News Service blames her death on a heart attack after falling in a toilet.

China has issued instructions for the arrest of the sect's founder, Li Hongzhi, who lives in the New York suburb of Queens. It asks Interpol to help bring him in, but gets a negative response. The state media put out stories about a practitioner who cut himself open with a penknife believing that he had the sacred wheel of the law in his stomach, another who killed his wife because of the Falun Gong's teaching, and 743 people whose deaths are blamed on the cult. Li is vilified as a charlatan who has milked his followers for money; the mainland media say the only thing anybody remembers about his childhood was that he played the trumpet – badly.

A former low-level employee of a state grain enterprise in Jilin province which adjoins North Korea, Li developed a big following with his lectures during the 1990s. The authorities say he was born in 1952, but Li dates his birth a year earlier, coinciding with the birthday of Buddha. He left China for the US in the spring of 1998, a year before the Falun Gong staged its sudden protest outside the leadership compound in Beijing. The *Youth Daily* newspaper reports that when police raided his former two-bedroom, two-bathroom flat in Jilin they found a big television set, an audio and video system, a leather sofa and a safe containing seven imported watches, rings, bracelets, jade earrings and gold-plated pens. In an adjoining office, beside a fax, a copying machine and a shredder, was a receipt for a Volkswagen Jetta. All of which is used to back up the charge that Li was sucking in money from the practitioners, who were said to have paid 92,520 yuan (US$11,000) for a three-hour talk he gave in 1994. It certainly couldn't have all been paid for from his salary at the grain office and his wife's earnings from her work at a public baths.

The creed which Li propagates involves deep-breathing and meditation exercises that claim to raise consciousness and to harness natural forces to the human body. It draws on a long tradition of Asian mysticism: one of the founder's portraits shows him in a dark suit, standing in front of the inverted swastika used in Zoroastrianism and other ancient religions. Li says it promotes good health and morality. There are also some more unusual claims associated with the movement, such as the ability to reverse the menstrual cycle and to enable followers to see out of the back of their heads, though it is not clear if they are put forward by the Falun Gong itself or associated with it by those who wish to discredit the sect. Li is said to have offered ardent practitioners the prospect of being able to fly to heaven by transforming the molecular make-up of their bodies. Asians will go to one heaven, Caucasians to another. A video made by Li and shown by Chinese authorities has the founder describing the earth as a rotten apple which has been destroyed 81 times, and asserting that he is the only person left in China who can save it.

A former follower from Hong Kong has circulated a report saying that the founder claims to be the Supreme Buddha of the Cosmos, with a status superior to that of all other deities, who is now presiding over the final 'clean-up' of the planet. After which, a new human race will appear, made up mainly of Falun Gong adherents. In the meantime, according to this report as published in the *South China Morning Post*, Li has revealed that he helped the Virgin Mary to reach Heaven after she spent 2,000 years going through various reincarnations on earth. He is also said to attribute the progress of computers to intervention by aliens, who have given a serial number to all human users.

Alien intervention or not, Li and followers have shown themselves adept at using computerised communications. They have set up websites, and operate by e-mail through servers outside China which are beyond the reach of the authorities. It is a very end-of-century meeting of an old Chinese cult of spiritual healing and modern information technology, and one which frightens a regime that faces a major problem in trying to extend its control to cyberspace. This is still a country where a businessman in Shanghai was recently imprisoned for supplying e-mail addresses to a Chinese-language electronic newsletter based in Washington.

One particular governmental worry about the Falun Gong is that it has practitioners in the administration and armed forces. The *Beijing Daily* says a former deputy director at the Ministry of Public Security, who is among those recently detained, protected Li from arrest when he was still in China, and helped him leave for the United States. A retired officer who was deputy director of the military's general health department has been identified as an adherent. Sources quoted by the *Washington Post* say a retired major-general on the general staff department was a practitioner. Thousands of soldiers are believed to have joined in its activities in the Dalian area of the north.

As well as trying to suppress the Gongists, the regime is maintaining its crackdown on political dissent this summer. Liu Xianbin, a 31-year-old organiser for the tiny China Democracy Party, from Sichuan province, has been charged with 'subverting state power' and will get thirteen years in prison. One piece of evidence used against Liu were letters he wrote to President Jiang and Prime Minister Zhu calling for the release of other members who had been jailed. A founder of the group who requested that it should be made legal the day Bill Clinton arrived in China for his visit in 1998 was sent down on a similar sentence. Two other members have received eleven-year terms. A dissident in Sichuan got twelve. In all, over 200 democracy activists have been taken in this summer, and thirty-five are still held, according to the Hong Kong-based Information Centre of Human Rights and Democratic Movement in China.

The Central Government is anxious to deal with opponents before the celebrations of the fiftieth anniversary of the Communist victory on 1 October, counting on protests from the West being muted by embarrassment over the bombing of the Chinese embassy in Belgrade. But it doesn't like its crackdown to become too widely known: a railway employee has been sent to jail for ten years for 'illegally providing intelligence to foreign organisations' about labour unrest – that is, telling foreign journalists about protests by workers complaining against not being paid or about corruption.

The fiftieth anniversary is also the occasion for a more general anti-crime campaign. Strike Hard is its name. The official press announces 35,000 arrests in July. *China Daily* says the aim is to 'eliminate latent threats to social stability' and to create a safer environment for the celebrations. The Public Security Ministry calls on citizens to denounce suspects and offers rewards for information leading to arrests.

Still, angry workers are reported to have blocked more train lines after not getting their pensions or pay. There have been fresh rallies against corruption and bad local government. One of those stories which probably isn't true but should be goes as follows. Instructions have been sent from Beijing to station masters in the industrial north of the country. If they see groups of workers heading for the capital, they are to stop the trains and order them to disembark. So you will be able to gauge the extent of industrial unrest by the number of empty trains arriving late from the north.

23 July

Lunch with a senior Hong Kong policy-making official. He asks why the media, and in particular the *Post*, are always so negative about the government, and why the *Post* has become 'so sensational'. His line is: of course, the administration makes mistakes, but a family should not hang out its dirty washing for all to see. Singaporean overtones are unmistakable. We're all in this together, so let's all pull together for the general good.

As for our supposed sensationalism, I ask him to give me an example. He cites a recent front page which featured three stories reporting government reversals in the courts. The main headline read: 'DAY OF DEFEATS FOR TUNG' and each of the cases was highlighted with a red and black bar. That certainly wouldn't have been regarded as sensational in a British broadsheet. Perhaps it just made its point about the government's discomfiture rather too well. As another senior official says: 'You may be right, but don't show us up so much.'

24 July

A long conversation with a rising Hong Kong Chinese solicitor. He had been doing well in London, but had wanted to come home to join in the development of the SAR. Now he is thinking of returning to

Britain. He is disillusioned with the way the government operates, with the lack of vision, with it not standing up for Hong Kong and with the way the old business establishment rules. And despite the recession, prices here are still so high that he reckons he could live just as well, if not better, in the UK. This is the kind of voice that provides a backdrop to the political, legal and economic debate – and which the government ignores at its peril.

25 July

We may feel hot and humid in Hong Kong, but the mainland media reports that the temperature in Beijing has gone above 40 degrees Celsius. What is striking is not the heat, but the fact that it was accurately reported.

For decades, the temperature on the mainland never officially rose above 37 degrees. There was a general belief that if it was any hotter, outdoor workers were entitled to a day off. So the official temperature report stayed below 37 degrees. Now the truth is out. Officials deny that there is any entitlement to a day off. The *China Youth Daily* says the new veracity is 'a very important step towards constructing the rule of law.'

31 July

Today is a routine Saturday at the *Post*, except that it is my last day as editor. The paper is in good shape. Though the sniping will never cease, we have established our independence in the post-handover Hong Kong. Pre-tax profit for the financial year that has just ended was equivalent to US$50 million, or 36 per cent of turnover. When asked why I am going, I reply that I have been given no explanation, but can only surmise that the Kuoks want somebody with whom they feel more comfortable.

The *New York Times* runs a 1,000-word piece under the headline 'A FREE-SPOKEN EDITOR WON'T BE BACK' and with a pull-quote declaring, 'At a tense time in Hong Kong, a voice is silenced.' The story says that the 'murky circumstances of Mr Fenby's exit have prompted a rash of speculation that he is a victim of Hong Kong's tightening political atmosphere'. It quotes the legislator Margaret Ng saying she 'strongly suspects that this is motivated by his wanting to be more independent than the owners are willing to be'.

That is enough for the government's information service to put in an urgent weekend call to the *Post* to make it clear that it had nothing to do with my going. If, indeed, there was an agreement that the editorship of the *Post* should be changed, it would have been done at a different level, or without any obvious reference to officialdom. Which tycoon would talk to the government information service about repositioning the pieces on his chess board?

The *Guardian* reports that attention will now be focused on the future of the *Post*. Its correspondent notes how the paper's independence 'helped to allay fears that the Hong Kong media would be muzzled once the territory returned to China'. *Newsweek* lists my departure as a sign of Hong Kong's 'fading autonomy', and an editorial in *The Economist* about the future of Hong Kong remarks: 'Worryingly, the editor of a newspaper that was sharply critical of the [legal reinterpretation] decision has since had his contract terminated.'

As for myself, I write a valedictory piece for the *Independent* on my four years at the *Post*. Later, I am told that it 'ruffled feathers' with the owners. Then it is time to do my weekly editorial page column. In the past, it has been called 'Letter from the Editor'. Only the title need change.

AUGUST

1 *August*

Whatever one's worries about the rule of law and accountability and the executive's power, a reality of one country, two systems is out on the street in Happy Valley, opposite the main racecourse. On the mainland, thousands of Falun Gong practitioners have been detained in recent weeks. But the Hong Kong government has authorised a demonstration today by some 200 adherents outside the office of the Chinese news agency, Xinhua. On a hot summer afternoon, they stand silently doing their movements, and disperse peacefully.

9 *August*

The *South China Morning Post* reveals that Beijing has rejected approaches from the Vatican for Pope John Paul II to be allowed to visit Hong Kong. It is a pointed reminder of how the one country part of Deng's formula works.

Apart from traditional communist distaste for Catholicism, the Papacy is in bad odour on the mainland because it maintains a diplomatic mission in Taiwan. The idea of a papal visit to Hong Kong was apparently seen by the Vatican as a means of enabling the Pontiff to preach on Chinese soil without needing to resolve differences with

Beijing. But Tung Chee-hwa says that this is a foreign affairs matter which falls under the authority of the Central Government. He adds that his own officials are united in disapproving of the idea, including the Financial Secretary, who is a Catholic.

15 *August*

Just in case anybody thought things were going to quieten down in Macau as the return to China approaches, a nail bomb kills two suspected Triads as they drive to the casino after a late night restaurant meal. A simultaneous arson attack damages two cars and a dozen motorcycles elsewhere in town.

Across the border, another gang boss, Ip Seng-kin, is tried for robbery and arms-smuggling. Known as Macau's equivalent of Big Spender, Hong Kong-born Ip and two associates are led from the court in Zuhai city with black hoods over their head after being sentenced to death. Back in Macau, the trial of his peer, Broken Tooth, opens with the defence lawyer storming out of the courtroom in protest at the way in which the trial is conducted. The joke going the rounds is that his client wants a quick verdict so that, if found guilty, he can arrange to escape before the PLA comes in and deals with him.

18 *August*

A major stock market flotation is being prepared in Beijing. Managers, consultants, auditors, bankers and lawyers fill a hotel owned by the China National Petroleum Corporation (CNPC), the world's fifth biggest oil firm. They work in specially fitted-out offices on the lower floors and sleep in rooms above. They are fashioning a new company with CNPC's prize assets, US$1 billion less in costs and one-third of its 1.5 million employees. Fifteen per cent of its shares will be floated in New York and Hong Kong in February. What is left unsaid is what happens to the remaining hulk of the old company with its million employees and assets the world does not want.

22 *August*

An airliner from Taiwan's China Airlines crashes in flames while landing at Chek Lap Kok airport during a typhoon. Investigators find that the Italian pilot did not reduce his speed sufficiently during the approach. The plane turned over and caught fire. Passengers hung upside-down in their seat belts, some for hours. The miracle was that only three died.

The typhoon, called Sam, is the first really serious storm to hit Hong Kong for several years. It kills one villager, buried under three metres of mud. Twenty-eight people are hurt. There are landslides and flooding in the New Territories.

27 *August*

The government announces second-quarter growth of 0.5 per cent. Is the recession over? After over-enthusiastic forecasts in the past, the Financial Secretary is cautious. But the green shoots of recovery seem to be sprouting all around. Malaysia announces strong expansion. Retailers in Thailand say trade was up 20 per cent in July. South Korea is bounding ahead. So is Singapore.

There is, however, another side of the slate. The unravelling of the giant chaebol groups in Korea is taking much longer than expected; Malaysia has been living behind a wall of controls; there is a major bank scandal in Indonesia; and changing the business culture in Thailand is going to take time. For Hong Kong, there is the question of whether China can maintain the growth it needs to power its way into the world economy and to avoid major social stresses that could threaten the system – and of what is going to happen with its stalled bid to join the World Trade Organisation.

30 *August*

Indignation is rising over a redevelopment scheme for the waterfront in Central which would mean the end of the old Star Ferry piers. They would be moved along the harbour. Nobody could claim that the current piers are things of beauty, but they are an integral part of Hong Kong life, particularly at rush hours, when passengers crowd on to the squat boats to cross the 1,480 metres between Central and Tsim Sha Tsui. The ferry is efficient, practical and cheap – HK$2.20 (28 U.S cents) for the upper deck and $1.70 (21 U.S. cents) down below for the seven-minute crossing. At any moment during the day, one or other of the thirteen boats will be plying back or forth across the water, riding on the wake of more powerful boats and making a crab-like approach to the quays on either side.

The view from the water in mid-voyage is spectacular, particularly at night when the lights are gleaming. Set up by a Parsee at the end of the last century and now run by a big conglomerate, the green and cream ferries have come to be a seminal emblem of the city, even if Richard Branson has recently taken over one and repainted it Virgin red. 'Here's the real Hong Kong,' writes the journalist and long-time local observer Kevin Sinclair. 'The smell of salt water (try not to look at the surface) and the odour of wet rope, the tang of diesel fuel, the clank as the gangway crashes down, the whistle to tell you you've missed the boat . . .'

The government has already changed its mind about a development and reclamation scheme in the harbour. Perhaps it can be persuaded to think again one more time.

SEPTEMBER

1—8 *September*

Architecture, culture, the economy, corruption, and China's great wild west.

Beijing has picked a design by a French architect for its new national theatre and opera house. The glass and titanium building is shaped, according to which simile you prefer, like a giant bubble or a squashed duck's egg or a space ship from a science fiction film. It will sit in the middle of an artificial lake in a park alongside the Great Hall of the People and opposite the Forbidden City in the centre of the capital. Inside the building, which will be reached through a tunnel under the lake, will be a 2,700-seat opera hall, a smaller concert hall and two theatres. Covering 100,000 square metres, the project will cost US$360 million.

The news has been confirmed by officials to foreign correspondents, but has not been announced domestically. The authorities might find it a trifle embarrassing to explain to their people why none of the twenty-four architects from China and Hong Kong who submitted designs was chosen.

On the economic front, the mainland Finance Minister is quoted as saying that he is 'not over-optimistic' about halting deflation despite a programme of fresh spending. The government is pumping in an additional 54 billion yuan (US$6.5 billion) in wages, pensions and unemployment benefits. All this means that the budget deficit has nearly doubled to reach an unprecedented 180 billion yuan (US$21.6 billion).

Some people have been spending regardless of deflation or anything else. A mainland prosecutor identified only as 'Du' has been found dead with his mistress at a luxury villa near the city of Shenyang in the north. It appears to have been a case of suicide. Du had been regarded as a model puritanical bureaucrat. He did not drink or smoke or go to karaoke bars. He had been with the prosecutor's department for thirteen years, and never earned more than 900 yuan (US$108) a month. But it now turns out that he had spent more than a million yuan of public funds on the villa and a luxury car for his mistress. 'The whole city was shocked by the news,' say the mainland newspapers.

On the other side of the country, the Central Government is reported to be imposing yet another crackdown on separatists in the vast Xinjiang region, on the frontier with Central Asia, with its dozen different nationalities, its great mineral resources and its 13 million Muslim Uigur people. It is an area of enormous contrasts: the urban expanse of Urumqi and the great Taklamakan Desert, where camel trains used to disappear in sandstorms; the painted caves of the Flaming Mountains and the Lop Nor test site, where Beijing let off its nuclear explosions. (A vineyard in a nearby oasis produces a pleasant light red wine; one hopes that it hasn't been nurtured on fallout.) The Turpan depression on the Silk Road is the second lowest point on the planet, and a tourist attraction for ancient sites nearby – a photograph in a hotel lobby of Bill Gates on a visit is even bigger than the picture of Jiang Zemin. Down the road, the Atex restaurant and dance hall is crowded with a bizarre mixture of local yuppies and increasingly sozzled old men in thick boots and fur hats. A local painter in two-tone shoes executes perfect waltzes and foxtrots with visiting ladies.

To the west, in the shadow of some of the highest mountains on earth, lies the great trading centre of Kashgar, the gateway to Central Asia, with its mosques and alleyways and huge Sunday market where the carpet traders track black-market rates for US dollars on cellular telephones while women walk round with big brown knitted veils completely covering their heads. In the nineteenth century, this was a key watching post for the British and Russians in the Great Game for influence over the approaches to imperial India. For twenty-eight years, George Macartney, a diplomat with a Chinese mother, presided over the British consulate, immortalised by the memoirs of his wife, whom he plucked from Victorian London to live in one of the more isolated of diplomatic posts at the end of a gruelling six-week overland journey across Russia and through the Himalayas. Today, the consulate is part of a modern hotel, as is the rival Russian mission where Catherine Macartney was taken aback by the drinking habits of the Tsar's representatives, especially when one poured champagne down her dress as he tried to make a toast.

A huge statue of Mao Tse-tung still points the way ahead in the centre of the city, but the religion here is Islam not communism. The mosque in the middle of town is the biggest in China. A sign in the courtyard advises visitors in English that 'breaking wind and speaking loudly is forbidden. The intimate action is not welcome in this mosque.'

Beijing has encouraged Han Chinese from other parts of the country to move to the region to try to alter the racial balance, but there has been no assimilation to speak of and most of the newcomers live in the capital city of Urumqi or are PLA soldiers. On a Sunday afternoon walk through the streets of Kashgar, I counted only half a dozen Han among the thousands of pedestrians, plus two driving by in a People's Liberation Army jeep. If you ask how many soldiers are stationed in the area, you get either a huge number or a shrug of the shoulders.

A Uigur joke goes as follows. An American, a Japanese, a Uigur and a Han are in a train compartment. The American gets up, opens the window and throws out all his cigarettes, shouting, 'Too many Marlboros.' A bit later, the Japanese stands up, opens the window and throws out several Sony tape machines he is carrying, shouting, 'Too many Walkmans.' A little further on, the Uigur gets up, opens the window and throws out the fourth man in the compartment, shouting, 'Too many Han.'

Chinese rulers have tried to assert control for two millennia. Following Muslim rebellions in the 1860s and 1870s, Xinjiang became an imperial province in 1884, but broke away again at the end of the Qing dynasty in 1911. For a while after the Second World War, it became the Eastern Turkestan Republic. Since 1955, it has been an autonomous region of the People's Republic of China. Now there is talk of economic revival, of opening up the Silk Road as a major land route between Central Asia and China. But a trip along the main Karakoram Highway through the shimmering lakes and vast open foothills of the Pamir mountains shows how primitive it remains. Great heaps of boulders that have slid down the slopes reduce the carriageway to single file in places. The road surface is rutted with deep crevices. Somewhere over the peaks are the Talibans of Afghanistan.

Beijing is deeply worried at the prospect that Muslim fundamentalists could stir up revolt in the region whose 600,000 square miles constitute one-sixth of the country's landmass. There are stories of groups from Afghanistan distributing audio cassettes in Kashgar; our trip westwards along the Silk Road in 1998 was halted after three hours' driving on the Karakoram towards Pakistan for fear of terrorists lying ahead. Last year, an internal instruction to China's security departments named the region's pro-independence movement as the greatest threat to national political stability. The region's Communist Party secretary worries that 'what happened in Kosovo today will happen in Xinjiang tomorrow'. Police recently raided a meeting of Uigurs alleged to have been planning to sabotage China's national-day celebrations on 1 October. Bomb blasts in Beijing have been blamed on militants from the far west.

This autumn brings a series of executions of Uigurs. Some were found guilty of manufacturing explosives or 'illegal religious proselytism'. Others were condemned for murder, robbery and arms offences. One group was accused of having set up a 'party of Allah' among migrants in Guangdong province across from Hong Kong. According to a Xinjiang newspaper, this group carried out murders in three mainland cities, and its leader was preparing to transport more than 260 detonators to Xinjiang. A Uigur accused of having killed two policemen and six civilians died in hospital this month after taking a three-year-old boy hostage and throwing a grenade before being shot by security forces.

The search for local heroes to put on a pedestal as approved role models led the central authorities to promote a Uigur woman called Rebiya Kadeer. Born into a poor family, she built a highly successful business career, urged Uigur women to follow her example and became a member of a provincial political body. But she married a former political prisoner who went to the United States. To make matters worse, she let her sons join their father. Her failure to come out against her husband lost her the political post last year. Now aged fifty-three, she has been arrested on her way to a meeting with an American congressional delegation carrying with her a list of political prisoners, and accused of revealing state information to foreigners. An official newspaper says one of her offences was to have sent clippings from Chinese newspapers to her husband, who is campaigning for Uigur rights from his base in Oklahoma.

5 September

Four lonely diplomats are holed up in the Wanchai district by the waterfront on Hong Kong Island. The area is a mixture of office buildings, residential blocks and girlie bars. However, the diplomats are unlikely to be visiting the Club Hot Lips, the Pussy Cat or the Club Venus. They have come to Hong Kong to open a consulate for North Korea.

The Central Government has decided to agree to the opening of the mission. It is also going to let Iran reopen its consulate, which was closed after the *fatwah* against Salman Rushdie. Both decisions, revealed by *Post* reporter Glenn Schloss, have caused concern, given Pyongyang's reputation for everything from drug-running to supporting terrorism, and allegations that Iran has used Hong Kong as a channel for arms shipments from China, including parts for missile and fighter plane guidance systems, nerve-gas technology and chemical weapons components. But, as in Beijing's refusal to let the Pope visit the SAR, the local government has no say in the matter, and the Tung administration remains characteristically quiet.

8 September

A postscript to the decline and fall of the Sally Aw empire, and
another sign of how nothing lasts for long in Hong Kong if it can
be turned into a property play. Li Ka-shing's Cheung Kong property firm, which bought the Tiger Balm Gardens from Aw last
December, is proposing to put up high-rise luxury apartments on
what was one of Hong Kong's top tourist attractions a decade ago.
A small part of the old gardens will be kept as a theme park, with
its temples and grottos and demon statues. The rest will be covered
by a 700,000 square foot residential development. The gardens had
been losing their appeal to tourists in the face of more modern
attractions: last year only 8 per cent of visitors bothered to see
them.

11 September

Bill Clinton is wearing a good-ole-boy smile as he greets Jiang Zemin
at a Pacific summit meeting in New Zealand. For his part, the
Chinese President calls his American counterpart 'my good friend'
before handing him booklets in Chinese and English setting out the
evils of the Falun Gong. Officials say relations between Washington
and Beijing are back on track. Jiang speaks of a strategic partnership.
Clinton reiterates support for China's membership of the World Trade
Organisation. On the diplomatic front, Beijing's approval of a new US
ambassador is taken as a sign that the deep freeze in relations after the
Belgrade embassy bombing is thawing.

Still, you have to ask how much has really changed. The two presidents clash on Taiwan. Pro-democracy activists are still being locked
up in China. And as for the strategic partnership, Jiang keeps inveighing against Washington for seeking to create a 'unipolar world' over
which it will hold sway. Last month, he attended a meeting in Central
Asia at which he exchanged bear hugs with Boris Yeltsin despite his
dim view of the way Russia has gone since the fall of communism.
China is to buy thirty Russian jet fighters. The Russian and Chinese
leaders are said to have agreed that Yeltsin will try to stop Nato

moving further eastwards while Jiang will attempt to prevent the formation of an 'Asian Nato' based on strengthened defence agreements between Japan and the US. China is also busy developing relations with oil-rich nations in Central Asia to assure itself of energy supplies, and to try to counter the spread of fundamentalism across its western borders. Jiang is about to pay visits to South-East Asia and Europe. China is, clearly, stepping out on the world stage, and is not going to depend on US approval.

12 September

Margaret Ng, the legal constituency representative in the Legislative Council and the hammer of the Secretary for Justice, is turned back at Hong Kong airport when she tries to fly to Beijing to attend a legal conference there. She put her name down for the meeting last month, but the airline has been shilly-shallying all week about confirming her flight. Today, arriving at the Dragonair counter in her black legal suit, white shirt and pearls, she is told that her visa has been revoked. The mainland frontier police have sent word that she will not be allowed in. As usual in visa-refusal cases, no reason is given. Ng holds a British passport, but that does not help her.

Around thirty other pro-democracy figures have been barred in the past. Two were stopped from flying to Beijing to talk to mainland authorities about the right of abode. In July, a Democratic legislator had his permit to enter the mainland confiscated and was detained for ninety minutes as he tried to cross the frontier for a weekend with his wife and daughter. Ng's case seems to be the most serious to date. The conference is not a political occasion. As well as sitting in the legislature, Ng is a practising barrister and a member of the executive committee of the Hong Kong Bar Association. Seventy other local lawyers have had no trouble getting to Beijing, and there is no question of the organisers having turned down Ng's application to participate. It is not clear where the ban originated. One report says that the State Security Bureau was in favour of allowing her in, but that the Hong Kong and Macau Affairs Office was against the idea and carried the day.

The decision raises obvious concern about Beijing's attitude towards its Hong Kong critics. There are those who think that the terrier-like Ng goes too far. But, under the Hong Kong system, she has the right to say what she thinks, to table a no-confidence motion against the Secretary for Justice or to lead a silent march against the decision to go to the National People's Congress for a reinterpretation of the Basic Law. A prominent American expert, Jerome Cohen of New York University, who backs the reference to the NPC, says he considered not giving his speech at the conference to protest at the banning of Ng. The Bar Association calls on the government to 'allay any fear that might arise that people in Hong Kong cannot express an opinion on a rule of law issue without fear of attracting some adverse reaction from the central or the Hong Kong SAR governments'.

On the other hand, a local NPC deputy says he thinks the problem is Ng's 'overall political stance'. The pro-Beijing newspaper, *Ta Kung Pao*, goes further. 'Those who hold different views and those who have acted to oppose "one country, two systems" and undermine the rule of law in the SAR are different in nature,' it writes. As Professor Cohen observes, however, a good application of one country, two systems would be to allow those who have been blacklisted by mainland immigration to cross the border. The legislator herself wonders if her case means 'the opening of a new phase of more naked and relentless attack on people like me. Once the kid glove is off, the rest will follow.' The episode casts an ironic light on the urgings of the Secretary for Justice that people like Ng should get to know the mainland legal system better: if they can't even get there, how can they gain a better understanding of the way things are done over the border?

From the summit in New Zealand, the Chief Executive observes blandly that travel arrangements to and from the mainland are at the discretion of the Central Government, and have to be respected. Tung Chee-hwa certainly has no reason to want to help Ng as a politician. But as a citizen of the SAR, does she not have the right to expect the government to go in to bat for her? The list of Hong Kong people who find themselves without open official backing in matters involving the mainland is growing all the time.

Evidently sensing the growing disquiet, Anson Chan telephones

Ng and then says publicly that she understands the concerns. She is sure that Tung will pursue the case at the first opportunity after he returns to Hong Kong. It is another case of the Chief Secretary stepping into the breach. But Ng says she is told by the Chief Executive's office that he is 'too tired and too busy' to see her when he gets back. She writes to him twice, but is told by the private secretary to the Chief Executive's private secretary that he will not be available for at least three weeks.

Matters are not improved when a mainland professor advises the NPC that even though the Court of Final Appeal is entitled to interpret sections of the Basic Law relating strictly to the SAR, 'this does not mean that it has the final interpretation'. Indeed, he adds, China's parliament has a duty to supervise Hong Kong courts, and to step in if it considers a verdict not to be in accordance with what it takes to have been the original intentions of the framers of the Basic Law. As a judge says after hearing this: 'So, all that will be left for us is to do what we are told.'

Amid all this, Anson Chan lines up to raise her glass with Tung in front of a large heroic painting of Mao at the first of many celebrations of China's impending national day. The Chief Secretary stands on one side of the platform; Tung, the head of the Xinhua news agency and Li Ka-shing on the other. The placing carries its own symbolism, intended or otherwise.

14 *September*

Willy Lam, the *Post's* China editor, reports that Jiang Zemin has taken over top-level responsibility for reform of state-owned enterprises from Zhu Rongji. One of the President's long-time associates from Shanghai, Wu Bangguo, will run the restructuring on a day-to-day basis. Wu is likely to be less forceful than the Prime Minister. On a trip to the provinces last week, he proclaimed that state enterprises were actually doing rather well. In another move to divert power from Zhu, a rising star in the government, Vice-Premier Wen Jiabao, is to look after development of the stock market and regional development.

Willy Lam's source says the Prime Minister is still in charge of 'macro-economic adjustments and controls'. But it looks like a big setback after a dreadful year. First Clinton let him down on membership of the World Trade Organisation. Then there was the bombing of the Chinese embassy in Belgrade, and the row over allegations about nuclear spying in the United States. All the while, deflation at home sapped the zeal for reform. Zhu can bang heads in the state sector till the cows come home. He can crusade against corruption, and announce plans to slash the ranks of the bureaucracy. He can receive the plaudits of the world for not revaluing the yuan. What he cannot do is to make Chinese consumers spend to provide the growth the regime so badly needs – or prevent booming harvests lowering the price of agricultural goods on the market.

How different from five years ago, when retail sales were rising by 30 per cent a year, and iron man Zhu was called in to clamp down on inflation. Once, consumer goods were such a novelty that nobody who could afford them cared too much about the price. Now the novelty has worn off and people shop around for bargains. Prices have fallen for two years, creating the belief that they will go down even further. The Chinese are also hoarding for the day when their iron rice bowl cracks, and they have to pay for services they used to get for free.

So the economy remains bogged down, and the inventories in warehouses build up. The number of unsold television sets was put at 15 million earlier in the year. In the boom city of Shenzhen, big household appliance stores are virtually empty. Signs proclaim the bargains on offer. A saleswoman tries to interest me in a video recorder. When I shake my head, she points hopefully towards a washing machine.

After cutting interest rates seven times in three years, the Central Government is now about to slap a special tax on earnings from bank deposits to try to dissuade saving. There is even an ironic suggestion that the best way out would be to create a scare about an impending currency devaluation: fearing higher prices as a result, people would start buying.

The Asian Development Bank forecasts growth will fall below the target of 7 to 8 per cent this year, and drop to 6 per cent next year, when it expects the trade surplus to be cut in half. Meanwhile, the huge problem of the black hole in lending looms over the financial system. Although the head of the Central Bank spent a lot of time in an interview drawing distinctions between really terrible and less awful debts, the bottom line is that 25 per cent of loans are non-performing, and many more are questionable.

On top of which, the Prime Minister's policies are being criticised for their internal contradictions. Reduce corruption, and you reduce spending by the corrupt, which feeds deflation. Cut the civil service, and you cut the spending power of bureaucrats. Ban time-wasting banquets paid for from public funds, and you reduce the earnings of restaurants and hotels.

Zhu has always appeared as a solitary figure without any power base other than his own policies. Now his isolation seems to be growing. One of his business protégés, who ran a go-ahead company called China Everbright, has been sacked. Rumours that the Prime Minister had himself offered to resign swept through the markets in the summer. Stories are doing the rounds that he has been ill, and had to go to a provincial city to recuperate during the summer. Zhu-watchers note that on a recent trip to the provinces, he restricted himself to talking about such general subjects as the environment, with no more of his 'kill, kill, kill' exhortations. His wife accompanied him, which is unusual. She was photographed with him, gazing up at trees by the Yangtze River. This, the watchers say, is a sign that she needs to be close by her husband because of his poor health.

Jiang must know, however, that his increasingly cherished place in history alongside Mao and Deng can only be achieved as a reformer. That means he needs Zhu, however many protective measures he may take on a temporary basis to placate the conservatives. So when the President returned from the Pacific summit in New Zealand this week, the official state photographic agency put out a colour shot of him and the Prime Minister in smart dark suits, white shirts and pale ties, shaking hands as if to tell everybody that they are as one.

Still, sources in Beijing say Jiang has singled out Vice-President Hu Jintao, whom he sent to attend the second anniversary celebrations of the SAR in July, as the coming man. Hu, trained as an engineer, made his mark when he was dispatched to help run affairs in Tibet. After holding a series of senior positions in Beijing from 1992 onwards, he became Vice-President last year. As befits a Jiang lieutenant, he looks more of an apparatchik than a man with clear policy views of his own. He has taken a significant step up the ladder by being appointed Vice-Chairman of the Central Military Commission, which Jiang heads. Hu is also reported to be acting as a mediator between Zhu and his conservative predecessor, Li Peng. At the same time, the propaganda department has told the media that coverage of fifty years of Communist rule should not let the achievements of the past two decades 'refute' the first thirty years under Mao. Editors have been instructed to mention the 'vigorous development' of the 1960s, notably China's atom bomb and long-range rockets.

This is all part of Jiang's characteristic spider's web, with himself sitting in the middle, minimising the risks and holding the strands. At a Central Committee meeting, for instance, he speaks the language of reform, but the communiqué notes the need to maintain 'dominant' state control over major industries. The constitution bars the President from serving a third term, so one line of speculation is that Jiang will hand over to Hu Jintao when his mandate ends in 2003 but will try to hang on to his command of the Communist Party for another five years. That prospect arouses opposition from both the more liberal and the hardline conservative factions. But the slogans about Jiang being at 'the core' of the leadership carry with them an implication that, whoever holds the presidency, the 'chief engineer' will remain at the heart of the regime. It is against such a background of personal ambition and scheming that the autumn and winter will be played out, with all the consequences this brings, not only for the mainland but also for the administrative region down south and for the wider relationship between China and the world.

15 September

A star of Hong Kong's boom years is stepping down. Having lost his own firm, Peregrine, a couple of years ago, Philip Tose is leaving the

American investment company, Templeton, where he found employment after the crash. At its height, Peregrine was a glamour finance house, working with Li Ka-shing and pioneering the floating of mainland 'red chip' companies on the local stock market. A dapper former racing driver with a glamorous wife and appropriate lifestyle, Tose appeared in the company portrait beside a big golden sculpture of the bird that gave his firm its name. He was a tough, fast operator who didn't like my newspaper at all. Twice he went after us for stories he insisted were libellous, once screaming so loudly on the telephone to a reporter that you could hear his voice from yards away. In each case, Peregrine failed to sustain its complaint, but left us with legal bills.

At one point after the economic crisis had broken, we held a lunch with Tose and his senior colleagues to get their views. They served up nothing but gloom and doom. Eventually I asked if there was anywhere that one could invest one's grandmother's savings in the region. A Korean–American called André Lee to whom Tose had bounced many of our questions said yes, there was a taxi company in Indonesia called Steady Safe, a good business with connections to the ruling Suharto regime and plenty of potential. At that, Lee got up to go to the airport, and the lunch broke up.

A bit later, Steady Safe turned into a US$250 million black hole. In October 1997, Peregrine ran newspaper advertisements denying rumours of potential losses. In December, Tose assured shareholders that 'the directors were not aware of any material adverse changes in the financial or trading position of the group'. But after a deal with a big insurance company fell through at the last moment, Peregrine collapsed.

Tose went to work for Templeton, which had held 10 per cent of his company. Minority shareholders began legal action against Peregrine over the reassuring statements issued before it crashed. The government hired a former member of Britain's Financial Services Authority to investigate the collapse.

I bumped into Tose recently at the opening of a Louis Vuitton shop in Central. He looked pale and was positively restrained compared to his bullish days; he even laughed thinly when I said that, given the legal bills we had to pay from Peregrine's litigation, the paper should be listed among the firm's creditors. André Lee is punting an Internet company in Korea. Other Peregrine executives are scattered round the financial world. Nobody is burdened with self-doubt. That is not the Hong Kong way, which is one strong reason why it bounces back so quickly from adversity.

16 September

The worst typhoon for sixteen years, called 'York', hits Hong Kong. The sky grows dark; debris flies through the streets; flat-owners batten down their balconies, scaffolding comes crashing down. There is widespread flooding. Four cargo ships sink or run aground. A hundred windows are punched out at immigration and tax headquarters, but officials insist there are no confidential papers among the documents blown out on to the street. Four thousands trees are uprooted. More than 14,000 homes lose electricity. Thousands of container trucks back up at the port terminals. Two hundred fish farms report serious damage. Yachts are overturned and washed up on to the shores of marinas. Schools shut, but the airport stays open; however, after the China Airlines crash last month, operators cancel all scheduled flights. A few crazy windsurfers go out for the thrill, and one doesn't come back. Plucky villagers in the New Territories refuse to leave their homes; one old woman dons a construction worker's hard hat to sit it out in her home.

The cost will be tens of millions of dollars. But apart from the surfer, only one person is killed – a security guard hit by flying debris – though nearly 500 are injured. By the next morning, most things are back to normal. Vegetable and fish prices are up by 20 per cent. If you want *choi sum* greens or kale, you pay double the usual rate. Normal enough in a traders' town.

17 September

No sooner has York moved away than another storm touches Hong Kong. The Taiwan Strait tension has spilled over on to us.

The idea of the SAR being attacked from Taiwan in the event of conflict between the island and the mainland may seem outlandish. But Hong Kong is part of the People's Republic now, and President Lee Teng-hui warns that if there is a mainland attack on his island, the consequences would be disastrous not just for Beijing and Shanghai – but also for Hong Kong.

The People's Liberation Army troops stationed here have been put on alert. Their commander says his men are 'ready in full battle array' in case the city comes under attack. He tells the *Post* that the alert is like a typhoon signal: 'it will go up according to the situation'. Armoured personnel carriers have carried out target shooting exercises with live ammunition, according to a mainland army newspaper.

The garrison consists of an infantry brigade and naval and air force units which are said by the *Liberation Army Daily* to be able to fight a 'high-technology regional war'. They have half a dozen cruise missiles, ship-to-ship missiles and shore-to-ship missiles. Their helicopters conduct regular 'city patrols', and troops practise landing exercises from them. General Xiong Ziren defines the priority for his men as 'ideological cultivation, the continuous strengthening of military skills, the requirement of abiding by the law, and maintaining the brave and majestic image of the army'. To celebrate its role, the garrison is opening a museum devoted to itself. At the inauguration, Tung Chee-hwa is photographed with his arm outstretched pointing a pistol at an unseen target. *China Daily* says the museum aims 'to deepen Hong Kong people's understanding of the motherland's military defence forces and the role of the PLA in the SAR'. But visits are only by prior arrangement.

The sparring across the Taiwan Strait has become sharper with news that more than 100 PLA officers on the mainland are being investigated on charges of spying for Taipei. A major-general from the Logistics Department has been shot for selling secrets to Taiwan. The conflict has also moved into cyberspace. Taipei says mainland hackers have broken into government networks on the island. One report puts the number of attacks at 72,000 in one month, of which only 165 were successful. Going the other way, hackers from Taiwan have got into mainland tax and railway networks. According to the *Liberty Times* newspaper, Taiwan's army has developed 1,000 viruses to use against the PLA if necessary. *The Economist* says the Pentagon reckons two computer viruses which damaged mainland computers at a cost of US$120 million originated from across the Strait.

China's former Foreign Minister, Qian Qichen, who remains an influential figure in the mainland's dealings with Hong Kong, turns the spotlight back to the SAR by warning the media here not to advocate the Taiwanese cause. This is an issue which senior mainland officials have raised from time to time in the past. As it happens, no newspaper or broadcasting station in Hong Kong backs independence for the island, but the Central Government cannot shed the fear of its newest region becoming a seedbed for pro-Taiwanese sentiment, propaganda and 'splittism'.

Naturally, the Tung administration is most anxious to avoid any such thing happening. The Chief Executive periodically warns against his domain turning into a base for anti-mainland subversion. Last year, immigration officers began to stamp the travel documents of visitors arriving from Taiwan with a warning that they should not embarrass the SAR during their time here. Now a storm has been set off by the appearance on Radio-Television Hong Kong (RTHK) public radio of the island's *de facto* representative here who masquerades as the head of its travel bureau, just as the mainland's representatives and controllers of the underground Communist Party used to masquerade in colonial days as members of a news agency.

In the broadcast, Taipei's man repeats the call by Lee Teng-hui for 'state-to-state' relations. This brings a rejoinder from the Hong Kong government spokesman that he would do better to confine himself to tourism matters, and a blast from a pro-Beijing politician that RTHK should not give a platform to 'splittist views'. As for the Chief Executive, he believes the activities of Taiwanese bodies here 'must be regulated by Vice-Premier Qian Qichen's guidelines' since it is a matter for Beijing, not the SAR.

That still leaves a large grey area as far as the media are concerned. If reporting is okay but advocacy is not, where does the first end and the second start? Editors here may make a clear distinction between the news columns and the opinion pages. But for those brought up in a system where the choice of stories and the placing of photographs are political matters, the distinction may be less evident. The *Post* has not been distributed on the mainland when it has run Lee Teng-hui's picture on page one.

18 *September*

China Daily says 115,000 people have been arrested on bribery and embezzlement charges since 1997. Over 3,000 of the corruption cases involve sums equivalent to US$110,000 or more. Nearly 12,000 smuggling cases have been brought to light this year.

This information appears in a story which leads with the case of a senior official in the coastal city of Ningbo who has been expelled for having helped his son and his wife in a series of illicit schemes running to a billion yuan. Xu Yunhong, an alternate member of the Communist Party's Central Committee, is the highest-ranking party functionary to have been excluded since Beijing mayor Chen Xitong. Ningbo, one of the original foreign Treaty Ports in the nineteenth century, seems to be quite a den of thieves. Prosecutors have also uncovered a multi-million-yuan racket there involving forty local officials. An even bigger corruption ring is being probed in Fujian province, elsewhere on the commercially driven eastern coast, involving up to 200 people and takings of up to 10 billion yuan.

In Shaanxi province, meanwhile, officers have made a pre-emptive strike against the government's instruction to the army to get out of business by turning PLA firms into private enterprises under their control. They then used the firms to raise large amounts of money. Some of this was funnelled into property development in China and some was sent abroad illegally.

19 *September*

Today, an extraordinary general meeting of the Democrat Party leadership in Hong Kong votes on whether to back the introduction of a minimum wage. In the past, such an idea would have run contrary to the Hong Kong tradition. But the economic crisis has changed that, and makes the debate a test of strength in the SAR's most popular political party.

The Young Turks who want the Democrats to take a more radical stance and shed their middle-class inhibitions see a minimum wage as both necessary and a vote-winner. They lose, but only by 114 to 94. They will be back. They say the party's mainstream group is trying to suppress them in 'June 4 Massacre' fashion. It is not a comparison Martin Lee can relish.

21 September

A huge earthquake kills nearly 2,500 people in Taiwan. More than a thousand buildings collapse, some toppling over intact on their sides. Some had been built by contractors who stuffed 'tofu' walls with empty plastic bottles and newspapers instead of concrete and bricks. Ninety per cent of electricity supplies are cut off. Corpses rot in the heat. The prices of high-tech electronic components rise internationally as factories in Taiwan stop working. Manufacturers elsewhere in Asia rush to gear up extra production.

International aid teams fly in from round the world. Hong Kong's contribution is an unhappy one. Its sixteen-man rescue team takes three days to make the hour-long journey to Taipei. When it arrives, it is told it is not needed; and its equipment is not what is required. Why did it take so long to be mobilised? Was it simply a matter of bureaucratic delay or was there some political hesitation given the state of cross-Strait relations?

When it comes to the mainland, those relations intrude with a vengeance. China offers aid. President Jiang Zemin says the people on either side of the Taiwan Strait are 'as close as flesh and blood'. But Beijing also instructs overseas Red Cross bodies to notify it before sending aid to the island. Taiwan says this holds up desperately needed help. China then takes it upon itself to thank foreigners for their assistance on Taipei's behalf, and compounds matters by asking the Taiwanese if they want the mainland to petition the United Nations, whose Secretary-General offers condolences to the people of 'the Taiwan Province of China'.

The Foreign Ministry in Beijing says that, however great its sympathy for the victims, the disaster will not lessen its hostility to Lee Teng-hui and his 'two states' policy. For its part, Taiwan insists that all it will accept from the mainland is financial help, not medical staff. Its message to the Chinese Red Cross is short and simple: 'Thank you. Please pass this on: "Don't bother." '

22 September

A meeting takes place at the United Nations in New York which many people in Hong Kong would have wagered against seeing. On one side of a gleaming table sit China's Foreign Minister, Tang Jiaxuan, and his staff. On the other side are three senior officials from Europe. One of them is the new Foreign Affairs Commissioner of the European Commission, Chris Patten.

The photographs of the encounter show the former Governor grinning as the Foreign Minister sits back and looks at him with a half-smile. They are discussing reopening discussions on China's membership of the World Trade Organisation, which the European Union has always been anxious should not become a purely American concern. The meeting ends with expressions of optimism that the black period after the Belgrade embassy bombing is past. Unlike the time he wore a tie with dinosaurs on it to show what he thought of the Chinese rulers, Patten sports red neckwear.

But the Foreign Minister shows some things haven't changed. While Patten hopes China will move forward on human rights, Tang says that putting human rights above sovereignty is a hegemonistic ploy amounting to 'a new interventionism'. Addressing the General Assembly later, he insists that any violation of the principles of sovereignty and non-interference would amount to a 'gunboat policy' which would endanger international peace and stability. President Jiang may be out to cut an international figure for himself and his country, but Beijing will go on locking up dissidents and keeping its tight grip on Tibet or Xingjiang for as long as it sees fit.

23 September

The economic recovery is further confirmed when the International Monetary Fund predicts that Hong Kong will grow by 1.2 per cent in 1999 and 3.6 per cent next year. The SAR is on its way to posting its first monthly trade surplus since the beginning of 1998. As officials keep reminding us, it is early days yet, but the figures are pointing the right way. The question is when the feel-better factor will percolate through to a population shaken by the first recession most of them have known, and the first interruption of a prosperity which many thought was inviolable.

24 September

Tung Chee-hwa does a U-turn and agrees to see the lawyer-politician Margaret Ng about the ban on her going to the mainland. His decision comes as 162 lawyers and legal academics send him an open letter describing the barring as 'a blatant example of political persecution and the Central Government's intolerance of dissenting voices'. The letter urges the Chief Executive to dispel fears that legitimate and lawful activity in Hong Kong could bring political retaliation from Beijing.

Not that the meeting does much good. Tung issues a statement afterwards saying that he told the legislator that Hong Kong was a pluralistic society, and that the government 'welcomes different opinions on issues of common concern'. He adds that he is committed to safeguarding rights and freedoms contained in the Basic Law. As for the point at issue, he says that the authorities in Beijing have given him to understand that the decision 'was made in accordance with mainland laws'.

Ng says Tung told her that he believed the ban was not connected with her opposition to the overturning of the Court of Final Appeal's verdict. So why was she kept out? 'I got the impression . . . that he rather thought I should re-examine myself as to whether I could become a different person,' she adds. 'I found that rather chilling' – an echo of the Cultural Revolution, when people were not told why they were being punished but were advised to reflect on their crimes themselves.

25 September

An interesting insight into the administration's standards of representativity. The SAR is sending a 200-strong delegation to Beijing for China's national day on 1 October. A list of names has gone to the central authorities for a decision on who should be included. The Secretary for Justice says those on the list were chosen 'not because of their political affiliation but [according to] whether they are representative of the Hong Kong community'. Many of them sat on the committees set up by Beijing to dismantle Patten's democratic reforms. Among nineteen current legislators invited, there are no pro-democracy politicians. Democrats who came out even before the Joint Declaration of 1984 in favour of China regaining sovereignty do not get a look-in. But locals who accepted knighthoods from Britain and cosied up to the colonial establishment are there as 'instant noodle patriots' who changed tack as 1997 loomed.

Naturally, the biggest single group in the party comes from business. Several of the Chief Executive's personal favourites are along for the ride. So is a representative of Jardines, which moved its domicile from Hong Kong in late colonial days and has not returned. The British law officer who played a leading role in the over-ruling of the Court of Final Appeal is invited. Whatever sophistry may be employed, it is hard to maintain that they are more representative of the community than politicians who win 70 per cent of the popular vote.

Though there are eighteen members of the media, including my successor as editor of the *Post*, neither of the two biggest-circulation Chinese-language newspapers is represented. Nor is the Director of Radio-Television Hong Kong among the ten broadcasting figures in the group, who include the chairman of Rupert Murdoch's Phoenix satellite channel. It's like the heads of commercial broadcasting organisations in Britain being invited to join an official delegation, and the Director-General of the BBC being absent. The speculation is that RTHK's recent decision to allow the Taiwanese *de facto* representative to defend

Lee Teng-hui's 'state-to-state' policy on the airwaves has made it *persona non grata*. Whether Beijing would actually have said anything on this score is beside the point. Tung Chee-hwa's self-defence mechanism is tuned finely enough to avoid any prospect of a gaffe.

28 *September*

Five hundred company bosses, mainly from the United States, fly into Shanghai for *Fortune* magazine's conference of chief executive officers of major world companies. Fleets of locally made Buicks meet them at the new airport and whisk them to the smart new hotels of the Pudong business district along streets decked with red lanterns. In the US$75 million conference centre, Jiang Zemin gives a twenty-minute address, saying Chinese enterprises 'must go out and temper themselves in the winds and storms of economic globalisation'. He stoutly defends China's human rights record, and says Beijing will not renounce the use of force over Taiwan – unconfirmed reports say the State Council has set aside funds to build two aircraft carriers to match the US Seventh Fleet in the Strait.

That does not stop this being a gathering of China bulls. 'I love China and I love the Chinese people,' proclaims one long-term enthusiast, Maurice Greenberg, of the insurance giant American International Group. But the backdrop is hardly encouraging. A report by the State Taxation Administration shows that only one-third of mainland enterprises with foreign investors reported profits in 1998, a drop of 5.5 per cent on the previous year. On government orders, a telecommunications group, China Unicom, has cancelled contracts with 40 foreign firms amounting to US$1.4 billion. Power contracts have been renounced because demand is too low to fund the payments due to the foreigners. Even Western consumer goods companies which have marched in like Protestant missionaries of the past bearing brand names instead of bibles may be given pause for thought by a Gallup poll showing the Chinese prefer domestic brands by a margin of four to one.

Ma Yu, a senior research fellow at the Academy of International

Trade and Economic Co-operation, worries about the 'severe challenge' of keeping up the inflow of funds which have gone to more than 150,000 enterprises, creating jobs for over 20 million people and importing much-needed technology and equipment – as well as providing a fast-growing source of tax revenue. Now, he calculates, contracts for overseas investments have fallen by 20 per cent in the first half of the year compared with 1998.

Speak to many on-the-ground managers of foreign investments in China and you will hear a litany of the problems of operating joint ventures, from simple red tape to outright fraud. Products are ripped off by Chinese partners. Lucrative sub-contracts are handed out to friends and relations. One overseas Chinese I know had a promising-looking agreement to build warehouses in a development zone. But his partners in the local city authorities did not link an agreed road to the site, so the warehouses remained empty. Eventually he sold his share to locals with friends in high places, after which the road materialised and the warehouses were in business. 'Officials have made it clear that China now has no shortage of every type of fraud imaginable: distribution fraud, bank fraud, forex fraud, tax fraud, customs fraud, letter of credit fraud, intellectual property fraud, grey market and parallel import scams,' the chief mainland representative of the investigators Kroll Associates writes in the *Wall Street Journal*. 'There is hardly a significant foreign company in China that has not been the victim of one of these types of fraud.'

It is not only individual companies that suffer. Singapore has just had a nasty surprise over a business park in which it invested heavily in Suzhou near Shanghai. The foreigners thought they were assured of President Jiang's personal backing, but the local authorities favoured a development of their own, and undermined the Singapore project, which has virtually collapsed. Probably with that in mind, the city state's Senior Minister, Lee Kuan Yew, takes to the platform at the Shanghai meeting to warn that unless the Chinese system can adjust, its legitimacy will be brought into question. 'The most pernicious problem of all is corruption that has become embedded in the administrative culture; hard to eradicate,' he adds. 'Not only will corruption severely impede economic progress, but more dangerously it is a political powder keg, a grievance around which anti-government sentiment can easily coalesce.'

There is an embarrassing reminder of mainland realities for the organisers of the conference, Time Warner. Two of its magazines, *Time* and *Asiaweek*, are banned from China as the meeting opens (so is *Newsweek*). Apparently the authorities do not appreciate the way their latest issues on the fiftieth anniversary of the Communist victory include articles by the Dalai Lama and dissidents Wei Jingsheng and Wang Dan, and accounts of prison camp life, the Great Famine and the unrest in the Far West. The chairman of Time Warner seeks to put a brave face on it. The company points out that its magazines are still available in Shanghai, on the conference's own Internet site.

One of the chief executives at the meeting boasts that his firm is 'an ambassador for China . . . much more effective than any diplomats'. He counsels global media companies to be aware of 'the politics and attitudes of the governments where we operate', such as in China. Journalistic integrity must prevail in the final analysis, 'but that doesn't mean that journalistic integrity should be exercised in a way that is unnecessarily offensive to the countries in which you operate'. It all depends what you mean by 'unnecessarily': Beijing's definition would hardly be the same as that of a US editor. What lends the remarks special resonance is that the speaker is Sumner Redstone, boss of the entertainment group Viacom, which claims to reach 43 million homes in China with its MTV music channel. Redstone's company hopes to bring the Nickelodeon children's channel and a second music service to China. It is also in the process of acquiring the CBS television network.

So, naturally the question arises of whether a Viacom-owned CBS would follow the pattern set by Rupert Murdoch dropping Chris Patten's book on Asia a couple of years ago for fear of offending Beijing. Would CBS have to weigh up whether reports about dissidents being jailed or the Falun Gong being oppressed or about the jockeying for power below Jiang Zemin might give 'unnecessary' offence? If a Hong Kong media-owner had made a statement like Redstone's, the cry of self-censorship would have rung from the rooftops. But such is the business sex appeal of American media magnates that his remark evokes only passing attention.

OCTOBER

1 *October*

National day in China. Time for Jiang Zemin and a finely tuned crowd of half a million to mark the fiftieth anniversary of the day on which Mao Tse-tung stood on a dais looking out over Tiananmen Square to proclaim the People's Republic of China. A giant portrait of Jiang making a speech is borne through the streets of Beijing on top of a lorry, setting him alongside Mao and Deng Xiaoping. In a gesture of sartorial symbolism, Jiang is the only member of the leadership to wear a Mao jacket at the ceremony. And he alone stands in the car which drives past the troops drawn up for review – a very conscious evocation of a celebrated one-man inspection by Deng at the last military parade in Beijing back in 1984. As he passes the troops, he calls out, 'Comrades, are you well?' and 'How hard you are working!' They chant in unison, 'Hello, Comrade Chairman. We are serving the people.'

The television commentaries go as far as to say that Jiang has moved ahead of Deng and Mao in maintaining stability, achieving economic growth, accelerating national unity, strengthening the PLA and establishing an activist foreign policy. Still, there is one obvious contrast to be noted. The classic painting of Mao addressing the crowd in 1949 depicts him in full oratorical flood, the Great Helmsman urging his people on to a new dawn. The portrait of Jiang on top of the lorry shows him in a dark suit, white shirt and red tie, holding a sheet of paper from which he is reading a report to the microphones of the 1997 Communist Party Congress.

Echoing the Soviet Union's parades in Red Square, China's military might is wheeled out. There is a fresh generation of nuclear missiles, a new fighter-bomber, surface-to-air rockets and recently developed artillery. PLA soldiers goose-step past the reviewing stand, followed by massed ranks of machine-pistol-bearing women from the capital's civilian militia in red outfits with short skirts and black boots. To make sure calls of nature do not interfere with the parade, some of the paraders are kitted out with adult-sized nappies. After the military, the civilians have their moment of glory. Children file by bearing boards proclaiming, 'Our motherland will be more glorious tomorrow.' Fashion models strut their stuff. Agricultural workers march by got up to look like wheat or sunflowers. And there is a bevy of brides and grooms in formal Western wedding gear. At the end, more children rush towards Jiang releasing red balloons and doves into the air.

One unnoticed sideshow takes place among the foreign guests. After hosting the *Fortune* conference in Shanghai, the boss of the Time Warner media empire, Gerald Levin, has travelled to the Chinese capital with a number of fellow American businessmen. Among them is Stephen Case of the Internet giant AOL. 'We stood together watching the tanks, the planes, and the fireworks,' Case recalls later. The next month, he telephones Levin to propose buying Time Warner in the biggest-ever takeover. The Beijing backdrop to the deal fits in neatly with China's new appreciation of the world of business.

The fiftieth anniversary celebrations reflect the robotic attitude of the leadership. Nothing spontaneous is permitted. The crowds are carefully drilled. The intense rehearsals with tanks rolling through Tiananmen Square conjure up chilling memories of 1989. The veneer of the occasion extends to the city itself. Apart from a general clean-up of buildings, a handful of Falun Gong adherents were dragged from Tiananmen yesterday as they tried to perform their exercises. Three hundred thousand unregistered workers have been cleared out of the city, and 18,000 vagrants detained. Tens of thousands of trusted inhabitants have been enrolled into neighbourhood watch squads, complete with red armbands.

Despite all the refurbishment along the main avenues, it is going to take a superhuman effort to turn Beijing into an attractive place. There are still pleasant parks and some fine relics of another age. The official guest houses and the leadership compound beside the Forbidden City are extremely agreeable so long as you can put up with the rhetoric served up by your hosts. In a pavilion by a lake, attendants in white gloves serve French wine while the breeze ripples through the trees and a minister discourses about the non-negotiability of mainland sovereignty over Taiwan. In a courtyard complex renovated by the Hong Kong businessman David Tang as the Beijing version of his Hong Kong China Club, one may admire the architecture and peer at the manuscripts on the shelves as an official from the State Council tells you that a giant container ship being launched by a Japanese firm is in fact a secret warship which can be converted into an aircraft carrier at a moment's notice with planes hidden below decks.

Some interesting alleys, lakes and gardens and small shops survive, along with the Forbidden City. There is the overwhelming expanse of Tiananmen Square, and, an hour's drive away, the Great Wall and the Ming Tombs. But this is an imperial city that reflects the character of its emperors, and the most recent breed has been more interested in power and material progress than in preserving the past. Mao destroyed much of its old character, tearing down historic districts, rearranging the city to fit his vision of communist modernity and installing smoke-belching factories. Fumes from a vast old-fashioned steel plant to the south add to the exhaust of huge traffic jams. Rows of featureless, shabby blocks of flats line the ever-expanding circles of ring roads. The destruction of the old continues relentlessly. Social and economic divisions grow wider by the year. Hordes of migrant workers collect garbage as upwardly mobile Beijingers crowd into the Hard Rock Café or take chauffeur-driven limos to play golf in the surrounding hills.

2 October

Canadian newspapers are running a story about an operation that 'tracked a myriad of companies linked to Asian tycoons to determine whether they were fronts for Chinese espionage activities'. The papers report that the study, carried out by Canada's Security Intelligence Service and the police between 1994 and 1996, also looked at 'hundreds of thousands of dollars' said to have been pumped into political parties to see if lawmakers were being influenced. As so often with such reports, there was no answer to the question it posed. One Canadian newspaper quoted sources as saying that 'political influence nixed the project'. The story was picked up by international news agencies and sent to Hong Kong, but no local paper used it despite – or because of – the presence of so many well-known names.

4 October

A Hong Kong man called Eric Ho from Shatin in the New Territories crossed the border to Shenzhen today. In a letter to the *Hong Kong Standard*, he tells of what happened as he and three friends walked back to the frontier train station at Lo Wu.

> We were suddenly surrounded by six men claiming to be mainland police. One of them showed his warrant card and said we were involved in a gang fight in Shenzhen the previous night.
>
> They demanded we go to a particular restaurant for an identity parade. I was suspicious and we refused.
>
> They shouted at us that they only wanted money and would stab us to death if we did not go.
>
> At a VIP room in the restaurant, they searched us and forced us to tell them our credit card passwords. I was punched by one of them in the chest.
>
> Unfortunately, my password was not correct and one guy with a northern Chinese accent hit me twice in the back with an iron hammer. He asked me for the password again. I could only tell him a possible one and let God decide my fate.

The robbers warned us that we would die if the password was still wrong. My friend was also beaten. One of the men went out to withdraw cash from my account.

A call was then received indicating that my bank password was correct.

After the call, two robbers indicated that we would be released as long as we had handed over all our money and belongings.

We handed over cash and mobile phones, and they let us go. We got to Lo Wu train station about 11.30 p.m. We were in a hurry to run to the Hong Kong side and report this brutal crime to the police.

We were told that our case was not unusual and that this sort of thing happened frequently across the border.

We were very lucky to have escaped greater injury compared with other cases.

The truth of that last sentence was shown a month later. A press photographer and a reporter who went across the border for a night out met a nineteen-year-old girl in the street. She gave them her pager number. They invited her to join them in a nightclub. She turned up with a female friend. The two women took the men to a flat in a village on the outskirts of town.

Waiting inside were three men with knives and iron bars. They told the Hong Kongers to hand over their money and valuables. When the photographer resisted, he was stabbed and left to bleed to death. The reporter was tied up, and forced to give his bank code number before the attackers fled with the two women. Two weeks later, they were arrested in a city up the coast when the nineteen-year-old's identity document was checked and found to be a fake. They still had the credit cards and jewellery belonging to the dead man.

6 October

Today is the Chief Executive's big day. Like British governors, he goes to the Legislative Council to deliver his programme for the coming twelve months in his Policy Address. This is Hong Kong's equivalent to the Queen's Speech. Chris Patten's final address was notable for setting down a set of benchmarks by which the SAR was to be judged. The colonialist overtones of this rubbed some democrats up the wrong way and the Council refused to pass the traditional vote of thanks. Not that this made any difference: what might be a resignation matter elsewhere, or at least cause for embarrassment, cuts little ice in executive-led Hong Kong, then or now.

As expected, Tung Chee-hwa sets out an environmental programme as his main theme. Having campaigned in the *Post* for four years for effective measures against pollution, I can only say that it is about time. Apart from the high health costs of bad air, businesses have become increasingly concerned at the deterrent effect on foreign executives they want to hire. There is a distinct illogicality in promoting Hong Kong as an attractive tourist centre while letting the environment deteriorate so badly. Tung's ten-year programme involves spending the equivalent of US$4 billion. The target is to raise air quality to the levels of London and New York. The import of diesel cars is to stop; owners of polluting diesel vehicles – mainly taxis and minibuses – will get financial incentives to fit cleaner engines; smoky vehicles are to face higher fines; there will be more pedestrian zones; cross-border co-operation is to be expanded; and work will start on improving the water of the Pearl River.

Tung's 142-minute speech also puts forward proposals to improve education, create sports and performance venues and enhance the look of the harbour. He will set up an urban renewal body that would be able to acquire old real estate and get it redeveloped without having to pay the large premiums currently levied; this could have a major effect on the property market and lead to the renovation of jam-packed inner urban tenements where living conditions are unworthy of a city as rich as Hong Kong. Looking across the border, he wants to explore ways of tapping into the potential of the Pearl River delta region.

Overall, the aim is to make the SAR into a 'world class city' and 'an Ideal Home'. This would mean fostering pride and confidence in the place, something the administration appears to consider achievable by gauche slogans rather than by encouraging civil society to develop. Improving the environment will certainly make Hong Kong a more pleasant place in which to live and work. But if its people feel that their home is losing its individuality as one country encroaches on their system, all the cleaning up of the air will not make them walk tall in the new century.

7 October

In an ideal world, the Chief Executive could expect his Policy Address to dominate the agenda for a while. But twenty-four hours later, he finds himself embroiled in a row with the Democrats on that most sensitive of issues – the 4 June vigil for the dead of Tiananmen Square. Tung has nobody but himself to blame. His taste for walking into minefields is a source of wonder.

The incident starts as he appears in the Legislative Council today for the traditional question-and-answer session after the Policy Address. The chubby-faced vice-chairman of the Democrats, Albert Ho, raises the matter of the mainland ban on various legislators, including himself. He asks the Chief Executive if he feels he has a duty to put their case to Beijing. Tung replies that he is 'very willing to try in that respect'. Instead of stopping there, he can't refrain from delivering a little lecture.

'I hope the Democratic Party and the democratic camp will improve their understanding of the country,' he says. 'I have mentioned my hope that you can prove your worth in every respect, but I've looked again and again and seen nothing.' When another Democrat asks what Beijing is looking for, Tung digs himself deeper into a hole. 'I haven't talked to Beijing leaders about the issue in this way,' he says. 'But I've talked to several of your leaders and I specifically mentioned that I hoped there could be a demonstration . . . I'm still waiting for that.' What does he mean by 'demonstration'? 'Perhaps you should ask your colleagues,' Tung replies.

This enables Ho to reveal to reporters that the Chief Executive had a secret lunch meeting earlier in the year with the veteran democracy leader, Szeto Wah, the key figure in the Tiananmen vigil and in the

Hong Kong Alliance in Support of Patriotic Democratic Movements in China. According to Ho, Tung told Szeto the 4 June commemorations should be stopped if pro-democracy politicians wanted to improve relations with Beijing. In particular, he asked Szeto not to hold this year's tenth anniversary event.

The revelation sets all the old alarm bells ringing about freedom of expression, and Tung's obeisant attitude towards those who chose him for his post. 'If that is what he meant by proving our worth and we did as he requested in return for permission to visit the mainland, I think Hong Kong's reputation as one of the freest cities in the world would be badly tarnished,' Ho says. In keeping with a recent pattern, the Chief Secretary jumps in to try to pour some oil on the waters. 'I am sure the Chief Executive does not mean to imply there ought to be self-criticisms,' Anson Chan says. 'Improving relationships by common definition is a two-way thing.'

But the Democrats have the bit between their teeth. The chance to steal Tung's thunder a day after his speech is irresistible. They grab the headlines. Which newspaper is going to rake over the details of the environment programme when presented with a story that has it all: secret contacts, freedom, kowtowing, and the most emotional event of the year? Even then, Tung can't stop digging a hole for himself. He insists he wasn't telling Szeto to stop the vigils, only repeating his theme of it being time to put down the baggage of 4 June. But how could the organisers of the vigil put down the baggage of the massacre and go ahead with the commemoration?

The whole episode shows either a startling naïveté or simple bull-headedness on Tung's part. The idea of the austere, dedicated Szeto Wah agreeing to stop the vigils in the hope of being allowed to visit the mainland is laughable. The whole lunch must have been a major exercise in non-communication. Szeto, who prides himself on his patriotism to China, if not to its current regime, didn't even like the Western food he was served.

The deeper danger of all this is that it will further worsen the already frosty relations between the administration and the major popularly elected political party. The Chief Executive's link-man with the Democrats, Paul Yip Kwok-wah, says talks between them will go on. He insists that the Tung–Szeto conversation was merely about 'conceptual and philosophical aspects of ruling Hong Kong'. But the reaction from the Democrats is unyielding. Martin Lee says he guesses Tung would like them to 'behave in such a way that the Beijing leaders will believe we are obedient children'. This sums up the administration's approach pretty well, but Hong Kong is not a place that got where it is today by keeping its head down in class. The trouble is that those who are running the class don't seem to realise this.

8 *October*

Apart from the alarm about being swamped by new mainland migrants, there is already quite a problem in coping with the existing influx of children from China, which averages sixty a day. A survey by the Education Department reports that between 15 and 20 per cent of these children are behind in mathematics and Chinese. The figure soars to 60 per cent where English is concerned. The government offers grants for sixty hours of tutoring for young immigrants. But as the principal of a school with one-third of its pupils from the mainland says: 'How can a student from a rural school who doesn't even know his ABC catch up with the rest of the class in sixty hours?'

10 *October*

Today is the eighty-eighth anniversary of the overthrow of China's imperial dynasty. The Double Tenth, as it is known, is a day of celebration in Taiwan, though this year's ceremonies have been truncated because of the earthquake. In Hong Kong, 200 people go to a former Kuomintang centre to pay their respects to the father of republican China, Sun Yat-sen, and 1,300 gather in a hotel to mark the occasion. In the Mongkok district in Kowloon, police take down a Taiwanese flag in the street. A spokeswoman says this is 'to protect the principle of one China'. The Chief Executive's special adviser adds that the decision is following the guidelines for relations with Taiwan set out by Vice-Premier Qian Qichen. Before the handover, hundreds of Taiwanese flags flew on the Double Tenth, but now one China rules.

11 *October*

A mainland newspaper reports that a vice-mayor in Guangdong province has been tried for siphoning off the equivalent of US$1.3 million to buy Hong Kong and Macau properties. He must have invested well as he more than doubled his money – which does not save him from a suspended death sentence.

13 *October*

Despite urgings from both the Democrats and the pro-Beijing DAB party, which increasingly fancies its chances at the polls, the Secretary for Constitutional Affairs makes it plain that there will be no speeding-up of the long march towards full democracy, which will be considered – no more – in the year 2007. It is all a bit reminiscent of the verdict of a spokesman for the foreign Treaty Ports in China in the 1920s, who declared that elected assemblies and democratic institutions had no place because the Chinese were 'manifestly incapable of self-government'. Then it was the foreigners who delivered such verdicts; now it is the masters of China and their chosen officials in Hong Kong who do so, maintaining that one of Asia's most advanced societies will not be sufficiently mature to face the issue for another eight years.

Inevitably, there are some sour comparisons with what is happening in Indonesia. There, to general acclaim, parliamentary elections have been held, East Timor has been able to vote on its future and a president will soon be chosen by the new legislature. Apparently the rulers of Hong Kong regard their people as being politically less mature than the inhabitants of Java, Sumatra or Timor. Nor is there any mechanism for amending the Basic Law drawn up at a time when politics in Hong Kong were in their infancy, the memory of Tiananmen Square was fresh in China's mind and democracy had not begun to unfurl itself over South-East Asia. The SAR is stuck in a time warp. This may be a source of comfort for both Beijing and the Chief Executive, but one can only agree with the legislator Christine Loh when she asks if Tung takes the people of the SAR and their representatives for simpletons.

19 *October*

A prominent pro-Beijing politician began to raise complaints eighteen months ago about the way the government was being criticised on the SAR's public broadcaster, Radio-Television Hong Kong (RTHK). He said at the time that the Chief Executive assured him the matter would be handled 'slowly, slowly'. Today, the slow movement goes into overdrive. An announcement is made that the Director of Broadcasting for the past thirteen years, Cheung Man-yee, is to leave the station to become Hong Kong's trade representative in Tokyo. The government insists there is nothing political in the move. It is indeed true that the Tokyo post carries with it a higher ranking, taking her annual salary to the equivalent of US$260,000. The Director, who is in Northern Ireland visiting one of her predecessors from British days, says she has been assured editorial independence will continue. The Chief Executive declares that this is fundamental government policy. Cheung's deputy will be appointed to succeed her as soon as the appropriate boards can meet.

Why then does the *New York Times* run a big story, and the Committee to Protect Journalists in New York call on the Chief Executive to act quickly to allay fears about the station being compromised? It is not just that Cheung Man-yee is a high-profile, popular figure whose looks belie her fifty-three years and who was part of the formidable 'handbag gang' round Anson Chan. After the handover, she came to personify media independence in a way that was all the more striking because of RTHK's status. A framework agreement with the government drawn up in 1993 gives its Director responsibility for fair, balanced and objective programming – editorial independence was added two years later. But its employees, up to the Director, are all civil servants.

Not surprisingly, hardliners in the pro-Beijing camp have long disliked the way that these government staff give air time to democrats and to critics of the administration. They wonder why RTHK is not whipped into line, shedding its BBC inheritance as the baggage of colonialism. In March last year, an old leftist called Xu Simin kicked up a storm by attacking the station for being anti-government and a 'remnant of British rule'. Recently, pressure has been building up. In August, a Hong Kong member of the National People's Congress called for RTHK to avoid propagating 'splittist' views. Soon afterwards came the appearance of Taiwan's representative to put forward his government's 'state-to-state' view of relations with the mainland. After that, the local NPC delegate suggested it might be time to bring in anti-subversion legislation. As for Tung Chee-hwa, well-placed sources say he was irked by the extensive RTHK coverage of the 4 June Tiananmen vigil. It was also noticed that he took two years to accept an invitation to appear on RTHK radio to answer listeners' questions; he did a similar programme for a commercial station eight months earlier. And Cheung Man-yee was not among the guests at the national day celebrations in Beijing.

All the while, Tung and his colleagues were passing on the criticism they heard to the station, and suggesting new jobs for its Director. Cheung turned them down, and seemed intent on seeing out the last two years of her term. Apparently she counted on a combination of her own status and reputation, her long-standing association with Anson Chan, and an awareness of the negative reaction at home and abroad if she was seen to have been pushed out. But now she has clearly accepted a deal, if only to ensure that her deputy succeeds her. She remains a civil servant and so cannot speak out, even if she wishes to. Politics apart, some wonder if the days of old-style BBC rectitude are numbered, as broadcast sensationalism and show business march forward hand in hand. A Chinese-language television station has just taken on a former Miss Hong Kong with no journalistic experience to present its main evening news programme.

There is talk of Cheung having been sent into 'internal exile'. Martin Lee declares 'the beginning of the end of freedom of expression'. To which the leftist Xu Simin, who started the row in 1998, expresses his hope that the station will now transmit 'constructive opinions' about the government. 'It should assist the SAR government and Hong Kong people, but has not done that,' he adds. 'There is an end to every banquet.' For RTHK, the proof will lie in what it puts out. Sudden changes are unlikely. The new boss is a good man, and a broadcasting professional. But will his reporters now think twice before asking piercing questions, and will producers find themselves forgetting to invite troublemakers on to the airwaves?

20 *October*

A story in the *New York Times* spotlights the price of following your religious beliefs in China if you happen to stray from the official path.

Seven weeks ago, a 37-year-old Christian called Gou Qinghui gave birth to a son. She lost her job as a bible teacher at a government-controlled theological seminary in 1994, and has been involved with 'house churches' consisting of Christians who meet privately instead of joining officially approved religious organisations. The regime is cracking down on them. An underground Catholic bishop was arrested this summer. Seven Catholics have been jailed for threatening social order.

Gou's husband is also a devout Christian and a pro-democracy activist. In the mid-1990s, he was detained for three years; he now lives in what the couple call 'soft imprisonment' under police scrutiny and deprived of the identification papers needed to get a job or to travel. In April, when Gou was five months pregnant, police arrived at her home with an arrest warrant, but her husband managed to dissuade them from taking her away.

Now, Gou tells Eric Eckholm of the *New York Times* that hospital officials in Beijing are refusing to provide a birth certificate for her seven-week-old son. That means the child cannot be registered, and will not be eligible to go to school or, later, to get legal employment.

'He's an innocent victim,' Gou says. 'I'm not really a political activist, I'm just interested in spreading the Gospel.'

21 *October*

The change in leadership at RTHK does nothing to prevent a half-hour panel discussion on the station about the right to demonstrate in the SAR, in which even pro-Beijing politicians come out in favour of free expression in the streets. Generally, protests in the SAR are small and well-behaved. Skirmishes on 1 October at the flag-raising ceremony for Chinese national day led to nothing more than two slight injuries to the forces of law and order and the loss of loudhailers confiscated from the demonstrators. Police, who meet the organisers of rallies in advance to agree the guidelines and the placing of the protest, usually turn out in force. On 1 October, a site was agreed 100 metres away from the ceremony. Around 100 police were deployed for sixteen activists.

Hong Kong's champion demonstrator, a pigtailed Trotskyite who single-handedly keeps the Che Guevara T-shirt tradition alive in this temple of market capitalism, has had to work hard to get arrested. He succeeded after standing up and shouting from the public gallery in the Legislative Council. Even then, the court only gave him a suspended sentence. So he went out for some more demonstrating and may end up in jail as a result. When I joined him in a television discussion, he smiled and said, 'It's become a way of life.' A secretary commented, 'He's like a little boy.'

The contrast between the freedom to demonstrate here and the clampdown in democracies when Jiang Zemin goes visiting them is ironic given the handover-era fears that freedom to protest would be scaled back in the SAR. Even the firebrand legislator Emily Lau admits that, in this respect, 'maybe we are a little bit better than the United Kingdom'. The Assistant Commissioner who speaks for the police on tonight's panel might surprise those who imagine that law and order here has become a Chinese matter since 1997. His name is Mike Dowie. He speaks with a broad Scottish accent.

22 October

The demonisation of Hong Kong as a front for mainland China is racing ahead in Senate hearings in Washington on the Panama Canal. Li Ka-shing, it appears, is a threat to US security. A quarter of a million people have signed a petition delivered to Capitol Hill expressing their disquiet.

The outrage runs as follows. Li's Hutchison Whampoa company controls a firm called Panama Ports, which has beaten several American companies to win fifty-year leases to run container ports at either end of the canal when the US withdraws on 31 December. As a result, Republicans are talking darkly about the waterway falling under Beijing's influence.

Li Ka-shing's links with the mainland are no secret; he has just opened a huge shopping plaza in the capital. From there, it is an easy jump for some in Washington to see him as the front man for the PLA. The Republican majority leader in the Senate, Trent Lott, thunders that 'US Naval ships will be at the mercy of Chinese-controlled pilots and could even be denied passage through the canal by Hutchison, an arm of the People's Liberation Army.' Ronald Reagan's Defence Secretary, Caspar Weinberger, warns that China has acquired a 'beachhead' in Panama, and calls for constant vigilance over the activities of the Hong Kong firm. While Beijing doesn't interfere with Hutchison on a daily basis, he adds, 'If there was something it wanted to do, this company would not be able to survive without doing just those things.' A former chairman of the Joint Chiefs of Staff, Admiral Thomas Moorer, says: 'My specific concern is that the company is controlled by the communist Chinese. And they have virtually accomplished, without a single shot being fired, a stronghold on the Panama Canal.' Later, he predicts a China–US clash over the canal which 'will need to be rectified with the blood of brave young soldiers, sailors and marines some day in the future'.

The smell of US domestic politics is in the air, with a Red Peril scare as a convenient weapon. The presidential hopeful, Steve Forbes, warns that 'having Chinese companies managing both ends of this strategic chokepoint . . . is simply unacceptable to American security'. A Republican congressman, Dana Rohrabacher, intones: 'If we do nothing, I can guarantee you that within a decade a communist Chinese regime that hates democracy and sees America as its primary enemy will dominate the tiny country of Panama and the Panama Canal.'

Another undercurrent is that Panama recognises Taiwan, not Beijing. The island's Evergreen group is also involved in the canal. But the mainland is wooing Panama, and one can imagine the reaction if this leads to diplomatic recognition. On top of which, sources not a million miles from Hutchison note that Caspar Weinberger, who is chairman of Steve Forbes' eponymous family magazine, used to work for the American company Bechtel, which failed to get the Panama licences. Bechtel denies any continuing link with Weinberger. Still, the suspicion in Hong Kong is that a touch of commercial sour grapes may be at work.

Li Ka-shing calls it all 'a very, very funny story'. Imagine, he goes on, that you owned an apartment at either end of the main tunnel under Hong Kong harbour. 'Can people say you are controlling the tunnel? How can we control the canal?' Anyway, he is on a roll, Hutchison having just made US$14.5 billion from selling its stake in the British mobile telephone operator, Orange, to Mannesmann of Germany.

There is a footnote when a member of the Forbes family pays a visit to Li. In the lift, he hands a copy of the latest issue of the magazine to one of Superman's lieutenants. It contains a piece by Weinberger raising questions about Hutchison and the canal. The embarrassment is entirely on the Forbes side. Li is photographed smiling even more widely than usual. With critics like that, who needs friends?

23 October

Lok Yuk-shing, the 63-year-old man from Hong Kong held in jail in China for 487 days without trial or being properly charged, is released and flies home. In the summer he was moved from prison to a guest house run by the Public Security Bureau where conditions were better. His family have paid HK$50,000 to gain his release, far less than the $4 million demanded by the Inner Mongolia officials when they went there to try to get him freed in the summer. Lok's former company, whose debts were responsible for his arrest, says it will consider reimbursing the family. But it declines any responsibility for what happened to its former employee.

Over dinner in a Shanghainese restaurant in Central, Lok tells of his months in handcuffs and leg chains in a cell with ten others on the edge of the Gobi Desert. 'A fellow inmate who was a northern gangster encouraged me to stay tough,' he adds. 'If I had given up or died in jail, my name would never have been cleared. The SAR government should speak up more for us.'

But the government, which said it would be 'inappropriate and impossible' for it to intervene on his behalf, remains as unforthcoming on the case as ever. 'We understand the mainland authorities acted in accordance with mainland laws,' a spokesman says. The government adds that it 'followed the case closely and related the family's requests to the mainland authorities'. For his part, Lok doesn't know what, if anything, the authorities here did to help him. Instead he says that if it hadn't been for the *Post*'s reporting and campaigning on his case, he would still be in prison. 'Although the police didn't say anything about it, the way they behaved showed me they knew that your newspaper and later other media were reminding people about my situation,' he adds.

As he returns and relaxes by looking after his plants and cooking, Lok sounds a true Hong Kong note. Would he go back to the mainland? asks our journalist Cynthia Wan, whose outstanding reporting brought the case to public attention. 'It all depends if there are any business opportunities there,' he replies. 'I'm not afraid to go back.' Still, he needs a bladder operation as the result of the poor diet he was fed in prison. To make sure the homecoming is not disturbed, his family lights a fire in a metal container at the door of his apartment to ward off bad luck and evil spirits.

The number of Hong Kong people detained on the mainland over commercial matters is a matter of some dispute. The government put it at forty-five earlier in the year, but now says twenty have been released. Of the forty-five, it reports that twenty had been in custody for more than six months. Other sources place the total as high as eight-five. One woman says her husband has been locked up since April in Henan province over a debt owed by his former company. She says mainland authorities asked for $2 million in bail for his release. The Hong Kong Inland Revenue threatened to slap a surcharge on her husband's unpaid tax bill, she adds.

The SAR Security Bureau says it is drawing up plans for a notification system so that it will know when Hong Kong people are arrested on the mainland. But will that enable it to do anything about their treatment, or to ensure that they are either charged or released according to Chinese law? The answer seems evident from the Bureau's insistence that the Hong Kong authorities cannot 'interfere with the mainland's judiciary system and procedures under the principle of one country, two systems' – even, it appears, when its citizens are being treated in defiance of mainland law.

24 *October*

Dressed in a long blue raincoat, his head thrown back in a broad grin, Jiang Zemin takes the blonde woman in front of him by the hand and sweeps her into an impromptu dance. Her husband smiles. The accordionist beside them concentrates on playing a local folk tune. The assembled officials laugh, and Jiang's dancing partner expresses her delight.

The scene is a small local museum near the country château of President Jacques Chirac of France. Jiang is his weekend guest. Arriving at the museum, the Chinese leader was presented with a 'China blue' accordion on which a few notes of a Chinese tune were played before the accordionist went into the song that got the visitor dancing with Bernadette Chirac. At a model farm later in the day, Jiang feeds a lamb from a bottle, noting the warmth of the milk as he does so. Clearly he is enjoying himself, though Chirac is attacked by human rights groups for coddling a dictator.

Jiang is on a lengthy tour of Europe, North Africa and Saudi Arabia. Many contracts are signed, or promised. The Chinese President outlines his vision of a multi-polar world, and damns the evils of the Falun Gong. At a state banquet in Lisbon, he sings a Chinese song without musical accompaniment.

Before crossing to France Jiang had been in London, where he stayed at Buckingham Palace and exchanged numerous toasts with the Queen. They are the same age, but how much else they have in common is a matter for doubt. *The Economist* remarked that: 'Britain has to deal with the China that exists, not the China it would like to exist. But does that really mean honouring Mr Jiang with a state visit? . . . For once it makes you feel sorry for the Queen, for being

used in this way.' Heavy-handed policing to ensure that demonstrators did not inconvenience the visitor went down badly, even if
they were taken for granted by the Chinese. 'For the past few days
the world has been treated to the bizarre spectacle of the British
police tearing the banners out of the hands of demonstrators who are
there, after all, to protest at the inability of the Chinese people to
stage just such demonstrations,' as the *Daily Telegraph*'s Christopher
Lockwood noted.

The Chinese spokesman observed that Free Tibet demonstrators
in London had 'long noses', an observation roughly on a par with the
Duke of Edinburgh's remark on a visit to China about the natives'
slitty eyes. But this being a time when everybody wants to avoid any
unpleasantness with Beijing, nobody objected to the spokesman's
characterisation, or to his blaming British imperialism for problems
in Tibet. There was also royal controversy when the Prince of Wales
preferred a private dinner engagement to a banquet given by the
Chinese.

Still, the visit to Britain, like the rest of the trip, was counted a
success, another Jiang step on to the world stage. Yet he drew no
crowds. If Mao had gone to London or Paris, the streets would have
been lined with true believers or those who were appalled with the
carnage he had wreaked – or simply those who wanted to see a historic figure. Jiang aspires to similar status but his constituency is
business-minded politicians. Though he insisted at one point in Paris
on the importance of maintaining communism, this tour is as good
a sign of the death of ideology as you could wish for – on both sides.

27 October

The Chief Executive can heave a sigh of relief. The Legislative
Council has passed the motion of thanks for his Policy Address. But
the vote is not quite as straightforward as government backers would
like to present it. The motion was passed due to the votes of representatives of the functional constituencies and of the hand-picked
election committee. A big majority of members elected by popular
vote came out against it. No wonder the administration is so opposed

to any speeding-up of democratisation in Hong Kong. Much safer to be able to count on the representatives of business and the pro-Beijing lobby.

29 October

China can be very prickly over what it sees as interference in the affairs of Hong Kong by other countries. Or it can be completely laid-back. The degree of reaction depends a lot on who is talking.

The Chinese Foreign Ministry Commissioner in the SAR, who used to be ambassador in London, is very het-up about a speech by the new American Consul-General which included mild remarks about democratisation, the rule of law and media freedom. This, says the Commissioner's Office, against a background of deteriorating relations with Washington, was inappropriate, irresponsible and unjustifiable.

Earlier in the week, another speaker from a foreign government told a dinner here that Hong Kong's political system should be changed to give politicians running in elections responsibility for fulfilling their campaign pledges. That would be the biggest upheaval seen since the establishment of the SAR, requiring, as the speaker said, an adaptation of the Basic Law.

Strangely enough, this speech drew no criticism from the Chinese, though it could be seen as a plain interference in Hong Kong's internal affairs. But the second speaker was the Senior Minister of Singapore, Lee Kuan Yew, whom the Chief Executive greatly admires. One can only imagine the reaction if such remarks had been made by the US Consul-General. It ain't what you say, it's the person you are that counts. One place, two reactions.

30 October

China's parliament, the National People's Congress, passes legislation outlawing the Falun Gong movement, which the *China Daily* has described as a 'devil cult'. Penalties start at three years for demonstrating or disrupting social order, and run all the way up to execution for using cult activities to attempt to subvert the socialist system or split the nation.

It is now six months since members of the movement suddenly materialised outside the leadership compound in Beijing. Despite the subsequent crackdown, police say the Gongists have staged 300 protests since April. The authorities allege that practitioners have breached national security by being in possession of twenty 'top secret' documents and thirty-nine others ranked as 'classified', some of which had been passed on to people abroad. But the definition of national security in China is so wide that almost anybody who knows anything can be accused of being a spy.

Nearly eight million books and five million videotapes produced by the sect have been seized in just two cities. Ten managers of printing presses have been arrested for turning out Gongist texts. The State Council has warned civil servants and workers at state-owned enterprises that they will be 'severely penalised' if they are practitioners. Inveighing against an 'anti-society, anti-science and anti-human-being' movement, Jiang Zemin compares it to the Branch Davidians of the United States and the Aum Shinri Kyo in Japan, and blames it for the deaths of more than 1,400 people, for driving others insane and for ruining families.

Broadening their campaign, the authorities have generally banned people from carrying out slow-moving, deep-breathing *qi gong* exercises in streets, railway and bus stations, government and military establishments, ports, schools and other 'important public places'. Qi gong groups must register with the authorities, and can only operate in small local units.

Officials say they are just after Falun Gong leaders, and will be lenient with the rank-and-file. Though the authorities in one part of Guangdong province have adopted a gentle approach by encouraging elderly practitioners to take up traditional dance and shadow boxing instead, police behaviour elsewhere shows what leniency means in Chinese terms. Three thousand practitioners have been detained in Beijing alone this week. Hundreds of police, in uniform and plain clothes, are patrolling Tiananmen Square. Some of those taken away in police buses have been kept in custody; some have been handed over to provincial security forces who have come to the capital to move them to regional detention centres. Still others have been driven to the outskirts of town and dumped there after being told never to return.

About 100 women have been punished in the north; according to a Hong Kong human rights group, twelve school teachers in the founder's home province of Jilin have been sent to labour camps. In neighbouring Liaoning province, a former senior housing official hanged himself after fasting in protest at the clampdown; his Communist party membership was removed posthumously. Elsewhere, functionaries have been told their performances will be judged on how well they wipe out the influence of sects.

In the capital, police are busy raiding shops for subversive Falun Gong literature, and combing small lodging houses for practitioners. Hotel operators who put them up are fined. Falun Gong practitioners report that a hostile article from the *People's Daily* has been posted on their websites in Europe. One man in New York says hacking has been traced back to the Public Security Bureau. In Shandong province, police stage a street bonfire of Gongist books and posters, while railway authorities in the south have taken to searching the luggage of passengers for sect literature or tapes.

The rhetoric from the official media reaches a frenzied volume. Beijing television warns that if Falun Gong had been allowed to continue freely, all the economic reforms would have been stopped. The Xinhua news agency calls the sect's challenge 'unprecedented in the history of the People's Republic in terms of the size of its organisation, its influence, number of illegal publications as well as the damages it brought to the society'.

A small group of practitioners bravely holds a clandestine press conference in Beijing, and insists that China's leaders would realise the merits of their beliefs if they only knew the truth. 'We just want a peaceful place in which to practise,' says a man from Fujian province. Two of those giving the press conference are former policemen. They say they were forced to choose between keeping their jobs and following the Falun Gong.

The American media report widely on the crackdown, and a row erupts when police question five reporters, including two Americans, who attended the press conference. Their credentials and residence permits are confiscated on the grounds that they violated regulations. President Jiang is angry: more than 1,000 police have been deployed to track the conference's location to a small Buddhist temple in the suburbs of the capital.

Whatever the truth about the Falun Gong, there is no doubt that China is home to more than its share of charlatans, nor of the extent of their appeal. Another group hit by police this month was founded by a former peasant who claimed to be able to see through solid objects and hear heavenly voices. He is said to have run sixty centres in twenty-two provinces, including an outfit called the China School of Supernatural Powers in Sichuan with more than 10,000 students. Then there is a newspaper report about the founder of a different sect, with a mere 900 followers, who promised he could help adherents reach enlightenment if they had sex with him, and raped at least four women. In Hunan province, a court has sentenced to death a self-proclaimed resurrected god who presented himself as a supreme being able to lead his followers to salvation. Disciples from fifteen provinces gathered for a congress he held in 1997. 'Nowadays, people blindly believe in gods and spirits,' he was quoted as saying. 'If you flaunt a divine banner, people believe in you and are willing to dedicate everything they have to you.' Growing rich, he bought expensive suits, a motorcycle and several mobile telephones. He also took some young women followers to bed. In his confession, he ruminated: 'If I were a god, would I be here today?'

Hong Kong is drawn into the repression of the Falun Gong in a minor but unexpected way. Like many other SAR firms, paging companies have moved a lot of their operations across the border where staff are cheaper. But it emerges that one paging outfit is not passing on messages which mention the Falun Gong. A company supervisor says that may be due to human error, transmission failure or reception problems. Or perhaps to staff on the mainland having heard about the ban on the sect and deciding that discreet censorship is the better part of valour.

The whole saga is adding to complaints about China's human rights record and its persecution of the home church movement. The Clinton administration makes its concern known, and the Senate Foreign Affairs Committee has adopted a resolution calling for an immediate end to repression of religious groups. Naturally, that brings a rejoinder from Beijing expressing 'strong resentment and firm opposition' to such a 'flagrant interference in China's internal affairs'. What a strange turn of events if a deep-breathing movement started by a clerk in a grain organisation now living in Queens ends up by causing more havoc for the regime than all the dissidents in China.

November

1 *November*

Mou Qizhong, once a star of the mainland business world, is on trial in the city of Wuhan. Ten years ago, he shot to fame by bartering 500 railway wagons full of food, clothes, shoes, thermos flasks and other products for four Russian passenger planes which he sold to China's Sichuan Airlines in a US$150 million deal. His motto was 'There is nothing in the world that can't be done, only that which can't be thought of.' *Forbes* magazine named him as the fourth wealthiest man in the mainland. He was going to blow a 48-kilometre-wide gap through the Himalayas to change the climate in north-west China so that arid land would sprout crops, dam great rivers to provide water supplies, lease Russian rockets to Western communications firms, and develop the fastest computer chip in the world. He claimed to be able to raise enormous sums in the West to buy into 13,000 state companies, and was going to build a 'Hong Kong of the north' on the Russian border.

Now, Mou is accused of having used phoney documents to obtain US$75 million in foreign currency. He is alleged to have got the money through a state import-export company in Hubei province which pretended to have imported goods and presented a local state bank with thirty-three credit documents. The bank issued foreign currency against the certificates. The import-export firm passed the money to Mou, with suitable greasing of palms in return.

His career epitomises the mainland's get-rich-quick tycoons who use political connections and bribery to borrow large sums from state banks and companies. Born beside the Yangtze in 1941 to the maid of his father's third wife, Mou was sentenced to death for a book he wrote during the Cultural Revolution, but was saved from execution by Mao's death and the subsequent policy switches. After building up a business by buying and selling clocks from the military, he spent another year in prison for speculative activities, but was able to borrow 7 million yuan in 1984 to launch the investment company that clinched the airliner barter.

In 1989, the bombastic Mou, a short man with a round head and deep forehead who bears more than a passing resemblance to Mao, denounced the demonstrators in Tiananmen Square before the outcome of the confrontation was evident. That won him points with the regime. He was singled out for praise in the official media and photographed with national leaders: like American executives, upwardly mobile Chinese love to show off snaps of themselves with those in power. Apart from anything else, it makes getting loans from state banks so much easier.

Mou traded on his connections for a US$75 million letter of credit from the Bank of China branch in Wuhan to import computers. In fact, the money went to finance a scheme to launch satellites on rockets from China's Central Asian neighbour of Kazhakstan. Mou does not seem to have made anything from the project. In fact, he was plunging further and further into debt. Eventually, three lieutenants welshed on him. Although his passport was confiscated, he tried to leave the country but was stopped at Beijing airport and charged with fraud.

According to one newspaper, Mou wrote a letter to the authorities after his arrest proclaiming that he and he alone could 'do in the East what oil barons and steel kings did in the West this century'. He also claimed to have an agreement to sell 5,000 tonnes of gold for a British company that would have earned him US$20 million. A best-selling book entitled *Great Swindler of the Mainland* quoted some of his business tips, among them: 'Use one daughter to marry eight men [i.e. borrow from eight banks for the same project]' and the more familiar 'If you owe the bank 10,000 yuan, you are their grandson. If you owe them 10 million, you are their grandfather.' The fraud charges could land him in jail for life.

2 November

Hong Kong's Disneyland agreement is signed. The Chief Executive poses with people in Mickey and Minnie Mouse costumes at Government House. 'I wish it was Confucius he was embracing,' says the businessman and socialite, David Tang. The government hopes the 125-hectare site will boost economic activity by as much as 1 per cent, and attract crowds of tourists. But the taxpayers will foot most of the bill. The deal is undoubtedly popular. Still, it is being presented as an infrastructure project just in case anybody gets the idea that the government is switching to an interventionist course.

4 November

Small and doll-like, with a helmet of black hair, Nina Wang could be a figure from a tableau. Standing in the middle of a reception given by a French bank tonight, she says her aluminium handbag is very useful for beating off attackers. Dressed in a bright red and green designer Chinese outfit with pointed shoes and a red clip in her hair, she laughs at her own joke. The crowd in the ballroom of the J. W. Marriott hotel gives her the celebrity-look once-over. She is one of those Hong Kong people everybody has heard of, but few have actually seen in the flesh. 'Is that Nina Wang?' says one. 'I thought she wore plastic mini-skirts.'

That was the Nina of old. In the days when she was ranked as the fourth richest woman in the world, she was famous for her short red vinyl skirts and bobby socks. In those days, with her hair in plaits, she bore more than a passing resemblance to a late-middle-aged version of the Icelandic songstress Björk. Short and feisty, rejoicing in the Cantonese nickname of Little Sweet Sweet, Nina has always cut an unusual figure in the buttoned-down male business world. Tonight, attended by a silent, smiling director of her company, she giggles a lot, but is no longer the tearaway who was photographed disco-dancing, and told her husband, Teddy Wang Teh-huei, that she would only join the board of his family firm if she could bring along her German shepherd dog.

Nina has built up quite an empire, not only in Hong Kong, but also in the mainland, the United States, Taiwan and Britain, where she owns a golf course and was involved in an unsuccessful pub game scheme. At one point, she planned to build a 522 metre-high Nina Tower in Kowloon. In America, she gave US$50,000 to the Clinton Birthplace Foundation to help restore the President's boyhood home in Hope, Arkansas. She also donated US$7 million to the Kennedy School of Government at Harvard to pay for courses for Chinese officials and soldiers. But she has just failed in a major cause – preventing her father-in-law from declaring her husband dead.

The Wang fortune was based on a business called Chinachem which her father-in-law started in Shanghai before the Communist victory. Moving to Hong Kong, Chinachem grew into the territory's biggest privately held property concern. In 1983 her husband hit the headlines for a different reason when he was grabbed by kidnappers and stuffed into a refrigerator in a flat near the old airport. Nina handed over a ransom of HK$85 million. Teddy was freed. The kidnappers were arrested and jailed.

Nina's husband went back to business, and made himself Hong Kong's fifteenth richest man, with a fortune estimated at HK$15 billion. Despite the kidnapping, he didn't bother to employ bodyguards. There were those who said he was too mean to spend the money. Instead, according to a story I was told by somebody who had known him, he had a radio transmitter embedded into the heel of his shoe so that he could always be traced. But he was grabbed again in 1990. The transmitter was useless: the kidnappers made him take off his fancy footwear before they forced him on to a fishing boat that headed out to sea. Had they been tipped off, my informant asked breathlessly; was this an inside job of some kind?

On the boat, Teddy was trussed up in a net with a metal weight attached to his feet. The kidnappers contacted Nina, who paid over some HK$260 million as a first instalment. She never saw her husband again.

So long as Teddy was not declared dead, his last known will could not be executed. This was a matter of some importance for Nina since she did not figure in it. To prevent her father-in-law gaining control of his son's estate, Nina had to disprove the idea that her husband was dead. This was a bit tricky, since a member of the kidnap gang had testified that over tea one day, a man he called 'the chief' had told him that the captive had been thrown overboard while the boat was being chased in Chinese waters by mainland frontier guards. But Nina insisted that Teddy had contacted her after the second kidnapping. She also claimed that he had given her power of attorney back in 1963, and had drawn up a new will after a riding accident. She spoke of a sealed envelope which might contain this fresh will. But nobody has found the envelope or the new will.

Now, after a hearing in chambers, Teddy's father, a frail old man wearing a beret, who has to be helped into court by two aides, is given authority to declare his son dead. So the will which does not name Nina can be executed. When I mention this to her at tonight's reception, she laughs and says something about the story not being over yet. Whatever happens, Nina is another of Hong Kong's high-level survivors, aluminium handbag and all.

5 November

Colonial days may have gone, but even the best known of the main-land 'princelings' in Hong Kong can get caught up in controversies in the former sovereign power. Larry Yung is quite a figure in the SAR, a well-built, immaculately dressed man with greying hair who is a prominent racehorse owner and keen golfer. More important, he is the son of a former Vice-President, Rong Yiren, who may be the richest man in the mainland at the head of a business empire called China International Trust and Investment Company, or Citic. The family were rich industrialists before the Communists won power, and decided to remain in China. Rong Yiren worked with Deng Xiaoping to open up the mainland market. He set up Citic in 1978.

His son runs its local offshoot, Citic Pacific, which is one of the biggest investors in the SAR. Among many other things it has a large stake in Cathay Pacific and Dragon Air airlines. In a rare interview before the handover, Yung said that the danger for Hong Kong was that greedy people would come down from the north and try to grab Hong Kong's wealth. That has not happened, but Citic has put up a shiny building by the harbour on the site of an old British naval base to show that it is here to stay. The *South China Morning Post*'s biggest shareholder, the Kuok group, has a substantial holding in Yung's firm, and occupies floors 20 to 22 of Citic Tower.

Yung's 19 per cent stake in Citic is worth US$1 billion. He has a spread in Vancouver, and spent an estimated US$7.5 million buying Harold Macmillan's 335 acre estate, Birch Grove, in East Sussex, complete with its own golf course and shooting grounds, where he slips on the mantle of a country gentleman for a few weeks each year. What would be more normal than for such a man to contribute money to a British rural organisation? Last month, Nick Rufford of the *Sunday Times* reported that Yung had given up to US$1 million to the Countryside Alliance, which is challenging plans to ban fox hunting. The *South China Morning Post* picked up the story. Yung was not pleased. Senior executives from the newspaper were called to the Citic offices to be told that the story was incorrect. As though Yung couldn't speak for himself, the Jockey Club wrote a letter to the *Post* saying that this prominent member denied having given money to the Alliance. Today the *Post* runs an item on page two noting that Yung has stated that he has not contributed to the Countryside Alliance and has not been involved in promoting its activities. The *Sunday Times* makes no apology.

6 November

The Hong Kong government has started to unload its shares in the territory's biggest public offering. After a major publicity blitz, more than HK$22 billion has been subscribed to a fund called TraHK, known as the Tracker, which contains a slice of the shares bought by the administration fourteen months ago to defend the currency. The offer has been sweetened with discounts and a loyalty premium. Pundits worry that it will draw liquidity out of the market, and that it does not include soaraway technology stocks. But the public has scented a bargain, and that is enough. After Disneyland, another boost to public confidence.

9–16 November

A thirteen-year saga is reaching its moment of truth in a huge, bleak building in Beijing. A ten-strong team from Washington sits behind a long brown wooden table at the Ministry of Foreign Trade and Economic Cooperation (Moftec). Opposite, the Chinese delegation is at an identical brown wooden table. Between them stands a row of potted plants. The two delegation leaders, sitting in the middle of their teams, are a study in physical contrast – the thin, intense Charlene Barshefsky with her trademark scarf round her neck, and the rotund, balding trade minister, Shi Guangsheng. Bill Clinton's economic adviser, Gene Sperling, is in the US delegation as a sign of how deeply the President is committed. At Shi's side is a serious-looking bespectacled man with a neat parting in his jet black hair: Long Yongtu has been involved in these negotiations from the start.

The subject at issue is American backing for China's membership of the World Trade Organisation, the body that sets the rules of international commerce. On the table are issues such as access to mainland markets, US quotas on imports of textile goods and how many years China can continue to be treated as a developing country. The implications go much deeper. China's economic reformers see WTO membership as a key element in pushing their programme. As well as forcing major changes in the financial and industrial structure to accord with what are essentially American-dictated ways of running an economy, membership would mean the mainland becoming subject to regulations set elsewhere, and to the rule of law. The Chinese would want to start availing themselves of freedoms granted to foreigners while competition from more advanced economies would lead to millions more workers being thrown out of jobs, initially at least. So conservatives like former Premier Li Peng take a leery view of joining the high church of globalisation, not only for its economic effects but for the threat it poses to the power structure built up since 1949. For its part, the United States could live without Beijing getting a seat at the WTO. But the benefits for American companies of a major opening-up of the Chinese market would be enormous, and agreement would be a great foreign policy prize for a president who needs as many laurels as he can gather in his last year in the White House. So the outcome of the Barshefsky–Shi talks at Moftec will mean much more than the easing of textile quotas or the lifting of limits on how many Hollywood films can be shown in Beijing or Shanghai.

This is not simply a Sino-US matter: the other members of the WTO will have to sign up to any agreement to let China enter the organisation. But if the Americans get a deal for themselves, and establish normal trading relations with the mainland, nobody believes the Europeans or anybody else would scupper a comprehensive arrangement for Chinese membership. Time presses because ministers from the WTO nations meet in Seattle at the end of this month to draw up the guidelines for a new round of world trade talks.

It has been a rough seven months since Bill Clinton pulled the rug from under Zhu Rongji in April. The President's regrets for what he had done were swamped by Kosovo, the bombing of the Chinese embassy in Belgrade and the tension over Taiwan and human rights, plus the allegations of Chinese spying on US nuclear secrets. In the late summer, however, Clinton sent Senator Diane Feinstein of California to deliver a handwritten letter to Jiang Zemin suggesting the resumption of WTO talks. A Chinese delegation visiting Washington gave a positive response. The President wrote again, and again got a good reply. When he and Jiang met in the early autumn at the Asia-Pacific summit in New Zealand, Clinton pressed the case for new WTO talks. Jiang agreed that the negotiators should convene.

The Chinese leader played a characteristically careful and calculating game, edging forward but avoiding giving the conservatives in Beijing a stick with which to beat him. Zhu had put himself out on a limb in the spring and suffered badly as a result. It is not in Jiang's nature to take any such risk, even if he can see that an agreement could burnish his place in history.

So when the negotiators Barshefsky and Shi met in Auckland the day after the session between their two presidents, the Chinese took a harsh line, halving the offers made by Zhu in some vital areas. Barshefsky ruled out any easing of Washington's demands: 'It's all up to China now,' she said.

Beijing went silent. Undeterred, Clinton telephoned Jiang on 16 October to draw attention to the looming WTO deadline. The Chinese leader said he was about to embark on a trip to Europe, North Africa and Saudi Arabia, and would reply when he returned. But he did not do so, playing hard-to-get like any object of desire.

Showing his persistence as a suitor, Clinton took the unusual step of sending a set of position papers to Beijing outlining six concessions which the US was ready to make. There was still no response. At the end of October, the new Treasury Secretary, Lawrence Summers, travelled to Lanzhou, capital of northern Gansu province, where a session of the Sino-US economic committee was being held. At a meeting with Zhu, Summers said Washington did not regard China's huge trade surplus with the US as an immediate problem, but that China really did need to open up its markets before long and that there was only a month left for WTO agreement.

On 6 November, Clinton was back on the telephone for a 45-minute conversation. Jiang indicated that an agreement should be possible. He is said to have got Politburo agreement that a deal could be made on three conditions: that China should enter the WTO as a developing nation with all the accompanying advantages of such status, that foreign access to finance and service industries would be gradual, and that the US would open its textile market and reject quotas.

Two days after Clinton's second call, Barshefsky's team fly to Beijing. They tell reporters they aim to wrap up the talks in a couple of days. They arrive amid some good omens for Sino-US relations: a new American ambassador has been approved and Beijing has agreed that the command ship of the Seventh Fleet can visit Hong Kong in December. But the planned two days turn into an epic knife-edge marathon of tough talking and shadow boxing during which neither side gets much sleep – one of the American team is said not to have closed his eyes throughout, though the Chinese have the bonus of being able to relax in sitting rooms at the ministry. The US delegation also has to contend with the thirteen-hour time difference with Washington. But no sign of weakness can be allowed. At one point, Barshefsky is seen to be nodding off over a meal. When a waitress jogs her elbow, she retorts: 'I'm awake.' She and Clinton's adviser, Sperling, seek solace in music, beginning each day by deciding on a song for the day. Among those they choose are 'Please Release Me', 'Ain't No Mountain High Enough' and 'Oklahoma'. They might have done better with 'The Long and Winding Road'.

Day One: At the opening session, Sperling refers to his own presence as a sign of the historic nature of the opportunity ahead of them. In April, he had been among those who counselled Clinton not to accept Zhu's offers. For China, Shi Guangsheng repeats the cliché about this being 'a win-win situation' for all concerned. After opening pleasantries, the two sides turn to financial markets and services.

Day Two: Sperling tells reporters that the talks are more substantial and more detailed than before. China has accepted the six concessions which Clinton sent in October. But it wants more. The negotiations are extended for an additional day. Everybody feels happy. Stock markets rise. In Hong Kong, a rumour spreads that a pro-Beijing newspaper has reserved a full page for the next day's edition for an important announcement. The guessing is that it will be about a WTO deal. It turns out to be a property advertisement.

Day Three: The climate changes abruptly as journalists stamp in the winter cold outside the Moftec building and the US embassy. A meeting scheduled for the morning is put off till the afternoon at Chinese request. The embassy tells reporters Barshevsky is 'discouraged'. At the ninety-minute afternoon session, the Chinese produce a new set of demands. Barshefsky looks grim as she rides off in an imported Lincoln limousine.

The vital telecommunications sector is one sticking point: China insists on limiting foreign ownership to 49 per cent, but the Americans want to be entitled to 51 per cent, as offered by Zhu. Another major difficulty concerns video and audio entertainment: the Americans want a much freer ride for Hollywood and US music companies than China is willing to concede. The two sides are also some way apart on mainland exports of textile goods.

'We came here hoping to make progress,' says Barshefsky. 'We are discouraged that progress has not been made at this point.' A spokesman says she will fly home in the morning. The White House spokesman briefs reporters that the talks are over. Still, the lights remain on into the night at the Moftec building, and Trade Minister Shi stays in his office. All is not quite as it appears: sources say a draft agreement has been shown to President Jiang who has approved it. Barshefsky asks to see Zhu Rongji. If this is refused, the US side will take it as a sign that the main proponent of a deal on the Chinese side has been sidelined, and so they might as well leave.

Day Four: Shi telephones Barshefsky at the Palace Hotel at 3 a.m. He urges her not to leave. An hour later, she is at Moftec. Then she is invited to meet Zhu in the leadership compound. This is, in Sperling's word, 'pivotal'. Barshefsky asks for a clear indication that China wants an agreement. Zhu says he wishes the negotiations to go on, that time is not limited, and that he seeks progress which will not put too great a penalty on the Chinese people.

Day Five: In the morning, it is all frowns. Both sides lay on the atmospherics, if only to let the world know the hill they are climbing. Neither the hardliners in Beijing nor the Republicans in Washington will be able to say that their side was a push-over. At one point, the US team leaves an Italian restaurant through the kitchen, going out of the back door to avoid the media. Their mobile telephones are switched off, and they let it be known that they are packing their bags for the second time. *China Daily* reports that the problem is the US is demanding too much.

Barshefsky and Shi have three meetings lasting a total of four and a half hours. After each, the Americans drive back to the embassy to confer with Washington. At one point, seven pizzas are brought round on delivery scooters. 'I feel like an expectant mother,' says Clinton, who has left the US for a visit to Turkey. In Hong Kong, Martin Lee writes to him backing China's membership, saying it would help the development of the legal system on mainland. His letter is distributed to Republicans, who regard him as a guiding light of freedom.

Day Six: The Americans cancel their breakfast booking to arrive early at Moftec. The Chinese are still obdurate. Barshefsky gives them 'an exceptionally strong response'. China's former Trade Minister, Wu Yi, a key Zhu ally, approaches her to say, 'Premier Zhu is here and he wants to talk.' Vice-Premier Qian Qichen is also on hand. The Chinese are ready to deal.

Barshefsky and Sperling see Zhu. Agreement is reached. On telecommunications, they meet halfway. There is also a compromise on video and audio entertainment. China gets an offer it can accept on textiles. The Americans go to the women's toilet to call Clinton in Turkey. It is the most secure place they can think of. But there is a problem at the other end. The President is in the shower. His National Security Adviser, Sandy Berger, goes into the bathroom to tell him a deal has been struck. Clinton takes the telephone. 'We were talking bathroom to bathroom,' Barshefsky says later.

At 1.40 p.m. the semi-official China News Service puts out a story saying that a bilateral agreement was signed ten minutes earlier. Moftec issues a denial. In fact, the Chinese still made a last effort, calling on Barshefsky in her hotel room to try to wring out some final concessions. She tells *Time* magazine she replied: 'Oh please. Too complicated. Can't possibly deal with it. What time is the signing?'

Back at Moftec, Barshefsky, Sperling, Shi Guangsheng and Long Yongtu put their names to the document as reporters rush into the room. An attendant tells the cameramen to get down off the chairs. Barshefsky and Shi clasp hands and smile contentedly. Their aides clap. Barshefsky calls Shi 'my all-time friend'. They are like two boxers who pummel the hell out of one another in the ring and then throw their arms round each other's shoulders in a display of camaraderie. To the television cameras, Sperling calls Barshefsky a 'most skilled and an excellent and smart trade negotiator'. To which she replies: 'I hope my mother's watching.'

Jiang receives Barshefsky in the leadership compound. They are pictured grinning broadly, sitting on dark brown wooden chairs with red flowers on the table between them. The formal signing ceremony in a pavilion at the Zhongnanhai leadership compound is attended by Jiang, Qian Qichen, Wu Yi and Barshefsky. From Turkey, Clinton says that China 'embraces principles of economic openness, innovation and competition that will bolster economic reforms and advance the rule of law'.

Clearly, much of the drama of the past days has been orchestrated at a high level. One report says that when a White House official told the reception desk at the delegation's Palace Hotel early on that the team would be leaving the following day, he was told by the Chinese that the reservation was for six days – exactly how long it took to clinch an agreement. But now the tension and the playing to the gallery evaporates. Jiang is all smiles as he takes Barshefsky on a little tour to show her the view of the lake outside the pavilion. Zhu Rongji is nowhere to be seen.

The deal gets a euphoric reaction in Hong Kong, even though the opening-up of China could pose major problems for the territory in the long term. If the mainland adopts modern commercial and industrial practices, builds up a twenty-first century financial system, develops its services and accepts the rule of law, the SAR's *raison d'être* could be gravely compromised. That, however, is for the day after tomorrow. Right now, shares boom, everybody feels happy and few wait to see the small print.

It is plain that China will not join the WTO in Seattle; the negotiating process over this year has taken too long for that, and agreements still have to be made with the Europeans. But it should be in the organisation in good time to join in the process of hammering out any new world trade deal which will go well into the opening decade of the twenty-first century. At the annual Central Economic Work Conference in Beijing this week, Jiang talks of using foreign capital to boost progress. Government departments are lined up in support, including the formerly recalcitrant telecommunications and agriculture ministries. The National Statistics Bureau produces an amazing instant poll to show that 93 per cent of urban residents followed the negotiations, 94 per cent say China deserves membership and 80 per cent think it will improve their standard of living.

Still, there are already discordant notes. Government departments are studying the deal for the possible infiltration of 'bourgeois-liberal ideas'. *China Business Information Times* notes that technical standards, anti-subsidy and anti-dumping methods could be used to restrict imports in several industries. The bumps on the road to the market were shown last month when the China National Offshore Oil Corporation was forced to withdraw a share offer because foreign banks thought the price was too high. One day after the agreement, the US Commerce Department approves retroactive anti-dumping duties on imports of Chinese apple juice concentrate. The AFL-CIO labour organisation says it will 'wage a full and vigorous campaign' against the agreement because of the threat to American jobs from more Chinese imports.

After their six days on the treadmill, the participants in the negotiations scatter, like rival gangs of cowboys who fight and then make up and ride out of town to their next port of call. The thirteen-year veteran of the WTO beat, Long Yongtu, heads south to Guangzhou to address a set of seminars. Tickets cost 1,500 yuan, but the demand is such that they change hands for 2,500 (US$300). When he speaks at the Sun Yat-sen memorial hall in the city, 3,000 people attend: business is the new song of China and he is one of its stars. Shi, the Trade Minister, goes to Canada to wrap up WTO negotiations with Ottawa. Zhu Rongji starts an official visit to Malaysia, swearing that Beijing 'will unswervingly stick to its programme of reform and opening up, and keep to the road that suits its national conditions'. Barshefsky and Sperling fly to Washington and launch into briefings to laud the deal, which will require Congress to grant China Normal Trading Relations (NTR) status before it can come into effect. Republicans are already making links with human rights. The administration clearly has a fight on its hands in an election year when relations with Beijing may be a factor in the race for the White House.

Though the detailed text of the agreement is not yet available, the broad lines commit China to cut tariffs progressively on both industrial and farm goods. Most changes are staged, but there is no escaping the magnitude of what the mainland has agreed to. Non-tariff quotas are to be abolished within five years. The duty on imported cars will fall from the current 80–100 per cent to 25 per cent by 2006. The oil and petrol market will be opened up. Foreign firms will be able to conduct local currency business. They will be allowed 50 per cent stakes in telecommunications two years after China joins the WTO. Foreign securities will be able to take 49 per cent stakes in joint venture fund management companies three years after accession. Investment in mainland Internet services will be allowed. In return, Washington has shown understanding on China's developing nation status and has given concessions on textiles.

There are some twists in the tale that may be less palatable to foreign investors and go-go mainland entrepreneurs. As a result of the agreement, preferential tax arrangements for overseas firms and for special development zones like Shenzhen will be phased out. That will create a level playing field, but the effect could be devastating as all those overseas Chinese investors find they have to pay as much to the state as domestic industries.

The big question is enforcement. Will China live up to its side of the bargain, or will it slide into non-compliance which will make a mockery of the past week? As sceptics point out, China has been the target of many more dumping complaints from the WTO than any other country.

After the signing ceremonies, Jiang is keeping his counsel. Perhaps he knows that the deal represents more concessions to the foreigners than China has known since the days of the Treaty Ports. There is no great speech to mark the occasion, no symbolic visit to a foreign joint venture factory. Even if he has played his hand brilliantly, the President remains profoundly risk-averse. Given the politics involved, he needs to box clever to keep his position on top of whatever transpires. So the great weathervane of the People's Republic makes a contradictory statement, insisting that reform will continue but extolling communist orthodoxy as he seeks to limit the dangers of this huge leap into the dark. Still, in the end, the leap has been made, and if it is carried through, China will never be the same again.

12 *November*

As a sign that economic reform does not signify any let-up in the control of the party and the state, trials of Falun Gong practitioners have started in Hainan province. A local sect leader who is accused of using the cult to violate the law, instigating protests and escaping from police custody gets twelve years. Three others are sent to prison for between two and seven years. The trial is televised in prime time. The presenter warns that 'anybody who violates the interests of the masses will certainly face the legal consequences'. One of the accused, wearing a short-sleeved blouse and with her hair pulled back severely, stares at the judges with a deeply sad expression, like a medieval martyr contemplating her fate.

13 *November*

More signs of recovery in the SAR. Over 5,000 people turn out for the sale of a new block of 550 flats, the biggest buying crowd seen for two years. Police have to use barricades to control them.

16 *November*

Elsewhere in Hong Kong, police are confronting a different kind of crowd, using tear gas against demonstrators armed with iron bars and a machete. One of the protestors holds a cigarette lighter to a gas canister and threatens to blow himself up. Others ignite barricades of flaming furniture and lob Molotov cocktails. Three of the 300 black-helmeted police are set on fire despite their protective Perspex shields and riot gear.

This rare instance of a violent confrontation is over the clearing of a village up towards the mainland border as part of an anti-flooding scheme. The villagers think they are not getting enough compensation or good enough alternative housing. One complains that the quality of the paintwork on the door of his new flat is not up to scratch. After the police, bulldozers go in and most of the houses come down. Villagers who were not arrested spend the night sleeping in the remains of their destroyed houses.

18 November

Another Hong Kong man held on the mainland is released. Peter Leung Wing-sum, forty-two, was kidnapped in Henan province in April after his former Hong Kong employer failed to pay a debt to a mainland ceramics firm. The assumption is that workers from the state-owned enterprise grabbed him. Leung says he was tortured, and fed once every two days as he was moved between different locations. 'It seemed like a movie,' he adds. 'I thought I might be killed if the mainland police failed to arrest the person they wanted [the former mainland manager of the company].' After four months, the manager was caught, and Leung was handed over to the local public security bureau, which held him for three months until an investigation cleared him, and a mainland businessman put up HK$100,000 bail.

The Hong Kong government says his release is a tribute to 'effective communication' between the SAR authorities and the mainland. It claims Leung was found in September thanks to its contacts with the mainland. But by that time, his wife had persuaded the Chinese authorities to allow her to see her husband. Leung says he is now relishing the taste of Coca-Cola and coffee. As he does so, a 36-year-old Hong Kong woman tells of the plight of her husband, a partner in a mainland joint venture to produce parts for television sets, who has been held for a year accused of deception. She has been asked to pay HK$27 million for his release. 'I phoned the government and the Chief Executive's office and asked for help,' she says. 'But they just told me there wasn't much they could do.'

In another case, a Hong Kong man has been arrested because of complaints about the failure of a bankrupt employment agency called Superwealth for which he worked. He was held in the late summer in a town in Guangdong province. Police there asked his relatives in

Hong Kong to pay HK$800,000 for his release. They reduced this to $600,000, which his wife raised by selling a house they owned across the border and borrowing from a finance company. Instead of freeing the man, police took him to a prison in another town where another $1 million was demanded. His wife says there is no question of raising more cash: she is having to borrow money just to support the family. A Public Security Bureau official on the mainland tells the *South China Morning Post*: 'We are acting according to the law.' In Hong Kong, the Security Bureau says it is contacting the mainland authorities, but an official there repeats the line that 'We are acting according to the law.'

There is a happier outcome in a long-running case involving a Chinese–Australian called James Peng who has just been freed from a mainland jail after being held for six years. Peng was abducted from a hotel in Macau in 1993, taken to Shanghai and sentenced to sixteen years. His lawyers say the charges were trumped up as part of a dispute with his business partner, a niece of Deng Xiaoping. His release comes soon after a visit to Australia by President Jiang. The rumour in Hong Kong is that in order not to embarrass either the Portuguese or the Chinese, Peng signed a statement that he had crossed the border from Macau voluntarily.

Beside these businessmen who got into trouble, Wu Man is a more equivocal figure. His case is causing some friction between Britain, China and Thailand, with the SAR keeping its head down. A Hong Kong resident, he is wanted on the mainland for crimes allegedly connected to the Big Spender gang. Like some three million other people in the SAR, Wu holds a travel document called a British National (Overseas) pass, a device used by London when it wanted to avoid granting citizenship but felt it had to save a bit of face by providing Hong Kong residents with something to use when they left home. Wu was travelling on his BNO papers in Thailand when police there picked him up and handed him over to the Chinese. He is currently in jail in Guangdong, where Big Spender was shot a year ago.

John Battle, the British minister with special responsibility for Hong Kong, who happens to be in town today, says the Thai immigration authorities have admitted they made a mistake in not telling the embassy in Bangkok of the arrest. The Chinese contend that Battle is 'completely wrong'. Everything is in order, they insist. All Battle can respond is that he will ask the British embassy in Beijing to make enquiries.

If he goes the same way as Big Spender and the Telford Gardens poisoner, nobody in Hong Kong is going to shed a tear for Wu. But the legislator Emily Lau, a staunch critic of Britain on the passports issue, has written to Tony Blair about the case. As she says: 'It is worrying if Hong Kong residents travelling on BNO passports are assumed to be Chinese and can be picked up in third countries.' The problem for Britain is that its fudge to give Hong Kong people a figleaf after deciding to slam the door on most of them leaves it without a leg to stand on in dealing with the unyielding mainland defence of its legal sovereignty.

And what about the Hong Kong government? Nothing is being heard from that quarter. Even a local deputy to the National People's Congress says the SAR authorities have not done enough to help those detained on the mainland. But the head of the Security Bureau hits back by having lunch with my former colleagues to tell them that the *Post*'s publicity about the detained grandfather, Lok Yuk-sing, and others hindered their release. Lok's own view that the media reports were more helpful than the government is waved aside. Still, his son-in-law e-mails me: 'I am glad to read news on Mr Leung's return to HK. *SCMP* helped not only ours & Mr Leung's families, it actually raised the public & government attention to this kind of unfair treatment to HK citizens. Hopefully we can see more HK citizens to be released in the coming future.' Regina Ip, the tough-cookie Secretary for Security, and I look past one another when our paths cross at a couple of receptions and dinners.

19 *November*

The Christmas decorations are up at Ocean Centre in Kowloon and Christmas songs are on the muzak in Central. For the past four years, I have been a guest at the launch of a big Christmas charity drive. The occasion is broadcast live, and I once got to sing a few bars on the air in company with some Cantopop stars and the Director of Radio-Television Hong Kong. Last year we did it with the Chief Executive's wife, who much enjoys such occasions. The ceremony is always a touch surreal as a children's choir sings of crisp and even snow in a shiny office plaza in the warm Hong Kong night. This year, no longer being editor of the *Post*, I'll miss the pleasure, and so will the RTHK boss, who is off to her new trade job in Tokyo. I doubt if the listeners will mind not hearing my out-of-tune carolling.

20 November

Another spectacular step in China's modernisation – the launching of an unmanned spacecraft. The dome-shaped *Shenzhou*, or 'Magic Vessel', went up on a Long March rocket from a satellite launch centre in north-western Gansu province. It landed twenty-one hours later in Inner Mongolia after orbiting the earth fourteen times. Among the objects inside was the future flag of Macau, dark green with a white floral design and light stars in the centre. Mainland newspapers were delayed to bring readers the news. President Jiang, who gave his personal stamp to the development of a manned space programme in 1992, chose the craft's name. He dons his military uniform to inspect the vessel when it is brought to Beijing. The next big step will be to send up cosmonauts: that seems on the cards for next year.

21 November

This being Sunday, Central is packed with maids. Today is Migrants' Day, and the weekly gathering is enlivened by a show in the bright winter sunshine. There are dances, singing, and sketches about the amahs' lives. One starts by acting out the saga of a young woman going through the formalities before leaving the Philippines. 'Birth certificate, identity certificate, death certificate,' says the commentary, to laughter from the crowd. After she arrives in Hong Kong, her employer puts her to work immediately, scolds her mercilessly and then sacks her for being five minutes late when her bus was delayed.

Another sketch begins with a woman tearfully handing over her daughter to a member of her family before flying to Hong Kong to become a maid; she puts on a piece of cardboard inscribed with the words 'Domestic Helper'. Her pantomime of cooking and cleaning draws fresh laughter from the crowd. There is particular merriment as she mimes the evening chore of taking out the dog with a newspaper in which to collect the animal's droppings. When she has finished her day, two companions join her. One wears a strip of cardboard inscribed 'Child Bride'. The other brings the house down by doing a raunchy bump-and-grind dance from the girlie bars of Wanchai. Then a fourth woman appears with the name of an employment agency on her piece of cardboard. They all grab placards from the ground and parade around to uproarious applause. On the placards are written 'No to 20% tax' – a reference to a proposal to make the amahs pay for cleaning up after them on Sundays. They seem likely to win on that one: as has been pointed out, if people in Hong Kong were forced to pay for cleaning up after them, what would the Cantonese have to contribute for despoiling the environment and littering country parks on Sunday picnics?

22 November

Visiting Beijing, Tung Chee-hwa hears from Zhu Rongji about worries over a loophole in the mainland anti-corruption drive – Hong Kong. Although the SAR is now part of China, there is no extradition agreement between the sovereign power and its region. Any such arrangement would immediately raise concerns that Beijing might haul back dissidents who have found refuge in Hong Kong. What worries Zhu is that the current state of affairs means that mainlanders suspected of corruption or fraud may be skipping across the border, and escaping mainland justice. To prevent that, a rendition agreement is being worked out. However it may help the anti-graft crusade, it is also likely to make some dissidents think about leaving the territory.

23 November

Not a good day for Macau's gangsters. The top Triad in town, Wan Kok-koi, a.k.a. Broken Tooth, is sentenced to fifteen years in jail for belonging to the underworld organisation, money-laundering, loan-sharking and telephone-tapping. Wearing a blue and white striped suit, he smiles and waves as he arrives in court. But when the sentence is announced, he jumps on to a bench and shouts, 'You've taken dirty money. All you guys took bribes. This is the worst verdict of the century.' Wan puts his fingers to his head like a gun and swears. Then he tells his mother: 'Don't cry. Don't be afraid. Steel yourself.'

Security guards click handcuffs on him and take Wan, forty-five, away in a convoy of vehicles to solitary confinement in a windowless cell in a new high-security prison. Relatives and associates in the crowded courtroom shout abuse when the judge announces that property worth millions of dollars seized after his arrest will remain confiscated. Eight of Wan's colleagues are sentenced to between eighteen months and ten years. In Beijing, where a calligrapher has just written the largest-ever Chinese character on a 1,999 square-metre piece of silk to celebrate the impending return of the Portuguese colony, Vice-Premier Qian Qichen calls the verdicts 'good for Macau's stability'.

The following day, a Eurasian former police officer called Artur Chiang Calderon, who is said to have been the *consigliere* of the gang, is sentenced to ten and a half years for criminal association, loan-sharking and illegal gambling. The shaven-headed Calderon, who was born in Peru and was forced out of the Macau police because of his links with Wan, smiles at the judge as the sentence is announced.

At least Wan and Calderon won't lose their lives. Another Macau gang boss who originated from Hong Kong is less fortunate. Found guilty of murder, armed robbery, kidnapping and illegal possession of arms in the neighbouring mainland city of Zhuhai, he is shot later in the day. A similar fate may well await another alleged Triad from Macau, arrested in Guangzhou in connection with the kidnapping of a Hong Kong man by a gang in the Portuguese enclave last year. They are alleged to have grabbed the man from his office, beaten him, bound, gagged and blindfolded him and demanded a ransom of HK$2 million. They eventually settled for HK$300,000 which was later stolen by a member of the gang. When the victim called out for help, he was killed. His body was dismembered and left in a rubbish bin. Nobody questions why a Macau gangster who killed a Hong Kong man is being tried on the mainland. Who cares?

24 November

Hong Kong's richest political party leader stands on the pavement of Garden Road leading from the Central District up towards the Peak where he has his home, waving at motorists returning home this evening. No, James Tien, Chairman of the Liberal Party, is not hitching a lift. In a dark suit with a yellow sash, he is after votes.

Tien is seeking election to Hong Kong's new district councils. Instead of relying on the usual distribution of leaflets, he is out on the streets. There is something faintly ridiculous about this very wealthy businessman waving at cars which thunder past in the dark, most of them unaware of his presence. But Tien needs to win this election. In the past, pro-business Liberals have depended on their connections to gain seats in the legislature for functional constituencies. But now they feel a need for a wider legitimacy. Two other prominent Liberals are also running in the council elections.

The hustings do not come naturally to a party which has been the epitome of U-turns and cosy deals. But Tien's pitch in seeking the Peak seat on the council is that he is a man who can get things done – though many of the inhabitants of the constituency are sufficiently well connected to get things done on their own. Tien reckons he knows 1,000 voters personally, and has also been hitting the telephone to whip up support. Every vote counts as the Liberals flirt with direct democracy.

26 November

We fly to the eastern city of Hangzhou for the opening of an art gallery and to see the city whose huge man-made West Lake makes it one of China's showplaces. Marco Polo found the market here stocked with 'roebuck, partridge, quails, fowls, capons, and so many ducks and geese that more could not be told' as well as red deer, fallow deer, hares and rabbits, giant white pears weighing 10 pounds each, oranges, mandarins, apricots and grapes. The city now has 1.5 million permanent inhabitants and a transient population of 800,000. It is not industrial or commercial on the scale of nearby Shanghai, but it is one of China's richest cities, and high-rise buildings tower at one end of the lake.

The beauty of the local women was such that emperors came here to select concubines. A senior official at the Xinhua office in Hong Kong before the handover used to punctuate dinner conversations by assuring us that there was no better city in China, with the 5.5 kilometre-long lake, a thirteen-storey pagoda, and an intricate set of gardens and temples to the memory of an imperial servant who was traduced and executed after saving his master. The epitaph on his tomb reads: 'If the state officials were not greedy for money and their military counterparts did not flinch at death, the whole country would be at peace.' And, the man from Xinhua liked to add as he raised his glass for yet another toast, the women of Hangzhou were still the most beautiful in the land.

An Indian on the bus in from the airport spends the journey on his mobile, conducting an intense negotiation in his native language between a mainland supplier and his office back in Hong Kong over goods unknown. English words – 'net price', 'final offer', 'best rate' – pepper his side of the conversation. At one point he exclaims, 'The price has gone to a dollar forty,' and snaps the telephone off in exasperation. At the hotel, he is still negotiating on the telephone as he signs in at the reception desk.

The weather is foul. Cold rain, fog and early dusk. My wife says it is a dry run for our return to London in January. After a gallery opening organised by Tung Chee-hwa's sister for a show of paintings by a Chinese artist, we walk along the lakeside to an official dinner for a couple of hundred guests. A sign outside a shop proclaims that it sells 'Antiques and their imitations'. In the restaurant, snakes lie sleeping in a glass case outside the cavernous main dining room. The meal, served by waitresses in mauve costumes, moves through sixteen courses: meats, chicken, lobster, soup, bamboo shoots, a local speciality of chunks of gammon with a thick layer of fat baked in little pots, rabbit cooked with chillis in tinfoil, crab, noodles, vegetables, dumplings, more lobster, salty and sweet consommés, pastries and fruit. To drink, there is beer and tea and rice wine that tastes like tawny port. There are many toasts. An elderly man in a dark suit walks by our table and introduces himself as the director of archaeological relics at the city museum. He hands me a card. It says he is a member of the National People's Congress. I do not ask him what he thinks about the over-ruling of the Court of Final Appeal.

The next morning, we visit the West Lake Dragon Well tea plantation outside the city which produces one of the best green teas in the country, sent to Beijing to be served for the leadership. In the entrance hall, there is a photograph of Queen Elizabeth in a yellow dress with a yellow hat looking as though she has just been bitten. 'She is surprised. Why is the tea so good, she asks,' a guide explains.

We start by being given a demonstration of tea-making (use water which is just below boiling point; put some leaves in the bottom of the glass and pour in a little water – never fill it to begin with since that is like saying goodbye; move the kettle up and down three times as you pour; the guests tap the table with two fingers to express thanks; the same leaves can be used five times during the day). Then we buy four extremely expensive tins of the lightest-coloured 'imperial' leaves. The prices are higher than at the hotel and the airport, but the attendants at the Dragon Well point out that they pack the tins in front of us, whereas elsewhere you might get a covering of good leaves on top and inferior growths below, or simply a counterfeit tin full of old rubbish. As usual, beneficial side effects are mentioned: the tea acts against cholesterol and cancer, and dissolves body fat; the used leaves can be mixed with egg white for a wrinkle-defeating face cream. Dried leaves put into a pillow help with sleep.

That night, we eat with two friends at a vast multi-storey restaurant which epitomises the flash of money in China today. There are thirty tanks in a side room from which to choose fish and lobsters – and the inevitable snake box. A young woman in a long black dress plays light classics at a white grand piano on an island in the middle of a pool of water in the centre of the room. Before taking a break, she glides through 'Auld Lang Syne'. A wedding party spends the evening taking photographs of one another. When I put my jacket on the back of the chair, a waitress hurries up and protects it with a plastic cover. The noise is enormous. Everybody seems to be having a good time. It is like a boisterous Saturday night in Kowloon.

In the street outside, the taxi drives off while one of our friends still has a foot on the ground. The driver laughs and says, 'No problem.' Back at the hotel, an elderly flautist is playing 'Ave Maria' in a bar decorated with photographs of Richard Nixon and lesser luminaries who have visited Hangzhou. Elsewhere in the city, four members of the China Democracy Party are reported to have been sentenced to between five and eleven years in jail for subversion. Among their crimes was the posting of information about their movement on an Internet bulletin board.

28 November

In the elections for Hong Kong's new district councils, the Democrats increase their seats from 75 to 83, but the real winner is the pro-Beijing DAB, which increases its representation from 37 to 83. In a telephone conversation, Martin Lee says he was about to call the result a defeat for the Democrats, but decided on second thoughts to describe it simply as 'a pass'. After all, they still got more votes than any other party.

The Liberal leader, James Tien, is rewarded for his waving from the pavement by being elected on the Peak. However, one of his best-known colleagues is surprisingly defeated, which may give the party second thoughts about plunging into popular elections.

The Democrats made some tactical mistakes during the campaign, and were hit by their stance over the rule of law which made it seem as though they are in favour of massive immigration from the main-land. Lee also complains about the large amounts of money he says the DAB is getting from donors who see it as a pro-administration group – a view which is borne out when the party indulges in some extraordinary voting U-turns in the Legislative Council to prevent the government from being defeated. It is clear that party politics in Hong Kong is now a two-horse race. Not, of course, that this reduces the overwhelming power of the executive.

The new councils replace two separate local government bodies which tarnished their reputations by their inept handling of crises such as the bird flu outbreak, and were stigmatised for the junkets undertaken by their members. But the new system represents a further dilution of democracy, since 100 members of the councils will be appointed by the administration.

A poll by the Hong Kong Transition project shows satisfaction with Tung dropping from 46 to 39 per cent, the lowest since the handover. Another poll has him at 56 per cent but this is still the lowest in the records of that survey. Dissatisfaction with the government rises from 46 to 53 per cent.

30 November

The right-wing, free-market Heritage Foundation from the United States comes to town with reassuring news for Hong Kong. The SAR is once again hailed as the world's freest economy. Last year, there was a warning that Singapore might be about to take the title. But a senior SAR official at the award dinner whispers that Hong Kong has acquainted the Foundation with various interventionist aspects of the way the Lion City is run.

The dinner in a French brasserie in the Conrad Hotel is an occasion for high-level celebration. As well as Tung Chee-hwa, the Chief Secretary and the Financial Secretary attend. One understands their pleasure. Still, there is something ironic about the award after the government's intervention in the stock market, the decision to go to Beijing to overrule the Court of Final Appeal, the Cyberport deal with Li Ka-shing's son, and the administration's assumption of the main role in financing Disneyland. Any of these may be defended, but when they are added to the government's ownership of all land and the pervasive presence of cartels, one wonders at the persuasive power of a flat 15 per cent income tax on the prophets of economic liberty.

Few local figures are ready to touch on such questions. But the night after the Heritage award, a thoughtful local businessman, Robert Dorfman, raises the eyebrows of his audience in a speech at another dinner in the Mandarin Hotel which enunciates a home truth the 'freest economy in the world' does not like to hear.

'Hong Kong's domestic marketplace is dominated by restrictive practices, especially in areas which impact on people's daily lives,' he says. 'Apart from the well-publicised areas like property, this is also true of many professional services, important parts of the retail sector, petroleum products and on policy on parallel imports. The reaction from established groups to innovators has often been to use their power to stifle the competitive threat rather than seeking to emulate and outdo it. We do not always practise the free-market principles we preach.

'Hong Kong is a community that has thrived on change. But there are formidable obstacles – such as a refusal to acknowledge openly that the problem of cartelised markets exists. Prominent interest groups – including the government in the case of the property market – are understandably reluctant to change a system that has served them well.'

But when I ask the main author of the Heritage Foundation report about the less than free market developments of the past year, and the underlying matters of land ownership and cartels, he pauses over his veal to say that his organisation could not detect a pattern.

DECEMBER

1 December

On the mainland, advertisements advocating the use of condoms fall foul of the law. The cartoons transmitted on state television show a contraceptive locked in combat with the Aids virus and other sexually transmitted diseases. The captions read, 'Avoid unwanted pregnancies' and 'Use a condom, no trouble.' The mainland has some 400,000 HIV carriers. But the State Advertisment Law rules that sex products cannot be advertised, so the cartoons are withdrawn. The organiser of the campaign, the Family Planning Propaganda and Education Centre, says it understands the decision.

3 December

The Court of Final Appeal delivers its verdict in the latest case involving the rights of migrants to settle in Hong Kong. As expected, the government wins this time, avenging its defeat in January. More important, bowing to the verdict from Beijing, the court recognises the right of China's National People's Congress to do as it wishes in interpreting the Basic Law, and to do so retrospectively to 1 July 1997. The rule of law in Hong Kong has now been made subject to the rule of a political body made up of people approved by the central regime. That is a bad enough attack on one country, two systems, but much worse is that this has been brought about with the active complicity of the government in Hong Kong. The United Nations Human Rights Committee in its first report on the SAR since the handover says it is 'seriously concerned' at the implications for judicial independence of the administration going to the NPC. The interpretation 'could be used in circumstances that undermine the right of a fair trial'. Or, as I write in a column in the *Post*, the recognition by the Court of Final Appeal of the unqualified right of the National People's Congress to interpret the Basic Law consolidates the most fundamental and dangerous shift in the short life of the SAR. The fact that it was widely expected should not be allowed to mask its significance.

Ever since the Joint Declaration in 1984, there was a general assumption that the courts of Hong Kong would continue to enjoy primacy, with the Court of Final Appeal taking the place of the Privy Council at the apex of the structure. Article Two of the Basic Law assured the SAR of 'independent judicial power, including that of final adjudication'. This was seen as key to the fifty-year guarantee of Hong Kong's system and way of life.

For those who lamented the turning back of the democratic clock on 1 July, the Basic Law appeared to provide comfort in the continuation of the rule of the law. Article Eight specified that the maintenance of laws in force in Hong Kong meant the common law. Now all this has been thrown into jeopardy. The comforting belief that if the NPC did exercise its powers on interpretation it would do so only on matters involving the mainland has been cast into doubt by the unqualified nature of the authority recognised by the Court of Final Appeal today. A mainland academic, Professor Wang Lei from Beijing University, says that any citizen has the right to ask for interpretation. So we could find losing parties in disputes between Hong Kong companies or individuals trying to approach the NPC.

They might get short shrift. That is beside the point. What matters is that the court meant to be Hong Kong's supreme judicial organ now acknowledges itself to be subject to appeal to a mainland political body. It is hard to see how this can be anything less than a major change in the system that was meant to be maintained until 2047.

That raises the intriguing thought that the judgment may itself be in contravention of the Basic Law. One can imagine the outcry from Beijing if Chris Patten had gone to the House of Commons to over-rule a Privy Council verdict against him. That would not have happened under the pre-handover system, so its equivalent should not happen now if the Basic Law is to be respected. But we know that the government has driven a cart and horses through a fundamental element in the system it should be preserving for the good of Hong Kong. The criteria for reference to the NPC promised by senior officials in the summer have not materialised – and it is hard to forget the assertion by a senior legal officer that reference can be made before, during or after a case. This leaves Hong Kong in a state of maximum peril, under arbitrary decisions by the government and with final adjudication no longer, in effect, in the hands of a local court, but subject to the dictates of Beijing's parliament.

The Basic Law was meant to remove doubts and to provide solid foundations for vital elements in Hong Kong's life and prosperity. Instead, the process started by the government after the January right of abode verdict has led to a significant moving of the goal posts, with all the attendant uncertainties. Whatever the administration says, the power of the executive over the judicial process has now been asserted and accepted. Is a change as fundamental as that not in contravention of the Basic Law?

The court is also hearing another major case which the government's lawyer, Gerard McCoy, says 'may be a defining moment in our constitutional law'. At issue is the action of two men who were con-victed of desecrating the Chinese and SAR flags after they cut a hole in the middle of the SAR emblem, blacked out the stars on the national flag with ink, and wrote the Chinese character for 'shame' on both during a procession from Victoria Park to Central on 1 January 1998. Their conviction was based on legislation rushed through immediately after the handover. The magistrate said flags were 'sacred' symbols of a nation which should remain respected by all Chinese regardless of their social, political or philosophical beliefs. But an appeal court then found that the laws were unconstitutional because they contravened international human rights agreements to which

Hong Kong is a signatory. The government says that laws protecting symbols of state over-ride the right to freedom of speech set out in the Basic Law, and that the rights of the community as a whole must be considered as well as the rights of individuals. Its barrister also extends his argument to claim that freedom of expression does not extend 'to allow you to be contemptuous of the Chief Executive in his existence as head of the SAR'. Counsel for the two men calls the government's argument 'the start to the road of destroying freedom of speech as we know it in Hong Kong because there is no limit to it. Once you start by saying that the state has the power to protect its symbols, you don't stop at the flag.'

Again, the court finds for the government. What takes many people aback is that the scholarly, reasonable Chief Justice quotes at length in his judgment from the sayings of Jiang Zemin. To which the chairman of the Basic Law Drafting Committee adds that the five stars on the SAR flag 'symbolise the fact that all Hong Kong compatriots love their motherland'.

But there is another point of view which is highly relevant, even if it would be seen as deeply subversive across the border. 'What if the flag itself is the message?' asks a column by a constitutional law professor, Yash Ghai, in the *Hong Kong Standard*. The Chinese national flag is the flag of the Communist revolution. 'One could say, unkindly but not inaccurately, that the Chinese national flag is the symbol of a political party, one moreover which has never been popularly elected in free and fair elections,' Yash Ghai goes on. So what sanctity does such a symbol have in a place where a different system is meant to hold sway?

9 December

Hong Kong's Antiquities Advisory Board has decided to allow an 850-year-old village in Kowloon to be razed to make way for a commercial development by Li Ka-shing's Cheung Kong company. The decision comes after a long fight to save one of the last relics of the rural past. The village of low houses and a red-tiled temple is already hemmed in by skyscrapers. Apart from the merits of preserving history, the decision flies in the face of a plan by the Tourist Authority to build up the

SAR's heritage appeal. But the Board decided that many of the village houses were too dilapidated to be suitable for preservation. Rather than suggesting repairs, it calls for detailed records to be kept of the village so that they may be used in a future development. In a Disneyland theme park, perhaps.

10 *December*

The WTO agreement with Washington has done nothing to make Jiang Zemin less suspicious of the United States. Today, he and Boris Yeltsin wind up a summit in Beijing with a ringing declaration against foreign interference on human rights. The Russian president expresses support for 'China's principled stand on Taiwan' and Russia is reported to have agreed to sell Beijing fighter jets worth US$1 billion. Jiang says that the impending return of Macau will make the Taiwan issue 'more pressing'.

And on the trade front, the collapse of the WTO's ministerial meeting in Seattle under the twin impact of hostile demonstrations and yawning differences between governments raises the question of just what kind of organisation China has signed up to join. The demonstrators have got Beijing in their sights. The main planner behind the Seattle protests warns, 'China: we're coming.' Anti-WTO groups are confident of mustering enough support in Congress to block Normal Trading Status for Beijing. Human rights, the environment, Tibet, religious freedom – there is no shortage of issues on which to hang China out to dry. Bill Clinton talks of China representing 'globalisation with a human face', whatever that means. But as the year draws to a close, Zhu Rongji could be excused for thinking that fate has got it in for him. After everything else, the WTO itself is under siege. It's enough to make a man pack his bags and go home to Hunan.

19–20 *December*

On the stroke of midnight, the red and gold starred flag of China rises over Macau. The ceremony on the stage of the brightly lit conference centre by the waterfront lasts just sixteen minutes. Outside, the weather is unusually cold. Only a thousand or so people gather for celebrations in the main square. Inside the vast hall, everything goes like clockwork. For those who were in Hong Kong on the night of 30 June two years ago, there is a certain familiarity. The proceedings have been choreographed by an American who organised the SAR ceremony, and now repeats it for Macau.

The new Chief Executive of the Macau Special Administrative Region calls it a joyous, proud and glorious moment. Portugal's president says Macau will endure as a meeting point of Europe and Asia. Jiang Zemin stresses that the implementation of one country, two systems in Hong Kong and Macau should pave the way for an 'early settlement of the Taiwan question and the complete national reunification'. The unimpressed Taiwanese point out that they are not a colony to be handed back.

Tung Chee-hwa is present in Macau as part of the mainland delegation. Anson Chan heads the Hong Kong contingent. As with China's national day celebrations eleven weeks ago, nobody from the pro-democracy camp is invited to join the 45-strong party. A couple of militants who come across on the ferry are quickly sent back home. Chris Patten attends in his role as a European Union Commissioner. The man described only recently by *China Daily* as a China-hating Cold Warrior is photographed shaking hands with Jiang Zemin, both smiling broadly.

The PLA sweeps across the border in armoured cars. Broken Tooth's lawyer tells the *South China Morning Post*'s Niall Fraser that his client, who is kept in his tiny cell for twenty-one hours a day, is in a deep depression. The lawyer has filed a 150-page appeal, and written to the United Nations Commission for Human Rights. But nobody expects him to get anywhere. A handful of local democracy activists are called in by police, and let go after they promise to behave. Police are more concerned about Falun Gong practitioners exercising outside the Lisboa Hotel and Casino on Jiang's route in from the airport. About forty are arrested, among them a six-year-old girl from Korea and a nine-year-old boy from Hong Kong. A man in a yellow windcheater is carried off by two policemen still in his meditating position.

Like the British during Jiang's visit in the autumn, the Macanese are anxious to avoid doing anything to annoy the chief engineer.

21 December

The number of Hong Kong civil servants recommended for disciplinary action by the anti-corruption commission has risen by 61 per cent so far this year. A third of them are police. The total of 300 is not high in absolute terms, and only 183 were, in fact, disciplined. But this was 28 per cent more than in 1998. The chairperson of the commission's ICAC Operations Review Committee thinks the increase may be due to the recession. Still, the trend is distinctly worrying for a place that has always prided itself on having a clean civil service.

22 December

An intense winter monsoon with a mass of cold air from Siberia moving across China has sent temperatures plunging. On the highest peak in the New Territories the thermometer has gone below freezing. Temporary shelters are opened for street sleepers. Thirty-four people die as a result of the chill. An 84-year-old grandmother is in a critical condition with burns after setting fire to newspapers in her home to keep warm.

26 December

The mainland crackdown on the Falun Gong is becoming even harsher. In Beijing, four practitioners are sent to prison for between seven and eighteen years. The sentences are heavier than those meted out to democracy activists, showing what the regime perceives as the bigger threat to its authority. The four were charged with organising and using the sect to obstruct justice, causing deaths in the process of organising the cult and illegally obtaining state secrets. Their trial was twice delayed when hundreds of Gong members gathered outside the court, and were removed on buses by police. The sentences are based on anti-cult legislation passed in the autumn by the National People's

Congress. At least some of the offences pre-date those laws. But who cares about a bit of retrospective justice when the President has thrown his full weight behind the crusades?

The contrast with Hong Kong remains striking, though the climate may be shifting. Nine hundred practitioners from around the world gathered in the SAR last week for a three-day session in which they performed exercises outside the headquarters of the Xinhua news agency and walked through the streets with big yellow banners. They did nothing to infringe the law, but the nervousness they aroused was palpable, amid fears by the authorities of Hong Kong becoming a base for what the mainland regime sees as subversion. 'What do they mean in getting overseas Falun Gong followers here?' asks China's Foreign Ministry Commissioner in the SAR, an urbane diplomat with a core of steel. 'Their aim is crystal clear, isn't it? It is because Hong Kong is part of China and Hong Kong is so close to the mainland. They can't deny it.' The Xinhua director says the SAR must not be used by the Falun Gong to infiltrate the mainland. Tung Chee-hwa refers to reports from Beijing that the sect had caused loss of life and social disorder. Practitioners must not act in any way against the interests of China, Hong Kong or one country, two systems, he adds.

For all the repression, Gongists are not going to give up. Their faith passes all understanding. An Australian–Chinese practitioner visiting Hong Kong tells of how she and eight others were arrested and taken to a detention centre when they arrived at the Beijing train station to express their worries about the ban on the sect. The fifty-year-old woman, now in a wheelchair, tells the *Hong Kong Standard* that she had suffered from concussion, impaired hearing and other ailments, but that her health had greatly improved since she took up Falun Gong. She had gone to Beijing as a mission to recognise what the sect's founder had done for her. After being held, she jumped out of a second-floor window in the detention centre, and says she lay bleeding on the pavement with a fractured knee for half an hour before police came out to help. She intends to return to the capital when she is well again. She expects this to happen within days because the cult's founder will visit her in a dream to heal her injuries. 'That is the usual way he communicates with his followers,' she explains.

30 *December*

One argument which the Hong Kong government likes to use against a faster pace for democracy is that the existing institutions represent the community. A good example of how it measures such representativity is given today when the Chief Executive unveils the list of ninety-eight members he is appointing to join the 390 members of district councils elected last month.

The government says the ninety-eight were selected in their personal capacity for their 'enthusiasm and familiarity' with community affairs. Evidently, Democrats and like-minded people lack those qualities. Despite having come top of the popular electoral poll, not one of them is on Tung's list. This means that the Democrats have a chance of getting the chairmanship of just one of the eighteen councils. On the other hand, Tung allocates twelve seats to members of the DAB, which finished second in the voting. Such is the Hong Kong way with democracy thirty months after the handover as we move into the new year.

THE YEAR OF THE DRAGON

While cities from Paris to Sydney shimmer for the coming millennium, Hong Kong has a horse race, some not very spectacular fireworks and a show featuring the singer Sarah Brightman. It is pretty downbeat compared with the past extravaganzas on which the SAR has prided itself, for the handover or Chinese New Year which will bring us to the Year of the Dragon in six weeks' time. Out of habit, a crowd has gathered by the harbour, expecting the usual pyrotechnic display. But even if they turn their gaze inland, they can catch little of the Happy Valley illuminations because of the wall of skyscrapers in between. You can watch it on television, of course, but it's not quite the same as oohing and aahing at the multicoloured cloudbursts and curtains of silver rain that usually mark festive moments in Hong Kong. 'If India could afford a proper celebration, what excuse does Hong Kong have?' asks a reader's letter in the *South China Morning Post*.

The hot New Year ticket in town is not to join the Chief Executive and the Chief Secretary at the Happy Valley racecourse, but for the Convention Centre, where several thousand people crush into a hall for a party underwritten by the younger son of Li Ka-shing, the cyber-tycoon Richard Li. The star is the American pop diva Whitney Houston, who has swept into Hong Kong at the head of a fifty-strong entourage. Li stands staring at the stage, a slightly shy smile on his lips.

The hall where Jiang Zemin and Prince Charles ushered Hong Kong back to China is full to bursting with the Hong Kong glitterati. Tung Chee-hwa comes on from Happy Valley and applauds politely as Houston swans about the stage. If the degree of security a person has around him is a measure of his importance, Li Ka-shing's son outranks Tung tonight. Ordinary mortals can get through the crowd to shake the Chief Executive's hand; when you venture towards Li, a burly Western guard in a dark suit keeps you at a safe distance. But then, anybody who has built an Internet company out of nothing to a HK$30 billion valuation within a year and is about to bid for the Hong Kong telephone system deserves all the protection he desires

By the time Houston launches into a series of lovestruck duets with her husband, the singer Bobby Brown, the Chief Executive has left, but the crowd stays on till dawn, downing oceans of champagne and shouting above the din. There are also the usual lavish parties in smart hotels replete with millennium dinners and dancing. On top of the Jardine's building, the senior executives are in their traditional kilts and trews as they eat breakfast and dance the old century away. A couple of hours' sleep and then it is time to cross the harbour for eggnogs at the Peninsula Hotel, accompanied by the police band in Scottish tartans playing 'Auld Lang Syne'. There may not have been much of a show for the people, but the rich and famous have seen in the millennium with some style.

At the same time, on the mainland, five Protestants are reported to have been arrested in Beijing as they prepared for a New Year prayer meeting. One, a doctor, was detained as he left the night shift at his hospital. In Fujian province, an eighty-year-old Catholic archbishop, who has already spent thirty years in jail for refusing to join the official Church, is re-arrested – one of eight senior prelates being detained on the mainland. In Jiangsu province, a nineteen-year-old man is given a three-year jail sentence for writing an open letter to President Jiang urging the regime to fight against corruption. In Wuhan, three organisers of the China Democratic Party are sentenced to between eleven and thirteen years in prison. In Tiananmen Square, fifteen Falun Gong practitioners are arrested as they meditate; in all, 5,000 devotees are now said to have been sentenced to administrative detention without trial. According to a human rights organisation in Hong Kong, an official in central China who practised Falun Gong has got four years in jail merely for having told other members of the cult about a critical speech by Jiang Zemin. The heaviest sentence yet against a Falun Gong member is reported to have been given to a retired air force general aged seventy-four who has been jailed for seventeen years at a secret court martial. Yu Changxin, a former ace pilot who had rank equivalent to a provincial governor, is the most senior person sentenced in connection with the movement. President Jiang is said to have been personally involved in deciding on the sentence because of suspicions that Yu masterminded the April protest outside Zhongnanhai which first brought the Falun Gong to public attention. But the Hong Kong human-rights group says he had nothing to do with the demonstration, and fellow generals are reported to be angry at the verdict.

Mainland journalists are instructed not to dwell on 'the dark side of society'. This is not always easy. *China Daily* tells us that children are getting taller, but the National Surveillance Network reports that 'excess weight has emerged as a major health problem for children, especially well-off urbanites who eat more high-calorie food'. Revelations about corruption and smuggling continue to pour out: a report to the National People's Congress says the number of cases investigated last year rose by 9 per cent to 38,382, and that 15,700 people were sentenced as a result. A ring which was uncovered in the port of Xiamen on the eastern Fujian coast is now said to involve goods worth between US$6 and 10 billion. As well as the usual oil, cars and weapons, the smugglers brought in telecommunications equipment under the auspices of the local government, and managed to build up debts of more than US$600 million to SAR and mainland banks with bad investments in Hong Kong property. Two hundred people are being questioned in the city; some have been held incommunicado by police in a hotel for six months. Among them are senior police and customs officers and two top local bankers. Reports in mid-January say the former wife of a member of China's twenty-two-strong Politburo is also suspected of having played a central role – though this is followed by a blanket denial of her involvement. Her former husband, who divorced her after police began the crackdown, is a major political figure in Beijing and a close associate of Jiang.

Wherever you look in the prosperous parts of China, the new century is arriving with a bang. The anti-smuggling campaign has boosted state revenue significantly. The Legend computer firm is about to start selling television set-top boxes with Microsoft software to allow users to access the Internet and trade securities through a Chinese brokerage. To assuage the people of the restive north-west, spending there is to be boosted on transport links, power, telecommunications, radio and television, and natural gas pipelines.

Jiang may have finessed them over the WTO, but the conservatives will not give up. An aged hardliner called Deng Liqun circulates a paper warning that the party could lose the basis of its rule in under ten years if the private sector goes on expanding. He deplores the fact that local officials are becoming more susceptible to the wishes of the private sector and foreign firms, warning that the way in which they are providing more and more of the tax revenue could increase their influence over the administration of the provinces. As the new millennium begins, tight controls are imposed on China's 9 million Internet users, prohibiting the 'publication of state secrets' on the Web: in China just about anything can be classified as a state secret. In another move to restrict new technology, some conservatives in the leadership suggest that the Windows system should be banned as a security threat.

For all the talk of reform, the state still controls between 60 and 70 per cent of firms with shares on the mainland stock exchanges. At a time when markets have been booming elsewhere in Asia, the Shanghai and Shenzhen indexes have fallen by 20 per cent in six months. The government is planning to close half the country's trust and investment companies because of their inefficiency. The *Economic Daily* reports that local opposition is delaying a key plan to swap the debts of state enterprises for equity. Last year, 400 billion yuan was meant to have been transferred, but in fact the total only amounted to 72 billion. Two state companies floated on the Shanghai stock exchange, one manufacturing motorcycle parts and the other tyres, have been undersubscribed by 18 and 26 per cent. And the Minister of Labour and Social Security says as many as 12 million workers in state-owned enterprises will lose their jobs in this year.

Despite an official growth forecast of 7 per cent for the new year, all this comes against a background of continuing uncertainty about China's ability to go on expanding fast enough to win Jiang's bet that the economic boom will ward off any threat to one-party rule. While income from exports rose by 6 per cent to US$194.9 billion in 1999, imports shot up in value by 18 per cent to US$165.8 billion – the figures boosted by goods which were previously smuggled in now being declared instead. As a result, the trade surplus fell by 33 per cent. Without strong demand in North America, which took 10 per cent more exports from China than in 1998, the economy would be heading for serious trouble.

In Washington, Bill Clinton launches an all-out campaign to get congressional agreement for the World Trade Organisation deal, but opposition to giving China Normal Trading Status is rising from both the Republicans and the trade unions. To show that trade is not its only concern, Washington announces that it will put forward a motion at the UN condemning China's human-rights record. Early in his presidency, Clinton sought to link economic relations and human rights. Now, the administration is putting them in separate boxes, and crossing its fingers that domestic critics will be placated. Beijing understands. 'I think these are entirely different things,' a Foreign Ministry spokesman says, knowing that the UN motion can be blocked by procedural manoeuvres. So the regime can go on locking up Falun Gong practitioners and Christians, and sending the Uigur businesswoman, Rebiya Kadeer, to jail for eight years for sending press clippings to her husband in America without any fear that this will give Bill Clinton second thoughts about the WTO deal – though a vocal number of Congressmen may have different ideas and Beijing's harsh line on Taiwan always risks bedevilling its links with the West.

Hong Kong, the turnout for the annual New Year pro-democracy march is pitifully small, at under 100 people. The pro-Beijing DAB party joins the Democrats in pressing for early discussion of political development. The party leader, Tsang Yok-sing, says: 'If there is one thing we can be certain about our present system of government, it is that the system is unsustainable.' But the government will not entertain any idea of change, however unrepresentative, unaccountable and incoherent the present set-up may be. On a phone-in programme, Tung Chee-hwa rules out the idea of introducing a ministerial system with politicians or recruits from the private sector taking on responsibility for policy. 'I feel the way forward is an executive structure with the civil service as its main trunk,' he says. 'The direction is not going to change.' As for democratisation, the Chief Executive intones the mantra of deep conservatism. Discussion of the issue can wait until ten years after the handover. The year 2007 will be the appropriate time 'to consider the next step in accordance with our development'.

To mark the New Year, the Hong Kong branch of the Chinese news agency, Xinhua, is renamed the Liaison Office of the Central People's Government. Democrats fear that the renaming may betoken more interference by Beijing. Martin Lee says Tung and senior officials sometimes ask Xinhua to help lobby members of the Legislative Council. 'Those words are irresponsible,' the Chief Executive responds. 'Of course there is no such thing.' Xinhua's role in running the Communist Party in Hong Kong remains unacknowledged, but it has become known that it has acquired a new senior official whose job is to investigate corruption by mainland companies here, in line with Zhu Rongji's concern that the SAR has become a bolt-hole for corrupt mainlanders sheltering behind the absence of an extradition agreement.

Hong Kong's economy is improving steadily. Retail sales rise by 12 per cent in January, the first increase in value terms since the crash of 1997. Richard Li is poised to make a spectacular US$38 billion takeover of Hong Kong Telecom from Cable & Wireless in a deal which will move control of the main telephone company from British to local ownership – with Beijing's evident approval. Not to be outdone by his son, Li Ka-shing is marching into cyberspace with a Chinese-language start-up that produces scuffles between would-be buyers and is oversubscribed more than 600 times when it offers shares to the public.

The stock market boom, fuelled by a dot-com craze, makes people feel happier, of course. Hong Kong is very good at bouncing from depression to euphoria, but the experience of recession still lurks in the popular psychology. The manager of a luxury goods store notes that clients are buying more reasonably priced goods these days – HK$1,000 silver chains rather than $10,000 gold ones. A senior executive at a big supermarket chain says price counts for more than it did a couple of years ago. Despite the crisis, adds just about everybody, Hong Kong is still too expensive. Back office services are being moved to the mainland or elsewhere in Asia. A sizeable Internet start-up keeps its headquarters in the SAR but moves all its programming work to Manila. 'I can get ten people there for the price of one here,' explains the founder. And why, wonders a pillar of the business community, is Hong Kong building a new container terminal when competitors over the border offer their services for a fraction of the price?

For all the talk about surfing the wave into the new millennium, and Richard Li's emergence as the face of the future, the real dynamic for change does not reach very deep, while the government has taken a paradigm shift away from its old rectitude. That has proved popular, and the businessmen who run Hong Kong can go on making enormous gains from the property system and from their privileged place in a low-tax structure. Politics has been shoved aside, at least in the sense that popular votes make a difference. For all the T-shirted appearances at community occasions by the Chief Executive and Chief Secretary, the administration becomes ever more distant, and is now losing some of its brightest members to the private sector, where the money is even better and there is not the daunting prospect of being grilled by the likes of Emily Lau and Martin Lee.

The prevailing political correctness of brotherhood and sisterhood with the mainland obscures the reality that China is Hong Kong's greatest competitor. The doctrine of loving the motherland sounds horribly like a rerun of *Babes in the Wood*. Officials may allude to it in private, but nobody in the administration could come out in public to say that if Beijing regards Hong Kong as a potential base for subversion, the SAR ought to see Shanghai as a very real base for undermining its position. Talk to people on the mainland, particularly away from the southern Cantonese belt, and you will not find much love for Hong Kong. 'You did well from mixing British colonialism with China's opening to the market,' a mainlander who combines official and private business said one night. 'Now you have lost the first, and we control the second. We need you to raise the money which we will spend for our future. When we have built ourselves up, we will not need you any more.' Then he laughed, and poured us both another drink. And then he laughed again, as if to signify that what he had just said was all a huge joke. But it was not. In a sign of the times, the big French telecommunications company Alcatel, which employs 10,000 people in the region, announced in January that it was putting its Asian headquarters in Shanghai.

As chroniclers of the Asian collapse and recovery like to remind us, the Chinese character for crisis contains ideograms for both danger and opportunity. The question is whether the danger is for Hong Kong and the opportunity for China. If that turns out to be the case, it will be because of what Hong Kong and China each does. On the one hand, a Chief Executive whose government kowtows at a time which calls for political leadership and audacity to match the leadership and audacity that made Hong Kong one of the world's great business centres; on the other, a Prime Minister in Beijing who is riding a dragon and a President who is playing politics at the very highest level.

For a brief time, there was the prospect that Hong Kong could become a world city. The Chief Executive still likes to promote a vision of New York for the Americas, London for Europe and Hong Kong for Asia. That is not an impossible dream. But it involves a great deal more than those in power in the SAR seem able to envisage. Above all, it means creating a far-reaching civil society that engages its citizens and the rest of the world. Disneyland and other palliatives are not enough. The chance was there: the reality may be that nobody wanted to grasp it, that Hong Kong retreated into itself after the handover and missed its destiny as it merely waited for economic good times to return. What is left is still amazing for a place with so few natural advantages – and the taste for a quiet life may be understandable enough when the rulers come from a family business or the civil service, and when rocking the boat could affect business. But in the end, the turn-of-century lesson is that the population which made Hong Kong what it is were not trusted by the old elite to make it something even more extraordinary.

It is easy to underestimate the role of democracy and accountability and the independent rule of law and a truly civil society – or to take them for granted where they have deeper roots than they do in the SAR. It is also easy to see Hong Kong in purely materialistic terms as a city where all that counts is financial success and keeping out of trouble with the sovereign power to the north. There's nothing to worry about, is there, as the British Foreign Secretary asked me almost imploringly on a visit in 1998. No, in one sense there is, indeed, nothing to worry about: life goes on, the city works, money is made and nobody is locked up for their beliefs. But the change of sovereignty should have meant more than the transfer of a small stretch of land to new ownership. The meeting of an essentially free place with an essentially unfree country gave the handover a very special resonance, and opened up possibilities of demonstrating the strengths and benefits of liberty in a positive rather than a passive manner, even if that meant confronting the prospects of disagreement and dispute with a central government which has always refused to brook dissent.

The game would have been hard and dangerous, but the potential prize was immense, building on the positive inheritance of the colonial period to forge a new relationship which would buttress and extend Hong Kong's unique place in the world. Instead, the way in which the SAR heads into the new millennium is a demonstration of what happens when challenges are ducked, corners cut, bulwarks demolished and coherence abandoned. Life can remain very pleasant and exciting, fortunes can be made and the stock market can boom. But dealing with the dragon to the north has been allowed to take its toll. The spirit which could have made something exceptional out of one country, two systems – with all the associated risks – has been stifled, without the people who could have given it life being allowed a chance to make the difference.

AFTERWORD

As the Year of the Dragon unfolded, mainland China reported eight per cent growth, and WTO legislation went through Congress. On the mainland, teachers, miners, factory workers and farmers protested over everything from unpaid wages to access to drinking water. Three thousand Falun Gong practitioners were reported to be locked up, and two dozen to have died in custody. The Uigur businesswoman, Rebiya Kadeer, was jailed for eight years for sending press clippings to her husband in America. More than 20,000 cases of graft were investigated. The fallen business star, Mou Qizong, got a life sentence for fraud while 200 officials accused of netting more than US$5 billion appeared in court in Fujian province. On one day in September, a former senior member of the National People's Congress was executed for receiving US$5 million in bribes and the arrest was announced of the former second-ranking national police official on corruption charges.

In Hong Kong, the head of the Housing Authority resigned over construction scandals. More than 30,000 people marked the Tiananmen vigil. There was a big row over academic freedom when an aide to the Chief Executive was accused of pressurising a leading university opinion pollster. A survey showed people thought corruption was increasing. A judge ruled that Beijing's interpretation of the Basic Law meant 5,000 mainlanders did not have the right of abode.

Home owners protested against low property prices. Tung Chee-hwa scrapped his housing development plans. Profits at Li Ka-shing's main company rose 326 per cent. His son, Richard, took over Hong Kong Telecom. Willy Lam, the China editor whose job had been saved in 1995, came under repeated attack from the owners of the *Post* after I left: he was finally replaced in November, 2000.

Public apathy for politics increased. Only 20 per cent of eligible voters turned out to choose members of the Election Committee which is likely to pick the next Chief Executive: conservatives and business figures dominated the results. Turnout at the Legislative Council election in September fell by ten points to 43.6 per cent. The Democrats – divided and increasingly seen as toothless watchdogs – dropped to 34 per cent from 57 per cent before the handover. Despite a scandal involving their vice-chairman passing a confidential document to a client of his public relations firm, the pro-Beijing DAB party took almost 30 per cent, double its pre-handover score. Polls showed that under 20 per cent of people wanted Tung to serve a second term, but President Jiang urged the SAR to put its faith in the Chief Executive. In the autumn, the Chief Secretary was instructed by the mainland that the civil service should be more supportive of Tung. Three months later, Anson Chan suddenly announced her resignation: though she insisted it was for personal reasons, everybody saw it as the biggest political change since the handover. The way was open for Tung to exercise full control, and for Hong Kong to fall even more under Beijing's sway. The patterns of 1999 reached into the new century. One country, one-and-a-half systems.